Legal Legends
and
Other True Stories

White Lodge Publishing

Legal Legends
and
Other True Stories

by
Theodore Ruoff, CB, CBE

London
White Lodge Publishing
1988

ISBN 1 85190 051 9

© 1988 Theodore Ruoff
Published by White Lodge Publishing
27 & 28 St Albans Place Islington Green London N1 ONX
Printed in Great Britain

Preface

Between 1952 and 1988 I wrote letters for the *Australian Law Journal* almost every month. Just a few of them were of serious significance. Most were in a light vein. Some had a message. But all of them were well received down under.

Therefore, knowing how much laymen and lay women (I refuse to use the uncouth word 'lay persons'!) enjoy reading about legal trials and tribulations, I have adapted (with the generous blessing of the Law Book Co Ltd in New South Wales) some of my Australian anecdotes for those very people in the UK. And if all our lawyers – on both sides of our learned profession – don't also like my legal legends, I shall be, to say the least, more than a modicum surprised.

Bragging aside, I truly hope that everyone who reads these true stories will enjoy them.

Finally, for the benefit of the lawyers and of such lay readers as may wish to pursue my sources, I have put the citations of decisions of the courts in an Appendix.

Theodore Ruoff

1988

I dedicate this book with gratitude to Joan Cossins, MBE, who, over many years, so faithfully and impeccably typed my letters to the *Australian Law Journal* which form the basis of all the true stories that follow.

Contents

Eating People is Wrong!

It was but a few weeks after I started to study the law that I was introduced to a case which will surely for ever enjoy legal immortality. I refer, of course, to *Regina* v *Dudley and Stephens.*[1] (Don't eat people, for eating people is wrong! Or, necessity is no defence to a charge of murder.) I am sure that most other lawyers, in the early days of their legal studies, were every bit as fascinated by this case as I was. Now I have read an immensely interesting account[2] of the circumstances of the murder and the subsequent trial which contains many facts and ideas of which, hitherto, I was entirely ignorant – and so, I dare say, were many other lawyers.

In 1883 the yacht *Mignonette*, fifty-two feet long, which carried a tiny dinghy measuring only thirteen feet by four feet by twenty inches in depth, was bought by an Australian lawyer named John Henry Want, and he employed, as captain, Tom Ridley Dudley (a God-fearing man) to sail her from London to Sydney for £200 – £100 down, and the rest to be paid on delivery. The remaining crew (after a number had been engaged and, one after another, had resigned on account of their misgivings about the hazards of the proposed voyage) were

1

Edwin Stephens, another God-fearing man (mate), Edmund James Brooks (able-seaman), and a seventeen-year-old cabin boy, Richard Thomas Parker.

The *Mignonette* was committed to sailing up to 16,000 miles round the Cape of Good Hope and thence along the southern hemisphere. Hazardous? Sir Francis Chichester's *Gypsy Moth IV* in which he achieved his circumnavigation was only twelve inches longer! But, of course, he enjoyed many results of the advance of modern technology that Captain Dudley could never have dreamed of.

Those who had declined to join the crew of the *Mignonette* were surely gifted with prescience for, not long after crossing the line on the 5th July, 1884, the yacht was stove in by heavy seas and the four members of the crew took to their minute and fragile dinghy. They were in a desperate condition because they had no fresh water and their only food consisted – just imagine it – of a couple of tins of turnips! After they had successfully beaten off a shark that attacked them, Captain Dudley imposed a harsh rationed regimen, five pieces of turnip being made to last two days.

At that time all sailors believed that sea water was poisonous and that to drink any of it was not only suicidal, but a sure recipe for madness, as witness the ancient mariner in Samuel Coleridge's poem –

'Water, water, every where,

Nor any drop to drink'.

Today, of course, we know that minute quantities of sea water can be imbibed with safety, especially if it is combined with some other liquid. To continue: on the 9th July Mr Dudley and his men contrived to catch a turtle. By the 13th July they had all begun to drink their own urine although, occasionally, they were able to gather a few drops of rainwater. But by the 16th July their food was finished and young Richard Parker, having drunk far too much seawater, had become violently ill and, of course, desperately dehydrated. By the 24th July he was comatose and the others then decided to accelerate slightly his death in order to save their own lives. It is not clear whether lots were drawn, but certainly, one morning, Captain Dudley, I think with the help of the mate, Stephens, cut the lad's jugular vein with a penknife. His blood was caught and drunk by all three survivors.

After these people had reached a safe haven, Captain Dudley, somewhat ungrammatically stated: 'I then offered a prayer for the poor boy's soul if were to commit such a rash act asked forgiveness from our Maker I then said it must be done it may save three lives so we put an end to his sufferings which was not a moments work and all was over himself never moving from where he lay.'

It is likely that poor Richard lasted no more than thirteen seconds. Thereafter the other survivors ate his heart and liver, although a large part of his corpse was jettisoned. Captain Dudley said: 'I shall never forget the sight of my two unfortunate companions over the ghastly meal we all made like mad wolfs . . . I feel quite sure had we not had that awful food to exist upon, not a soul would have lived.'

On the 29th July 1884, after the wretched survivors had drifted or sailed over 1,000 miles, they sighted a sail, were taken aboard the German barque *Moctezuma*, and reached the port of Falmouth on the 6th September 1884.

Today, it is interesting to observe Captain Dudley's next move. Immediately after his arrival he explained, as he was by law required to do for the primary purpose of securing the safety of vessels at sea, without any trace of fear or inhibition, how it had become absolutely necessary that one member of his crew should be sacrificed to save the rest of them and that the lad, Richard Parker, being by far the weakest of them all, had been killed for this purpose. This quite extraordinary candour was borne of the simple fact that, at that time, all those who went

3

down in their ships to the sea, recognised universally that such a practice was both acceptable and universally accepted without question.

In short, when Captain Dudley and his associates were arrested and charged with murder, they were shocked, outraged and even disgusted at what they regarded as a jejune (although they would not have used that particular word) assessment of their behaviour. Indeed, some ninety pages of this remarkable book are devoted to the then current recognition of the legitimacy of this extraordinary custom because it was clearly the settled practice of sailors to eat one another when they became starved at sea although, as you may well imagine, this was scarcely a way of life that was likely to commend itself to Her Majesty's judges. Brooks, by the way, turned Queen's evidence.

It was a tragedy for the accused, as well as for the cause of justice, when such a devious, overbearing and, indeed, thoroughly dishonest judge as Baron Huddleston, who was so well accustomed to bullying juries, should have been chosen to try Captain Dudley and his friends. Although he was the son of a merchant sea captain, the Baron sought, through his most prejudicial opinions, to counteract the fact that every single captain under whom Dudley had earlier ever served, gave evidence in his defence.

Baron Huddleston set about reserving a 'special verdict' on a point of law for the Court of Crown Cases Reserved (before the establishment of a Court of Criminal Appeal), and by devious means this mendacious judge deprived the jury of any chance of coming to a decision themselves about whether the accused seamen were guilty of murder, guilty of manslaughter, or simply not guilty.

Moreover, as I believe, he was dishonest in the account he gave the jurors of the text of the special verdict which was to be referred. One simple example of the way he fiddled the text is that the jury had stated quite unequivocally that Dudley and

Stephens 'would have died if they had not had this body to feed on'. Without telling the jury, the Baron interpolated the word 'probably' between 'would' and 'have' in this sentence.

There is the further point – if you will allow me slightly to over-simplify a somewhat technical argument – that the Court of Crown Cases Reserved had no jurisdiction whatever until there had been a conviction! This caused some slight worry to some of the judges under Lord Coleridge.

However, counsel for the defendants pleaded a case for necessity, as he cited *inter alia* Cicero's predicament of the two drowning men on a single plank that could support only one of them. Perhaps extreme circumstances place men outside the law's ambit. Perhaps, too, in desperate conditions, a man's actions are not truly voluntary. Perhaps, again, it is wrong to give a majority all the benefit. Above all, perhaps the utter frailty of human nature needs to be taken into account.

Counsel for the accused persons also cogently pleaded a lack of jurisdiction because, whereas the Court had, by statute, a power to try a case of murder arising on the high seas on a British ship and whereas the *Mignonette* was such a vessel, the dinghy was not a British ship under the Merchant Shipping Act 1854, which clearly defined a ship as including 'every vessel used for the purpose of navigation not propelled by oars'.

The Court rejected this cogent argument and Lord Coleridge announced that 'we are all of the opinion that the conviction should be affirmed'. But what conviction had there been which needed to be ratified? His Lordship could not bring himself to refer to this as a 'verdict' (which is something that juries render) so he somewhat evasively called it 'a judgment'. Subsequently, without donning the black cap, he sentenced Dudley and Stephens to death with a recommendation to mercy. Three days later the sentence was commuted to six months' imprisonment.

Comments and correspondence in the national press were

in general greatly favourable towards the prisoners and *The Daily Telegraph* deplored the passing of sentence of death. Its leader writer went on to say: 'It is a trial of the judicial temper, if lunch be too late, and for dinner not only to be delayed, but altogether withheld, would involve a departure from composure, which would make Bracton and Hale very untimely. What if breakfast, lunch, dinner and supper, too, were to be denied for a whole day, two days, or even a week?'

Dudley and Stephens were released on the 20th May 1885, one year and a day after they began their fateful journey to Sydney.

A Tale of Two Goldfishes

At midsummer 1952, with the temperature about 100°F (give or take a couple of degrees), I went by rail from Adelaide, on the coast of South Australia, to the Dead Heart at Alice Springs. Of all the many things that made me open my eyes in wonderment as I passed through the sort of country where, to some extent, 'there aren't no Ten Commandments, an' a man can raise a thirst,' none did so more than the empty beer bottles. There they lay, scattered, in their tens of thousands, where they had been discarded on both sides of the track, at almost regular intervals of 5 yards for each one of the 953 miles of my journey. Remembering a young enthusiast from a seaside resort in South Australia, who had told me he earned threepence for every bottle he collected from the beach, I hurriedly calculated that an expedition to salvage this precious commodity would immediately produce the gross sum of

$$£953 \quad \times \frac{1760}{5} \times 2 \times \frac{3}{240}$$

(call it something under £9,000).

Just imagine my chagrin on being told that the sun's fierce rays had rendered the glass brittle and useless!

The Melbournians have a 'bottle-o' man and one used to be able to, and, for all I know, still can buy and sell second-hand clothes in Paddy's market, Sydney. But nowhere in that prosperous country have I ever seen what in my boyhood was a common sight in London, although it has since become less so. Yet even today, in the poorer districts, you may come upon a man trundling a long flat hand-barrow and calling out, in an indescribably hoarse cockney voice, 'Ennyole-i-on?' or, 'Ragger-bo,' or emitting similar sounds intended as an invitation to the public at large to sell him any unwanted iron, rags or bones.

Some thirty years ago one of these dealers was summoned before the stipendiary of a court in the East End of London on an information preferred by the local town clerk. The dealer had handed over a live goldfish to a boy in exchange for some old bits of cloth and he was charged under s. 154 of the Public Health Act 1936, which provided that 'no person who collects or deals in rags, old clothes or similar articles . . . shall . . . sell or deliver, whether gratuitously or not, any article of food or drink to any person, or any article whatsoever to a person under the age of 14 years.' (Maximum penalty: £5 fine).

The history of the statute shows that half a century ago rag-and-bone men often traded toys and other articles to penniless children in exchange for discarded clothing. These playthings were often carried on barrows mixed up with a horrid mess of filthy cloth and rotting bones and by this means, amidst a teeming population, vermin and contagious diseases were spread. An earlier Act had prohibited rag collectors from giving children 'any article of food or any balloon or other toy.'

The question for decision was simply, 'Is a goldfish an article?' The 1936 Act did not define 'article' and there was no suggestion that a live goldfish might be prejudicial to the health of a child. It is a well-settled canon of construction that if a penal statute is so ambiguous as to be reasonably capable of two meanings, the more lenient one which does not attract a penalty should be applied. No one in ordinary conversation would refer to a goldfish as an article and that word ordinarily means something inanimate. Hence, summons dismissed (*West Ham Corporation* v *Markham*[3]).

Emboldened, no doubt, by this satisfactory result, another East End rag-and-bone merchant shortly thereafter bartered another live goldfish to another lad, also under fourteen, named Lesley Cullen. This man knew what glittering inducements goldfishes are in the eyes of small boys and he knew, too, that if he foolishly handed over a fish in a bowl, that bowl would be an article, and he would be in trouble. Therefore, he and his fellows, with the ingenuity of their trade, insisted on small boys supplying their own gallipots and pans ready filled with water. Yet, despite his careful foresight and wise precaution, this dealer was summoned by a sanitary inspector before the local bench of magistrates. He did not appear, but wrote a polite note to the court, saying he was sorry if he had done wrong and explaining how he had heard a rumour that some court or other had already decided that a goldfish was *not* an article. In due course this trifling point came under the review of the Divisional Court presided over by the late Lord Chief Justice Goddard (*Daly* v *Cannon*[4]).

Counsel argued that John Black's Irish pig was 'an article or thing' (*R* v *Armagh Justices*[5]), and so was the Welsh horse that was auctioned in *Llandaff &c Co* v *Lyndon*[6]. Although Mr Justice Byles (famous as the original author, in 1829, of 'Byles on Bills') sat on the bench in this last case, he refrained from giving judgment. Was there some significance in his silence? The citation of the case provoked Lord Goddard into a recollection of how this lover of horses used to ride to Court on a white mare which, as you can guess, was universally – and, one might add, inevitably – known by the name of Bills.

The upshot of the goldfish case was that the Court thought the magistrate's decision in the first case I mentioned 'exceedingly sensible.' 'I cannot contend,' said Lord Goddard, 'that our judgment will add a great deal to the jurisprudence of this country . . . . If it is thought that goldfish spread disease . . . it would be quite easy for Parliament to alter the law on this point. . . . I think that it is a straining of language to say that a goldfish is an article.'

No doubt rag-and-bone man William James Cannon is still doing a roaring trade in the Ilford district, for as George Herbert once observed 'Great businesses turn on a little pin.' No doubt, too, some cynical and some economically minded persons would like to echo Pope's words – 'What mighty contests rise from trivial things!'

Nevertheless, there will be others who will think there is some satisfaction to be found in the fact that no question is so small that the learning and the authority of the Law cannot be brought to bear upon it.

A Lady Locked in a Loo

Every practising lawyer who has the time to pause and reflect about his or her daily work may well remark upon the extraordinary impact which unheeded trifles have made upon our law, particularly in the realm of contract and tort. By the same token, a concatenation of humdrum happenings may at any moment lead any one of us haphazardly into a tangled web of danger or difficulty and thence into litigation.

A bursting hot water bottle scalds someone and a leading case is born. The highest tribunal in the land is called upon to allot blame for the presence of a rotting snail in a bottle of ginger beer – although, as a matter of history, it now seems to be accepted that if, after the preliminary point of law had been decided, the facts had been proved, no snail would have emerged from any bottle, let alone one that had sometime been encapsulated in a non-alcoholic container. A barrel of flour descends from the upper storey of a warehouse upon the head of an unfortunate passer-by and, as every tyro in the law has long been required to learn, *res ipsa loquitur* – the cause is obvious; it speaks for itself, as clearly as does Newton's law of gravity.

That, at least, used to be the classic answer in an

11

examination paper. Perhaps, however, examinees ought now to offer a modified opinion because it seems that if someone walks on the opposite side of the road from a four-storeyed building that is being reconstructed and he is knocked senseless, apparently by a falling brick, he will not be able to recover damages if it is proved that the precautions which the builders took rendered the possibility of such an accident happening so remote as to be improbable.[7] 'Improbable' was one word that was bandied about as well as 'inexplicable' – this despite the wire · netting, the tarpaulin sheeting, and the chap posted in the roadway to warn passers-by. Yet the brick did fall – probably dislodged by the vibration of drilling. Even the sedate columns of the report in *The Times* carried a sub-heading; 'Brick strikes man: what it *said*', for the plaintiff contended that the brick itself spoke just as did the famous barrel of flour.

Then take this simple incident. On a January morning in 1960, after breakfast a Mr and Mrs Sayers left their home some twenty-five miles or so out of London, intending to catch a bus into town at 8.32 a.m. They may well have been on their way to hunt for bargains at the winter sales in the West End stores. Having some twenty minutes to spare, Mrs Sayers, who was a lady of thirty-six, unfortunately decided to leave the safety of her husband's side in order to visit a public lavatory. In doing this she was, most mercifully, ignorant of the fact that she was entering into a legally binding contract and certainly oblivious of the consequence that she was taking the first step in a long walk that was going to end in the solemn atmosphere of the Court of Appeal.

> Who can hope to be safe? Who sufficiently cautious?
> Guard himself as he may, every moment's an ambush.

Entering the lavatory, which was owned and operated by the local authority, Mrs Sayers went to the furthest cubicle and, slipping a mere penny (halcyon days!) into the slot provided, she opened the door, went in and was then aware that the door had slammed to behind her and that, as there was no internal handle, she was without any means of reopening the door from her side. Finding herself thus unwillingly incarcerated in a loo and there being no attendant in the building she sought to attract attention. Lord Justice Morris graphically describes her plight thus:

'What did she do? First of all, she did her best to operate the lock. She tried with her finger to see whether there was any way of making it work. There was not. She then tried to get her hand through the window. She was unable to do that. She then banged on the door. Nobody came. She shouted. There was no response. Ten or fifteen minutes went by. The situation could not have been an agreeable one. What did she then do? It appears to me on the evidence that what she did was to explore the possibility of climbing over the door. That I cannot think was unwise, or imprudent, or rash, or stupid.'

I expect that her thoughts switched during those seemingly endless ten or fifteen minutes, from her own predicament to her husband outside, picturing him, no doubt, impatient at her overlong absence, apprehensive that they would miss the bus and so have a full hour's wait for the next one if, indeed, they had not already missed it, and probably stamping in the cold of the chill January air, but not yet sufficiently alarmed to come in search for her.

Lord Evershed took up the story. 'A woman goes to a public lavatory and finds that she is immured in it. She finds, after ten or fifteen minutes, that the obvious and proper means of attracting attention has been entirely without avail. Shouting and waving through the window has produced no result at all. It is an extremely disagreeable situation in which to find oneself; and it seems to me to be asking too much of the so-called reasonable man or woman to suppose that he or she would just remain inactive until her husband, or someone else, chose to come and look for her and find her . . . '

It was in these circumstances that Mrs Sayers tried to see if she could possibly escape over the door or make her presence known over it. She stood with her left foot on the seat of the lavatory. With her left hand she seized the pipe from the cistern. Her right hand she put on top of the door and her right foot rested on the toilet roll and the small fixture in which it was inserted. She had (says the official report) 'got so far in the belief that she would be able by a feat not too acrobatic to get out over the door, which was seven feet high, with a space about two feet four inches between its top and the ceiling'. But having arrived in that position she decided 'in truth the manoeuvre was beyond her capacity' and so she started to climb down again. In passing; even the Duke of Wellington is reputed to have said that a test of greatness is to know when to retreat and to dare to do it.'

In her descent Mrs Sayers allowed some of her weight to be on the toilet roll and her balance to depend on it. Alas! Impelled by a wicked fate, the innocent toilet roll rotated and disturbed her equilibrium so that she fell down and was injured. As the Master of the Rolls later observed: ' . . . . In getting back to *terra firma* again she should have appreciated that she could not properly and ought not to allow her balance to depend upon anything so unstable as a toilet roll and a fixture of a somewhat slender kind'.

So it came about that she commenced proceedings in the local county court claiming damages first, because – as she averred – the owners of the lavatory had warranted that the cubicle was safe. Secondly, she based her claim upon negligence.

Although the county court judge found the defendants guilty of a breach of duty, he decided that the risks taken by Mrs Sayers out-balanced that.[8] He spoke of her 'very hazardous undertaking' and her 'exceedingly perilous manoeuvre'. He said that she 'was not in any sort of danger, nor indeed in any real discomfort. She knew or ought to have known that at 8.32 a.m. her husband must come and find out what had happened to her.

The only consequence would have been the wrath of her husband and an hour's delay'. In the result he considered the damage too remote.

On this the Court of Appeal found that in seeking a possible way of escape, Mrs Sayers had acted entirely rationally. As the Master of the Rolls said: 'I cannot for my part think that she could be condemned for having failed to see from the start that the whole thing was impossible; and, secondly, it seemed to me to be quite clear that there was no damage suffered by her from anything that she did in what I call the first stage of the operation . . . The damage was suffered by her after she had realized that the attempt could not be carried out, and while she was trying to return to the ground.'

For these reasons the Court of Appeal held that she was not the author of her own calamity but that, in putting her foot, in her descent, on the rebelliously rotating toilet roll, she was guilty of a sufficient degree of contributory negligence to require her to bear one quarter of the blame for the accident. Is it not evident that

> The massive gates of Circumstance
> Are turned upon the smallest hinge?

Brilliant Cross-Examinations

It was in 1962 that one of the greatest of the English legal giants, Lord Birkett, P.C., a potent yet gentle magician of the spoken word, went to his rest. Norman Birkett died suddenly only two days after making a compelling speech in the House of Lords which, as a result, turned aside one of our modern Juggernauts, the powerful Manchester Corporation, from overrunning the wild natural beauties of Ullswater in the Lake District, by converting it into a reservoir.

He is known everywhere as one of the judges of the Nuremberg Tribunal. He is famed, as was his almost inevitable opponent, Sir Patrick Hastings, as one of the two greatest crossexaminers of his age. And, following his relatively early retirement from the bench his mellifluous voice over the radio weaned millions from all kinds of other programmes.

His construction of a simple sentence, his diction, the timbre of his speech, were spell-binding. He could compel men to think the way he wished them to do because he fully understood the workings of the mind of the ordinary man. Small wonder is it that one judge once said that his powers of persuasion 'were a positive menace to the administration of justice' – although he was universally acknowledged to be the straightest and fairest of advocates. He was at once correct but compelling, scrupulously restrained, but devastating, courteous and sincere, but irresistible.

Although primarily renowned as a defender, Norman Birkett's most famous role was probably that of the prosecutor of Alfred Arthur Rouse for murder in the early 1930s. In the small hours of a winter's day a remote English country lane was lit up by the flames from a burning car. When the blaze died down, the charred corpse of a man was found inside. The car was Rouse's, but it turned out that the body was not. Rouse was a commercial traveller who, as the embarrassed putative father of a number of children, scattered around England and Wales, might well have conveniently disappeared, and the prosecution alleged that he had deliberately undone a brass nut in the car's engine so as to allow petrol to leak out between the tank and the carburettor and thus cause a fire, which he had started, to burn with extreme intensity.

A crucial witness for the defence was a supposed expert, an automobile engineer, who was called to refute the suggestion about the intentional loosening of the brass nut. Norman Birkett rose to cross-examine him and asked, in his most mellifluous and cordial tone:

'What is the co-efficient of expansion of brass?'

'I don't know', replied the *soi-disant* expert.

This was the first and only and completely discrediting question in the cross-examination which I shall return to later.

Such unpretentious methods are a thousand Lord Chancellor's feet away from those employed not too long ago, as exemplified by my old friend, Mr Dooley.[9] You may remember that his 'distinguished barrister' asked a wretched witness: ' "To begin with ar-re ye or ar-re ye not a man iv th' most dissolute morals?" "Answer yes or no", says th' Coort. "He admits it", says th' lawyer. "Ye were dhrunk in 1892?" "I can't

raymimber', says th' millyionaire. "Put it down that he's always
dhrunk", says th' lawyer. "Where did ye get ye'er money? Ye
don't know? Th' jury will take note iv th' fact that he prob'bly
stole it. Ye're father is dead. Did ye kill him? I think so . . . " '
and so forth.

It has been judicially stated[10] that 'it is only by cross-
examination that a witness's evidence can be properly tested,
and it loses much of its effectiveness in counsel's hands if the
witness is given time to think out the answer to awkward
questions; the very gist of cross-examination lies in the
unbroken sequence of question and answer'.

But occasionally, very occasionally, the first question,
even though it be drawn as a bow at a venture, can be
devastating, as it was with Birkett's at the Rouse trial. It may
prove to have an irresistible penetrability. It may, of course, fall
short, even in the hands of a master. 'Questions', wrote Lord
Birkett, 'should not be asked at random. They should have a
clear purpose behind them'.

Think of the poisoner, Seddon, who, three quarters of a
century ago, killed his spinster lodger with arsenic got from
soaked flypapers for the sake of terminating not only her life but
also an annuity on her life which he had not long before arranged
in exchange for a few golden sovereigns.

'Did you *like* her?'

Did he, Seddon, *like* poor, sick Miss Barrow? This was
not the first, but the second question put quietly and courte-
ously in cross-examination by Sir Rufus Isaacs to the murderer
in reference to his victim.

'Did you *like* her?

'Did I like her?' repeated Seddon, licking his dry white
lips, whilst he tried to gather his thoughts, then hesitated, and
eventually broke down.

If he had answered 'Yes', how could he have explained
away the miserable pauper's funeral that he had arranged for

her? If he had said, 'No' – well, perhaps, he would have been a little safer if he had said, 'No'. Nevertheless, the question posed a Morton's fork.

The first question? It was Sir John Simon who, in all kinds of exceedingly complex issues touching company frauds, nearly always opened his cross-examination of the principal witness by asking, in a sweetly reasonable way:

'Was this an *ordinary* business transaction?'

Always, the witness was placed upon a Morton's fork by such a simple, but cogent, question.

The first question! In the original trial of Oscar Wilde for criminal libel the very first question a legal giant of an earlier generation, Sir Edward Carson, asked the defendant in cross-examination, was:[11]

'You stated that your age was 39. I think you are over 40? You were born on the 16th October, 1854?'

Wilde (staccato): 'I have no wish to pose as being young. I am 39 or 40. You have my certificate and that settles the matter'.

Carson: 'But being born in 1854 makes you more than 40?'

Wilde: 'Ah! Very well'.

This opening exchange enabled Carson to lead up to the age of Lord Alfred Douglas, the son of the defendant, whose dubious association with Wilde was the root cause behind the three notorious trials. But it did more. It discredited Wilde, although in a slight way, from the start. And it exposed him as a poseur – he himself introduced the word 'pose'.

Almost at the culmination of the ensuing two days of cross-examination, during which Wilde, for the most part, more than held his own, Carson asked him a simple question about Walter Grainger, a waiter, aged 16.

Carson: 'Did you ever kiss him?'

Wilde: 'Oh, dear no. He was a peculiarly plain boy. He

was, unfortunately, extremely ugly. I pitied him for it'.

Carson: *'Was that the reason why you did not kiss him?'*

Wilde: 'Oh, Mr Carson, you are pertinently insolent'.

Carson: 'Did you say that in support of your statement that you never kissed him?'

Wilde: 'No. It is a childish question'.

Carson: 'Did you ever put that forward as a reason why you never kissed the boy?'

Wilde: 'Not at all'.

Carson: 'Why, sir, did you mention that this boy was extremely ugly?'

Wilde: 'For this reason. If I were asked why I did not kiss a door-mat, I should say because I do not like to kiss door-mats. I do not know why I mentioned that he was ugly, except that I was stung by the insolent question you put to me . . . '.

Six times more Carson ruthlessly put his question in different forms until he had unnerved Wilde. So, after two days, the bubble of Wilde's banter was burst in two minutes. Even so, who can deny the value of the first question?

Some years after Sir Edward Carson had left the bar he returned to the courts for the purpose of hearing young Norman Birkett cross-examine a certain Captain Peter Wright who had brought a libel action against the son of Lord Gladstone (the famous Liberal peer) for whom Birkett was appearing. The second Lord Gladstone had called Wright a liar and a coward because he had alleged that the Grand Old Man, whilst affecting, in his public life, to have the highest principles, was leading an immoral life in private. Carson watched Birkett cross-examine the plaintiff for over ten hours, spread over two and a half days, a brilliant effort which resulted in victory for his client and a complete vindication of the high moral qualities of the G.O.M. Despite this, Carson thought that Birkett should have asked the plaintiff just three questions before sitting down.

These were:

Q: 'Have you a Mother?'
A: 'Yes'.
Q: 'Do you love her?'
A: 'Yes'.
Q: 'Would you have said the same things about your mother that you said about Mr Gladstone?'

It is, of course, problematical whether even the great Carson would, by this means, have succeeded as did the youthful Birkett by a longer route. Personally, I believe that Carson over-simplified the possibilities of cross-examination in this context.

These true accounts remind me how adept that old egg, Humpty Dumpty, was at cross-examination. He had to deal with a bright, straight-forward little girl of seven or eight and he took a 'Dooleyish' advantage of her childish innocence when he said:[12]

" 'However, this conversation is going on a little too fast: let's go back to the last remark but one'.

'I'm afraid I can't quite remember it', Alice said very politely.

'In that case we may start afresh', said Humpty Dumpty, 'and it's my turn to choose a subject – ' ('He talks about it just as if it were a game!' thought Alice).

'So here's a question for you. How old did you say you were?'

Alice made a short calculation, and said, 'Seven years and six months'.

'Wrong!' Humpty Dumpty exclaimed triumphantly. 'You never said a word like it'.

'I thought you meant "How old *are* you?" ' Alice explained.

'If I'd meant that, I'd have said it', said Humpty Dumpty. "

Thousands of famous cross-examinations have followed

that pattern. But to return to the Rouse trial, consider what was the clear purpose behind Norman Birkett's very first question.

'What is the co-efficient of expansion of brass?'

Many years after he had posed that vital question, Lord Birkett was invited to say what would have been his next question if the automobile engineer, who so badly fluffed the first one, had given the answer correctly.[13]

" 'What (he actually asked) is the co-efficient of expansion of brass?'

The witness might have answered : '0.0000189'.

Birkett (supposing the witness had so answered): 'And copper?'

Witness: 'A little less, I think, but I am not certain of the exact figure'.

Birkett: 'And aluminium?'

Witness: 'I don't recall it at the moment but my diary will soon tell me'.

Birkett: 'Please don't trouble. Let us go to more important things . . .' ".

But in fact, as I have said, the first question proved to be a winner.

Watery Molly & Other Simple Fees

If Geoffrey Chaucer is to be believed, in the fourteenth century the transfer of land and houses was as easy and as certain a process as it has ever been in the history of the world. I so say because he wrote about his Sergeant of the Law that:

'Al was fee simple to him in effect,
His purchasing mighte nat been infect.'

No one, in short, could impugn the title of a purchaser for whom he, as a reasonably competent professional adviser, had acted. And, when all is said and done, what could be simpler and more certain than the ancient ritual of feoffment with livery of seisin? The man who was selling what we now call virgin land invited his purchaser to the site and in the presence of witnesses (who, in the future, and in case of dispute, might become what we now call jurors) solemnly handed over a sod of turf, with appropriate words, in token of the whole field. A twig represented an orchard; a clap and hopper, a corn mill; a net, fishing rights; a horseshoe and nails, a forge; a sheaf of wheat, the title to tithes; and, in the case of a dwelling-house, the seller clasped the knocker on the door. With the appropriate symbol in his hand he would say, 'Enter into this house (or orchard, or forge) and God give you joy.'

Today, under the unregistered system of conveyancing, in places where it still subsists, you may discover a considerable variety in methods of transfer and great complexities are sometimes also to be found. For many years in the course of my work at H. M. Land Registry, I enjoyed a bird's eye view of unregistered conveyancing such as is available to no practising lawyer, and I have often been struck with the variations that occur from county to county, so much so that if, today, I were to be shown a conveyance from which all references to the location of the land had been obliterated, I believe I could tell whether it was situated in Essex or Middlesex, Yorkshire or Lancashire, Devon or Surrey. In Surrey the posthumous influence of Mr Tulk[14] is marked and most land is now heavily burdened with restrictive covenants. I remember once examining the title to a single dwellinghouse in the county of Surrey on which covenants running into some 20,000 words had been imposed by 27 separate deeds. In London, by contrast, restrictive covenants are almost unknown. In Manchester, for hundreds of years, land was seldom sold for cash. Instead, the consideration was nearly always a rentcharge, so that many titles are cluttered with overriding and improved rentcharges and a complicated tangle of numerous and recurring informal apportionments and exonerations, which scarcely any conveyancer in the south of England is able to comprehend.

Writing of the technicalities of conveyancing brings to mind a true story about that great English conveyancer, the late Sir Arthur Underhill. He was consulted by a solicitor from a village in the outback of Wales in the days before 1926 when, in unregistered conveyancing, it was necessary to use strict words of limitation in order to convey freehold land. In the idiosyncratic manner of those who, for a long while, have lived and worked in isolation from their professional brethren, this Welshman had, for no particular reason, over a period of 30 years or more, drawn every conveyance in favour of a purchaser 'in simple fee' instead of the customary 'in fee simple' and had got away with it – until, that is, a former client for whom he had acted on a purchase some years earlier, asked him to conduct a sale. Another solicitor, an Englishman, and, hence, by definition in this Welshman's book, a foreigner, from one of the big cities represented the purchaser and he objected that, at best, all the vendor had power to convey was a mere life interest. Indignant, and even cock-sure, this Welshman went all the way up to London to consult no less a person than Underhill himself.

'I'm afraid', said Sir Arthur, 'he's right'.

'But', protested the Welshman, 'I've been doing this all my life. No one has ever taken such a shabby point against me before and all I've done is to change the order of the words'.

'My dear sir', retorted the great man, 'what would *you* say if you had given me £50 to buy you a chestnut horse and I turned up with a horse chestnut?'

In some countries 'flying freeholds' (or flats) are thought to give rise to tiresome, if not insoluble, problems. I am thinking especially of South Africa where many lawyers claim that the law does not permit the horizontal division of land. (As if they had no underground mines there!) 'Flying freeholds' have been known in the Albany, in London, since at least 1803 and they are now such a commonplace here that many thousands of them are created every year and are registered at H. M. Land Registry. They cause no special difficulties.

But have you ever heard of a *moveable* freehold? I learned about this legal curiosity some 40 years ago but was a little incredulous about its existence. Later on, however, I had an opportunity of examining the title to one of three of these 'lot meadows' that exist in Oxfordshire – I doubt whether there are any others anywhere else. Their characteristic quality is that the ownership of the fee simple shifts from one plot to another each year, in a manner reminiscent of the Saxon and Norman systems of cultivation, where the common land of the manor was cultivated in strips by tenants in free socage (or even by villeins) for two years and then allowed to lie fallow for the third. Certainly these moveable freeholds are of exceedingly ancient origin and they appear to have been overlooked by those responsible for drafting the revolutionary Birkenhead Acts of 1922 to 1925.

Just outside Oxford, but within the city bounds, are three large meadows lying beside the River Thames, which is, of course, locally named the Isis. Parts of these fields produce good hay and, later on, grazing for cattle, but other parts are liable to flood so that the value of the land varies according to its distance from the river and, presumably, it was for the sake of fairness that, in ancient times, the owners agreed to draw lots annually in order to determine which portion of the total area should be allocated to them each year. At this point I must stress that there is no question of co-ownership: each owner is an absolute owner of the fee simple of a piece of land, the position of which changes yearly. The traditional method of allocation is quaint and is fully described in a lengthy and factual statutory declaration, which I have been privileged to read, and which was made some fifty or more years ago by one of the 'meadsmen' (as these owners are called) who had regularly attended the ceremony for forty earlier years. In passing: one of the Oxford Colleges (being, of course, a corporation) is a meadsman.

Each field is divided into three parts which are bounded by grass tracks. Each part is, in turn, divided into thirteen strips of equal area which can be identified on the ground. Originally there must have been thirteen owners and the ownership of each of them was represented by a ball, made of cherry wood, slightly smaller than a modern golf ball, with a name painted on it. The names of the balls are William of Bladon, Gilbert, Watery Molly, Geoffrey, Boat, Dunn, White, Parry, Harry, Boulton, Freeman, Green and Rothe. Today, there are still thirteen balls, but not necessarily thirteen owners, for a meadsman may own (either through purchase or by inheritance) more than one ball, or even a part of a ball.

On a certain day in July every year, the balls are brought from a nearby farmhouse in a bag and a long procession of meadsmen, attendant labourers and onlookers makes its way to a corner of strip No. 1 of the first division in a field known as Oxhey Mead. The meadsman with the bag of balls holds it up so that the contents cannot be seen and someone – perhaps a distinguished visitor – is invited to draw the first ball. If, for example, he draws Watery Molly, the man holding the bag verifies the fact and he calls out, 'Watery Molly'. Then the meadsman who owns that ball or, more usually, his agent or employee, steps forward and claims 'I am Watery Molly' and, taking up a scythe, he cuts a few feet of hay on the first strip. Next with a knife he cuts his initials: or those of his master) in the turf laid bare by the scythe. A number of those present then walk in single file down the sides of strip no. 1, tracing its exact boundaries by trampling down the hay and revealing the corner posts.

Then the next ball is drawn. 'William of Bladon'. 'I am William of Bladon'. Again the corner of the plot is scythed, the initials cut, and the boundaries trodden and so the process continues until all thirteen strips in the first division have been allocated. All the balls are then returned to the bag and the thirteen strips of the second division are allocated similarly. Finally, the third division is shared out and that completes the annual ceremony at Oxhey Mead and the mowing of the hay begins. After the last Monday in August, Oxhey Mead is stocked and the ownership of each of the thirteen balls carries with it the right to graze fourteen head of horned cattle over the entire field.

At one time two other adjoining fields were also dealt with by similar methods on the same day and I can imagine that it would be a lengthy and thirst-provoking business on a sultry

English July afternoon. It is therefore amusing to read in the statutory declaration I mentioned above that 'it is a tradition in the village that originally Oxhey Mead, West Mead and Pixey Mead were drawn for on the same day till the time of a certain vicar of Yaraton, who succeeded, about the year 1817, in securing Oxhey and West Mead should be drawn for on different days, mainly because of the numbers of mowers that were brought by the single drawing into the parish, such mowers being Irish, and the drunkenness and fighting that followed at the end of the day'.

There are, of course, many other oddities in conveyancing methods in other parts of our country. There is one ultra-simple form of landholding that is occasionally found in the remoter parts of the county of Essex where they have no deeds and never go to the trouble and expense of employing a solicitor. The tenure of the land is sometimes referred to as 'Keyhold', for the vendor merely hands over the keys of his cottage to the purchaser in return for cash. They have almost got back to the pristine simplicity of the feoffment with livery of seisin and the purchaser is quite secure – unless, of course, the vendor tries to go back on his bargain, or the purchaser attempts to sell the land on the open market!

An Upset Cup of Tea

Australia is a thirsty, as well as being (or, more likely, because of being) a sunburnt country and Australians are renowned as drinkers, often of ice-cool beer but not least as drinkers of tea which, as Thomas de Quincey once remarked, 'will always be the favourite beverage of the intellectual'. Tea is a wonderful *refocillant* and any self-respecting tea drinker must shudder at the notion of Samuel Pepys drinking chocolate in the morning to revive himself after having, in his phrase, come home 'foxed' the night before. Not that the refocillative qualities of this refreshing, cheering, uninebriating liquid, tea, render it merely a substitute for Alka-Seltzer.

This is the simple story of an upset cup of tea over which tears were spilled in two courts.[15] The scene is a remote village in Westmorland where, some quarter of a century ago, there was one of those vestigial curiosities of the English educational system – a village infant school wherein twenty children between the ages of five and eleven were, in a single room, divided into three classes, presided over by a single schoolmistress. This worthy spinster, enjoying near anonymity in the name of Jones, had the sole care of her pupils throughout a long day.

29

Her only means of transport, a little local bus, took her into the village at eight o'clock in the morning although the children did not arrive until nine. At one o'clock some of them went over to the village hall for their lunch and Miss Jones devotedly gave up her own free hour to looking after them and then, from 2 p.m. onwards, took up her teaching duties again until it was time to go home.

In these circumstances it is scarcely surprising that her employers, the Westmorland County Council, allowed her to make herself an occasional cup of tea. Although, tea-drinking spinsters are often associated with tittle-tattle –

'Her tea she sweetens, as she sips, with scandal . . . '

– in Miss Jones' case it was a pure desire for refocillation that drove her to tea and the county council, in view of her many responsibilities, not to mention some measure of self-sacrifice on her part, quite properly allowed her the use of an electric kettle.

One warm June afternoon, no doubt with a sense of relief, she put the kettle on to boil whilst the children were out at their break. Little Janet, aged six, stayed in because she wanted to read to her teacher. Although this might sound like an act of childish self-ingratiation, the learned judge who later on had to consider Miss Jones' tea drinking, called it 'a homely little scene'. Then, realizing that the children might be boisterous on returning to their classroom, the worthy Miss Jones switched off the kettle before calling them in from play.

In they trooped and she made them sit down in their places before actually making her tea. This she did – and I can't believe that it was a good cup of tea – by pouring the water, presumably no longer boiling, straight on to the leaves in her cup.

She was going to wait for it to brew before adding milk and she drew the cup towards the front of a four-foot-high cupboard on which it stood. This was natural enough for she was not tall and it would enable her to pour in the milk more easily. She had her hand on the cupboard, near to the cup of tea, when young George came up and had to be corrected and whilst she was dealing with him, dear little Janet sidled up behind Miss Jones, crept underneath her arm, turned round and put up her hand.

How often a child who is seeking to be noticed, hugs an adult's skirts and pushes and insinuates herself into the limelight in just this way, twisting from side to side! Alas! Poor Janet's hand was caught in the saucer and tipped it up. The cup fell over. And the hot tea cascaded over her arm, and neck and scalded her. The whole incident reads just like one of those moral tales for Victorian little dears – something rather less severe, perhaps, than the story of Augustus (who wouldn't take his soup and faded away), or Johnnie (who sucked his thumb and had it cut off), or Matilda (who played with matches and was reduced to a heap of ashes).

Be all that as it may, the thought of scalding tea sent my thoughts scurrying back to a scene eleven years earlier when I was charmed by a crocodile hunter into leaving the relative security of The Alice (Alice Springs, in the centre of the dead heart of Australia) and travelling to Darwin with him. I had already 'gorped' (as our friends in Yorkshire say) at the sight of some stark naked aborigines on walkabout as they stalked, almost majestically, at the roadside, clasping their twelve-foot spears at their shoulders and carrying their woomeras and thuruntha yunthas (with which to launch their spears) in the other hand. Then, after some hours of thirsty travel northwards – for it was in the first mid-summer week of January – we came upon three young men who were collecting dingo pelts. Whatever may be the position today, even those few years ago the hazards of life in the friendly Northern Territory demanded that we should stop and pass the time of day with them. They were, inevitably, boiling a billy and into it one of them threw two enormous fistfuls of tea leaves, which were then allowed to boil for the ensuing quarter of an hour, being occasionally stirred with the plyers with which the steaming can was handled. As the liquid grew blacker (almost to the point where you could stand a spoon upright in it, as in sergeant-major's tea!) we got thirstier and thirstier, until someone added a handful of gum leaves to the sizzling liquid which was then dispensed to us all. I was by then so parched that I would have gladly swallowed anything wet. Yet I felt something of a ninny because, dry as I was, my mug was so hot that I could not even manage to hold it in my hands, although the others were already refocillating themselves, putting their lips to their mugs and sipping the steaming brew. My friends – God bless them! – were gently pulling the leg of an unsuspecting 'pommy' by handing him a tin mug whilst they themselves cheerfully and successfully drank out of far cooler enamel ones!

But to continue with Janet and Miss Jones. Janet, by her father, sued the Westmorland County Council in negligence and, in the assize court, was awarded, by today's standards, considerable damages. The suggestion that the defendants were negligent in letting Miss Jones make tea in the classroom was quickly dropped but the judge held that, although Miss Jones was not negligent in making the tea, she was negligent in putting her cup so near to the edge of the cupboard.

In the Court of Appeal, Lord Denning, Master of the Rolls, said that it was agreed that the test to be applied to Miss Jones was that of a reasonably careful parent in the same situation, with this difference, that she would be a reasonably careful parent with a family of twenty. Miss Jones had agreed that if she had gone away from the cupboard it would have been wrong to have left the cup so near its edge. But she was actually on the spot and her hand was outstretched to the cup. She could not reasonably have anticipated that Janet would squeeze under her arm, turn round, and pull down the scalding liquid.

'I can understand (said his Lordship) that if a mother had

been the unwitting cause of such an injury to her child she might blame herself and say, "I can't forgive myself for leaving that cup of tea like that". But anyone standing alongside would surely say, "You cannot blame yourself. How could you have thought that the little girl would come up like that?" ' It was a pure accident and the conscientious and careful Miss Jones was not to blame.

I have no doubt that when a greatly relieved Miss Jones heard the result of this appeal she straightaway refocillated herself with a nice cup of tea whilst reflecting, perhaps, in the words of T. S. Eliot, that –

> Youth is cruel, and has no remorse
> And smiles at situations which it cannot see.
> I smile, of course,
> And go on drinking tea.

Embranglement

Words! I don't know nearly as much about them as I should like to but I do love their infinite variety of shape, colour and purpose. They are the tools of the lawyer's trade, whether as advocate bent upon persuading other people, as judge resisting over-persuasiveness, as draftsman of statutes, striving to pin down the exactitude of an idea, or merely as humble practitioner seeking to impart a modicum of comfort and common sense to some poor bewildered and, perhaps, inarticulate layman.

I should like to bring to the reader's notice, the word 'brangle', and may I say at once that it is just as easily comprehensible as the simple statement –

Twas brillig, and the slithy toves
Did gyre and gimble in the wabe;
All mimsy were the borogroves
And the mome raths outgrabe.

A simple statement? Of course it is. It was written by an imaginative man for an imaginative little girl who fortunately never had the chance to be intellectually telly-paralysed and who, in consequence, felt, even if she did not perceive, precisely what the author meant. Those of you who go in for litigation will have sensed, long before you have read thus far, just what embranglements are, for you have witnessed so many of them. Some of your clients become involved in them because, in their commercial documents, they use words which, according to the late Lord Wright, 'could not be regarded as other than inartistic and might appear repellent to the trained sense of an equity draftsman'.[16] Even so, as Lord Simonds once observed in a case where an important business transaction had been carried through in a manner 'too indulgently described as slapdash', 'No doubt there are rules or canons of construction applicable to careless and slovenly, as to other, documents'.[17]

Although the Oxford English Dictionary labels 'brangle' as obsolete except in dialect use, it gives its origin as a combination of a brawl and a wrangle. It may have some kinship with a 'branle', that is, a wavering. 'Embranglement', of course, is the sort of perplexity that Alice suffered from when, in trying to walk towards the Red Queen, she lost sight of her in a moment so that only when, a little provoked, she drew back and started walking in the opposite direction, she found herself face to face with Her Majesty.

I fancy some of us lawyers occasionally find ourselves in a similar predicament when, ignoring the wonders of modern technology, we overlook the fact that the Clapham omnibus (with our inalienable friend, the reasonable man aboard) has a reverse gear.

Perhaps Lord Bramwell was suffering from self-embranglement when, in considering one of his earlier judgments in a later case, he said: 'The matter does not appear to me now as it appeared to appear to me then'. But seeing that the O.E.D. appears to sneer at dialect, I will indulge in it by saying that it wouldn't be jollick to pursue the point too far.

'Jollick', by the way, is current usage for 'descent' in the wonderful county of Dorset. They are real people down there and I know a small village where the words over their war memorial read simply in the local dialect:

'Do'set men doan't shame their kind.'

I have mentioned the O.E.D. The so-called Shorter edition in two fat tomes is frequently quoted in court in preference to the vaster complete work that fully fills a long shelf, and in the House of Lords, in a rating case concerning a temple of the Latter-Day Saints (or Mormon Church), Lord Evershed was content to rely on the Shorter dictionary for the meaning of the word 'worship' in relation to a place of 'public religious worship'. [18] A correspondent of *The Times* complained that whereas the Shorter O.E.D. 'has its uses in the home as a compact work of reference for those addicted to scrabble and other word games', he deplored its use 'as the definitive source for the elucidation of a meaning in our highest court of law'. Incidentally, I should hate to play a game of scrabble founded upon such a weighty work! Yet, as another correspondent has pointed out, the definition of 'worship' in the Shorter edition 'is precisely the same, to the last syllable and comma, as that in the Oxford English Dictionary', although the latter devotes four and a half columns of 'ripe scholarship' to the meanings of 'worship'.

But to return to brangling, the successful lawyer always avoids becoming embrangled. Yet if there is no other way out of a difficulty he may seek to put others into a branglement. Techniques have changed over the years and I am reminded of some of the old methods of pleading that were employed before the Judicature Act 1873 came into force.

A certain Mr Karslake once acted for a trustee who had foolishly parted with trust moneys at the instance of an unusually importunate female beneficiary who was subject to a restraint upon anticipation. In drafting the interrogatories he asked:

'Did not the defendant fall down upon her knees, or on one, and which one of them, and implore the plaintiff with tears in her eyes, or in one, and which one of them, to advance the said or some other and what sum of money, or how otherwise?'

Then there was a famous lawyer (his name escapes me)

who, in a paternity suit concerning twins, pleaded on behalf of the putative father that 'he denies that he is the father of the said children or of either of them'. Surely men with such forethought and fastidious carefulness of language would never allow themselves to become embrangled.

Finally, I should like to tell you *pour encourager les autres* (I am not, like Voltaire, being sarcastic) how, as an inexperienced young solicitor, I had an encounter with a brangler. I suppose that sooner or later most young lawyers come up against the pompous bully who seeks to beat them down and embroil them by the sheer weight of his words. I met such a one, easily old enough to be my father, and it was not long before I realized instinctively, not only that his law was shaky, but that he was propping up his spurious arguments with exceedingly long words which were supposed to impress me. I confess I did not then know the meanings of all of them. Nor, I began to suspect, did he. During a pause, I asked him with a boldness which, even at this distance of time, gives me a slightly prickly feeling:

'But don't you think we ought to aim at complete *dirapulative nugency?*'

The trap closed. His instant agreement revealed his fraudulent state of mind. The phrase was, of course, an utterly meaningless invented sound, straight off my rather dirty cuff.

If you don't like my resuscitation of old words, at least they are better than some of the pretentious new ones. Personally, even after some thirty or forty years, I have failed to become reconciled to rodent extermination executives, refuse officers, and lady cleansing operatives. Even the old solicitor's managing clerk (with certain differences, it is true) has become a legal executive and now our milkman is in danger of being turned into a mere milk purveyor. And in one of the United States of America the local cop has suffered transmogrification into a community relations officer.

A Testamentary Tangle

The humerus and ulna of coincidence may not be as lengthy as people suspect.

In 1956 a young doctor named Rowland was appointed as a medical officer in the South Pacific where, as he knew, he would be required to travel in small ships to numerous islands in the archipelagos. He was twenty-nine and his wife, who had been a nurse, twenty-six, and before leaving England they made their wills. For this purpose they bought printed forms which contained the words, '*The Barrister Will Form is strictly protected by copyright*', but, as the Master of the Rolls observed some years later, if the use of the word 'barrister' was intended as a recommendation to induce people to make their own wills, it would be better ignored.

Dr Rowland had only something under £3,000 to dispose of and he left it all to his wife. He went on to state: 'In the event of the decease of [my wife] preceding or coinciding with my own decease I give and bequeath all my estate to [other relatives].' Mrs Rowland had only some £20 to £30 to dispose of and she left it all to her husband, and went on to say that in the event of her husband's death 'preceding or coinciding with' her own she left all her estate to her brother's child.

In passing, presumably this printed will form was drafted by a member of the English bar, in which case he had at his command the inexhaustible riches of the English language, susceptive of exactitude as they are. Why then (in view of the undoubted intention of the parties) could he not have used some such phrase as: 'If my wife shall predecease me, or if she shall die within [three] months after my death, then in either of these events, etc.'? – words which are well recognized as meaning what they say.

But to continue: in July 1958, Dr and Mrs Rowland, in the course of duty, left a village in the Solomon Islands as passengers in the *Melanesian*, a vessel of only 130 tons, bound for a distant atoll. The following day this little ship radioed her position. Thereafter, there was silence. Nothing more is known of her save that one body (out of 64 persons on board) was subsequently found with a lifeboat, a raft, some lifebuoys and many pieces of wreckage. At a subsequent commission of inquiry there was evidence that the only body recovered had died, not from drowning but from some other cause, such as loss of blood from being eaten by a shark. Death in those waters does not normally occur from cold or exposure but rather from being eaten by fish, and the conclusion of the commission was that the *Melanesian* sank suddenly with all hands.

It was in these circumstances that, in February 1962, Mr Justice Buckley held that the deaths of Dr and Mrs Rowland did not 'coincide'. Subsequently (in a case never officially reported) the Court of Appeal was invited to upset his judgment.

In this connexion it is noteworthy that in 1925 Parliament enacted[19] that, in all cases where . . . two or more persons have died in circumstances rendering it uncertain which of them survived the other or others, such deaths shall (subject to any order of the court), for all purposes affecting the title to property, be presumed to have occurred in order of seniority, and accordingly the younger shall be deemed to have survived the elder'. The words in parenthesis are important; they indicate that the court may hold that deaths were simultaneous or occurred in a different order from that described in the section.

The clear purpose of the above presumption was to avoid the inconclusiveness that had bedevilled a number of earlier cases. For example, in October 1853 a man and his wife and their three children were bound for Australia in the emigrant ship *Dalhousie* when she was wrecked off Beachy Head. The sole and fortunate living witness of this catastrophe testified to having seen all five of them swept by a wave off the quarter deck into the sea. The question of survivorship was an important one in relation to the wills previously made by the husband and wife, and a doctor gave evidence that regardless of age, or sex, or indeed, health, asphyxia would have killed all of them at the same instant. Yet the court held that in the absence of positive evidence of survivorship the matter was incapable of being determined,[20] although I should imagine that the man in the street – for whose benefit all laws are ostensibly made – would have found it impossible to doubt that all members of the family died simultaneously. He would, perhaps, have been less clear in his mind about the case of the husband and wife in the *Melanesian* which was presumed to have been lost at sea with all on board, where there was no jot of evidence about the nature of the calamity which overtook her and her passengers and crew.[21] Still less would he have been dogmatic about the instant of death in the case of the missionaries (also husband and wife) who were believed to have perished in a general massacre of all foreigners carried out in North China on the 9th July 1900.[22]

One might be forgiven for imagining that the statutory presumption I have quoted would have provided an ideal solution to problems concerning the order of deaths due to enemy bombing during World War II. Not so. It is true that when a man and his wife were sleeping in the same room during an air raid and, after the explosion of a bomb, only scattered remnants of their bodies were found, it was held that they had died simultaneously,[23] yet in other incidents where the corpses were discovered intact, although suffering from multiple injuries, the courts held that it was impossible to say that the deaths occurred at the same instant.[24] In cases of these kinds 'the basis of belief may range from mere conjecture through all degrees of probability to absolute demonstration – possibility, probability, certainty'.[25] Even in the House of Lords, where the macabre instancy of the decapitation of two men by the knife of a double guillotine was argued, the law lords failed, by two to three, to set the seal of certainty on the bombing problem.[26] As Lord Justice Harman put it: 'Those angels reputed by the schoolmen to be able to dance on the point of a needle made their appearance.'

But to return to Dr and Mrs Rowland, Lord Justice Russell considered that the normal and natural meaning of 'coinciding with' was 'simultaneous', so that Dr Rowland's references to 'preceding' and 'coinciding' in his will were merely a verbose reference to 'not surviving'. If the evidence had been that the two of them were below decks in their cabin and the vessel plunged abruptly to the bottom of the sea (he said) the view might be taken that their deaths were, metaphysics apart, coincident in point of time. But he simply did not know what had happened to them. Counsel had suggested that this testator had meant something wider, such as 'on the same occasion and by the same cause', but his lordship considered the problem, not as one of Dr Rowland's possible intention, but of the language actually used by him. His phrases meant the same whether he and his wife travelled daily between Sussex and London by the same train or car, or sailed at Cowes together, or were doctors in a fever-ridden area, or missionaries among cannibals, or lived beneath the slopes of an eruptive Mount Etna, or simply lived quietly under the shadow of nuclear warfare.

Lord Justice Harman remarked that it was not even

known at what date, within a week, the *Melanesian* went down, nor was the whereabouts of either Dr Rowland or his wife at that time certain. One or other of them might easily have survived the sinking of the ship, and the event was too uncertain to infer a simultaneous death. Although it had been attractively argued that the testator and his wife, by setting out on the adventure offered by this post in the Southern Pacific, contemplated the very event of a common calamity, that was not the event for which their wills provided. The Court of Appeal accordingly held that their deaths did not 'coincide'.

This decision caused some sharp and stinging barbs to be loosed off in the press against lawyers so that, even in the dignified columns of *The Times*, one incensed correspondent complained that 'the average layman believes that the law is made for lawyers' and that 'if lawyers are so smugly content with such an astonishing decision it seems that, whatever the danger, the layman must rush in'. Another wrote: ' . . . It is not for nothing that a judge has anticipated arriving on the other side and meeting, not the sound of trumpets, but the stony glances of frustrated testators.' And another: 'The intention of the testator was so clear that the meaning he attributed to the word "coincide" could not reasonably be misunderstood.' Yet another wrote of 'the legal mind, keen for ambiguity, sensitive to the possible effects of a precedent'. And another, writing about the impact of equity upon the common law, remarked, not without some mixture of metaphor, that 'after a few centuries, the arthritis of the host common law was fully communicated to the commensal equity and parliament declared the two systems to be jointly fossilized by the Judicature Act, 1873. Since then there has been little room for intelligent common sense and any layman who approaches our courts with a problem of interpretation casts his bread upon the waters. It rarely returns'.

Jibes like these were scarcely aimed at Lord Denning for, in a dissenting judgment, he disassociated himself from the view that if deaths are separated by any measurable interval, even by so much as a few seconds, they do not 'coincide'. Counsel had argued that a couple might die simultaneously in an airplane which exploded in mid-air but not in one which hit a mountain side, killing everyone in it. If ever there was an absurdity this was one. The supporters of that argument invoked as their authority the ordinary man. Such a man (so Lord Denning thought) would be amazed to find such a view attributed to him. The fallacy of it seemed to be that it proceeded on the assumption that in construing a will, one had to consider *not what the testator meant, but what the meaning of his words was* (my italics!). That might be the nineteenth-century view, but it had been the cause of many mistakes. The whole object of construing a will was to find out the intention of the testator in order to see that his property was disposed of in the way he wished.

Thus once again Lord Denning who, after five years as a law lord, was, by way of demotion in 1962, appointed Master of the Rolls, demonstrated that he preferred a common-sense approach to legalistic logic. His demotion to a sphere of wider influence certainly worried some lawyers who live by splitting hairs. But of course no difficulties about testamentary dispositions would ever arise if only laymen would take the trouble to consult *competent* lawyers.

TAILPIECE

When Lord Denning's appointment as Master of the Rolls was announced his wife was asked by a friend, 'Which part of the country do they hunt in?'

The Wayfarer's Dole

'Please may I have the Wayfarer's Dole?' I begged, poking my head through the hatch at the porter's lodge in the ancient, square, four-storeyed gatehouse of the Hospital of St Cross, a couple of miles or so outside the City of Winchester.

'And please may *I* have the Wayfarer's Dole?'

My companion, an eminent Australian silk, faithfully repeated the words which, for over 800 years, have ensured that every traveller who passes that way shall have, on demand, a horn of smooth brown ale and a hunk of home-made white bread of a wholesomeness far surpassing that of the insipid steam-baked loaves which all too many shops commonly supply. St. Cross is one of our oldest charities.

In our Welfare State many thousands of minor local charities of great antiquity still survive. Often, in years past, while perusing title deeds, I have come across a perpetual annual rentcharge in terms such as these:

'Thirteen shillings and sixpence halfpenny a yeare to provide 2 dozen wheaten loaves each Sunday and a broiling fowle atte Christmas for 6 poore widows of this parish for ever . . .'

44

So then let me take you with me and my Australian friend to Winchester, by turns a Celtic stronghold, a Roman city, and, subsequently, the capital in which many Kings from Canute to the Angevins held their Courts and their Parliaments. Entering by the West Gate from the roof of which, when requisite, the city's fourteenth-century defenders poured molten lead upon their beseigers, we saw the bare remains that Cromwell's heavy artillery left of the fortress built by the Conqueror. From here, Rufus started out upon his last fatal hunt in the New Forest. His bones lie in the nearby cathedral, together with the arrow that killed him. To this place came Richard the Lionheart after his captivity abroad. Here, in the great hall, where Her Majesty's judges still hold their Courts of Assize, there hangs, high above the bench, a vast circular table divided into segments painted with the names of twenty-four Knights and reputed, though doubtfully, to be the very Round Table of King Arthur himself. Here, in the wall, is a 'King's ear' – a cunningly contrived little tunnel through the thick masonry which enabled the King to listen from the ease of his private apartment to the debates of his Parliament. Leaving the castle, we passed God-Be-Got house which belonged to the wife of Ethelred the Unready (she later married the Dane, Canute) and so, in the precincts of the cathedral, came upon the gravestone of a young soldier whose death from a violent fever is commemorated in this doggerel –

Here sleeps in peace a Hampshire Grenadier
Who caught his death by drinking cold small Beer.
Soldiers be wise from his untimely fall
And when vere hot drink Strong or not at all.

When in course of time the memorial decayed, officers of the garrison erected a fresh stone –

An honest Soldier never is forgot
Whether he die by Musket or by Pot.

Within the cathedral we saw the six mortuary chests

which rest high up on the massive side screens that enclose the choir and contain fragments of the bones of many famous kings and bishops, some of whom died far more than a thousand years ago.

I had promised my companion that we should climb the tower of the cathedral, passing inside the vaulting of the nave, so as to see the original beams – each a whole oak trunk which, at a guess, I should say measured 3 × 3 feet square – that support the roof. Bishop Walkelin, who built the cathedral just after the Conquest to replace the existing church of A.D. 645, was desperately short of timber. Therefore, he approached King William I. In the result he was granted as much as he could fell and carry away from part of the royal forest in four days and nights. Full of guile, the bishop assembled every woodman up and down the country and with their help stripped the area bare except for a single tree – the Gospel Oak under which, even then, St Augustine was reputed to have preached. When next William rode past he was not amused by this trick.

Today, – in sharp contrast with earlier years – in this nice little, tight little, over-populated island it is not normally possible to get permission to wander at large in the labyrinth of an ancient building where one could so easily become lost. I approached first, an under-verger, then the head verger himself. They were short-handed; no guide could be provided. 'But', I explained in some desperation, 'my friend lives 12,500 miles away. We have specially come down today from London to explore your cathedral and he returns home next week. I myself know the route through the tower and nave. Can't we go up alone?' (Indeed, my brother and I were once conscripted to round up and collect in a safe place the vertigo-struck stragglers on a large conducted tour.) I was thankful as well as surprised when the great key was handed over to me.

Immediately, my Australian friend and I started to climb the steep, twisted stone steps of the spiral staircase in one of the

towers of the south transept, where there is scarcely room for a
man of normal stature to pass even when he stoops sideways,
and crept along the tiny passage, at triforium level to where I
knew the entrance to the tower was. Suddenly and unexpectedly
we came up against a bricked-up doorway where (I thought)
there should have been an opening. Thereafter for three
quarters of an hour, by a process of careful elimination, often in
darkness, we groped our way up every winding flight of well-
worn steps, through every narrow passage and every possible
opening in the rugged walls, striking matches now and then to
pierce the blackness, but all in vain. Dead ends everywhere! Hot
and somewhat shamefaced, I left my friend and returned to the
head verger to confess that I had lost my way. Without a word of
reproof he climbed back with me and set us on our way. Yet I
had been right the first time for if only I had turned sharply
aside at the original blank wall I should have been able to feel the
wooden door opening on to the belfry staircase at my side.

Afterwards, in the first real sunshine of that particular
year, my Australian friend and I walked the two miles to St
Cross, where we arrived feeling something like *bona fide*
travellers.

'Please may I have the Wayfarer's Dole?'

Whilst being served with our bread and ale we were
regaled with the story of how, in 1136, Bishop Henry of Blois (a
grandson of the Conqueror) founded this hospital for 'poor men,
feeble and so reduced in strength as rarely or never to be able to
raise themselves withouth another's aid,' who were to be given
'garments and beds suitable to their infirmities, good wheaten
bread daily of the weight of 5 marks, and three dishes at dinner
and one at supper, suitable to the day, and drink of good stuff'.
For good measure one hundred other indigent men and all
wayfarers were also provided for. To this day there are eighteen
inmates who, by reason of the colour of their mediaeval
garments, are called the Black Brothers. Besides them there are

nine Red Brothers who wear claret-coloured robes and who benefit from an additional foundation of Cardinal Beaufort (1445) of 'an almshouse of Noble Poverty' for those who 'once had everything handsome about them but . . . had loses'.

As we listened I was getting agitated, because my Australian friend was a teetotaller and we had pre-arranged that after he had taken the single sip of his ale that courtesy demanded, I should drink the remainder. The story went on and on and the hospitable porter showed no sign of leaving us alone. Then a brief turning of the back gave me my chance. Seizing my friend's ancient horn cup, I pushed my own empty horn towards him, and gulped down his drink in one long swallow.

The Disposal of Corpses . . . and Eyes

Perhaps twice in my life I have come across a novel in which a down-and-out student succeeds in persuading a benevolent hospital board to advance him £10 in return for the right to receive his corpse after death. But then, I am not a great reader of fiction. I wonder: does it happen in real life? Although I venture to think that it does not, it would be interesting, as an exercise in legal draftsmanship, to try to set down all the precautions that could and should be devised to ensure that eventually (in ten years' time? fifty years?) the anatomy school will receive, in proper condition and in due time, a decent, whole, healthy-for-preference, dissectable body.

One hundred and sixty or so years ago William Burke, a squat jumble dealer and hawker of rags and cat-skins, and William Hare, his gaunt ghoulish companion, and their two women, ensured that the Anatomy School in Edinburgh always had a plentiful supply of material for its students.

It was in 1827 that an old tenant of theirs died suddenly on their hands, owing £3 for rent – a mean way of behaving, which drove this avaricious pair half crazy with anger and despair, until, that is, one of them had the brainwave. No sooner had the undertaker nailed down the coffin than Burke and Hare prised it open, removed the contents (replacing a sack of bark) and sold them to Dr Knox for £7. 10s. 0d (or £7.50, in today's currency).

The recovery of their precious rent and, especially, the net profit of £4, suggested to their vulturine minds that they should immediately go in for the resurrectionist business and plunder graveyards in a big way, but they found an easier and safer means of obtaining saleable material. One after another an old man, an old woman, or sometimes a young woman, members of the floating population of the Scottish capital, were decoyed after nightfall into their miserable hovel, plied with liquor, suffocated or strangled, smuggled out, and their corpses sold for £8, £10 or even £14. It is said that one female victim, 'the possessor of a flawless body that was famous in the whole night life of Edinburgh', was recognized on the dissecting table by a student who, less than a week earlier, had spent the night with her. Despite this bizarre identification which might, so easily, have destroyed for ever the horrid trade of Burke and Hare, their business continued to flourish and success so drugged their senses that they began to work openly in daylight.

> Up the close and down the stair,
> But and ben with Burke and Hare,
> Burke's the butcher, Hare's the thief,
> Knox the boy that buys the beef.

When at last the ghastly evil was uncovered, for reasons of expediency, only Burke was brought to trial, even then complaining that Dr Knox owed him money on the last corpse.

Unquestionably, these body-snatchers helped to bring into being the Anatomy Act of 1832 which, in the language of literature, is introduced by a preamble that recites that: 'Whereas a knowledge . . . of healing and repairing divers wounds and injuries to which the human frame is liable cannot be acquired without the aid of anatomical examination: And whereas the legal supply of human bodies for such anatomical examination is insufficient fully to provide the means of such knowledge: And whereas, in order further to supply human bodies for such purposes, divers great and grievous crimes have been committed, and lately murder, for the single object of selling for such purposes the bodies of the persons so murdered . . .'

The law does not permit a man to dispose of his dead body by his will otherwise than in strict accordance with statute,[27] and this particular Act, under considerable safeguards, permits an executor or other person having lawful possession of the body of any deceased person, 'not being an undertaker or other person interested with the body for the purpose only of interment', to allow the corpse to undergo anatomical examination. But if the deceased in his lifetime expressed a contrary wish, or if the surviving husband or wife or any known relative requires the body to be buried without examination, then buried it must be. The statute also allows a person to direct an anatomical examination of his body after his death but there are many protective provisions and a body which is removed for examination must first 'be placed in a decent coffin, or shell' and eventually interred within six weeks of the date of removal 'in consecrated ground or in some public burial ground . . .'

So it comes about that the Royal College of Surgeons' Museum, next to which for 40 years I daily worked, and which contains many interesting specimens, is reputed to be a public burial ground.

Today, surgeons and research scientists find themselves severely hampered by the limitations of the Anatomy Act and there has been much talk of setting up a committee of leading doctors and lawyers to see what can be done to help those who do homografting – the grafting of living tissues from dead bodies on to live ones – and they want to be enabled to establish, not only skin banks, but also bone banks. One change in the law that has been suggested is that it should be made possible for doctors to invite a patient, on his entering hospital, to sign a *pro forma* authority disposing of his body absolutely in the event of his death, although I should have thought that psychologically such an approach might have an unsteadying effect on the patient on the eve of a serious operation and might breed an undue post-operational pessimism.

In the matter of eyes we have made some progress, as witness the Corneal Grafting Act 1952, which, on the one hand, provides that 'if any person, either in writing at any time or orally in the presence of two or more witnesses during his last illness, has expressed a request that his eyes be used for therapeutic purposes after his death, the party lawfully in possession of his body after his death may, unless he has reason to believe that the request was subsequently withdrawn, authorise the removal of the eyes from the body for those purposes'. On the other hand, the person lawfully in possession of the body may authorize the removal of the eyes unless he has reason to believe that the deceased had expressed an objection, or the surviving spouse or *any* surviving relative objects to that being done. In passing, it is interesting to note that from time to time one or two healthy living people offer one of their sound eyes in their lifetime to save the sight of other people.

> Full many a glorious morning have I seen
> Flatter the mountain-tops with sovereign eye,
> Kissing with golden face the meadows green,
> Gilding pale streams with heavenly alchemy.

A few brave people are willing to share such an experience at great personal cost with those less fortunate than themselves. But when, many years ago, a question was asked in the House of Commons on this point, the Parliamentary Secretary to the Ministry of Health replied: 'The law on the matter is not certain, but I am advised that it is at least possible that, for a surgeon deliberately to remove a sound eye from a living person, even with that person's consent, might be held to be a criminal offence. In any case, it seems most unlikely that surgeons would be willing to perform the operation.' And I would add that once the practice became sanctioned it is possible that some hideous commercial bargains could be struck.

On one occasion – again, many years ago – in the House of Lords, a noble lord called attention to the long list of patients awaiting cadaver eyes and asked whether, in the hope of increasing the number of donors, the government of the day would issue an explanatory leaflet to the public. For example, at Moorfields, the famous eye hospital, there is a waiting list of never less than 100 people who, through delay, are condemned to eighteen months of unnecessary blindness. The noble lord who replied pointed out the great difficulty and delicacy of the situation in going into a hospital and asking patients who are very ill whether they will give their eyes, because it is tantamount to suggesting that they are on the point of death. On the other hand, what happens at the moment is that a patient dies and before his healthy eyes can be used to give sight to the living blind – they must be excised within six hours of death – his relatives have to be asked for permission.

Thus, in one breath a bereaved mother or sister or wife has to be told of the death of the loved one and asked whether his eyes can be removed immediately. It puts the doctor in an unenviable position. Perhaps, as was suggested in the House, when people go into hospital and are asked to sign an agreement for post-mortem, words should be added to the form that they are willing, in the event of death, and provided their relatives have expressed no objection, for their eyes to be used for therapeutic purposes.

The whole question is a delicate one. Today, there are at least 110,000 blind in this country, and allowing for the 30,000 others who are at present partially blind, it is likely that there will be at least 200,000 by the turn of the century. Of course I don't know how many of these unfortunate – but never despairing – people could be cured by corneal grafting.

―――――――――――――― ● ● ――――――――――――――

Who Tells the Truth?

On one of his visits to London, Billy Graham, the famous American evangelist, told his vast audience, as he pointed to his tongue: 'This little muscle lying behind your teeth is responsible for sending millions of people to hell – and millions more to heaven!'

More than thirty years ago, a Departmental Committee under the chairmanship of the late Lord Evershed, were seeking what they called 'the magic key to the door of cheaper litigation.' To this end they reviewed the law of evidence in several countries. They made the remarkable comment that 'the emphasis which under our system has been placed upon the sworn testimony of witnesses in the witness box should be qualified today by the fact that . . . the sanctity of the oath has lost much of its force. A witness in 1953 (*a fortiori*, in 1988) is no longer impressed with the fear that if he swears falsely he will go to hell, as were his father and his grandfather before him. Prosecutions for perjury are rarely undertaken.'

When, as sometimes happens, children of tender years are required to give evidence, the prosecuting counsel commonly asks searching questions with a religious flavour so as to demonstrate that the child is aware of the need for truthfulness.

Baron Brampton told a story, now more than 130 years old, of how a boy was asked 'the usual sensible questions which St Thomas Aquinas himself would have been puzzled to answer; and being a mere child of seven – or at most eight – years of age, without any kind of education, was unable to state what the exact nature of an oath was.' Mr Justice Maule intervened with: 'What will become of *you*, my little boy, when you die, if you are so wicked as to tell a lie?'

'Hell-fire, sir.'

'Do you mean to say,' asked the judge, 'that you would go to hell fire for telling *any* lie?'

'Hell-fire, sir.'

And to every similar question that was directed towards testing his rectitude the child confidently answered, 'Hell-fire, sir.' Upon this his Lordship observed to counsel; 'If you and I believed that such would be the penalty for every act of misconduct we committed, we should be better men than we are. Let the boy be sworn.'

I came across a contrasting incident in *The Times* of 9th January, 1850. Two men and a woman were charged before Alderman Humphrey at the Mansion House with having committed a desperate assault upon a policeman who was rescued after some of his fellows had been called to the place by cries of 'Murder' – a word which the correspondent claimed was in general use in that vicinity, but which was repeated in a tone that showed that it was really meant.

A fourteen-year-old lad, rejoicing in the name of George Ruby, who at the time was taking his father's supper to him in a warehouse, was put into the witness box for the purpose of identifying the chief culprit. He looked astonished when the Testament was handed to him. The following catechism ensued:

Ald. H. – Do you know what an oath is?

Boy. – No.

Ald. H. – Do you know what a Testament is?
Boy. – No.
Ald. H. – Can you read?
Boy. – No.
Ald. H. – Do you ever say your prayers?
Boy. – No, never.
Ald. H. – Do you know what prayers are?
Boy. – No.
Ald. H. – Do you know what God is?
Boy. – No.
Ald. H. – Do you know what the devil is?
Boy. – No. I've heard of the devil but I don't know him.
Ald. H. – What do you know, my poor fellow?
Boy. – I knows how to sweep the crossing.
Ald. H. – And that's all?
Boy. – That's all. I sweeps the crossing.

Of course, the Alderman refused to take the child's evidence.

It is my belief that Charles Dickens read this account (or perhaps he was present in court), for chapter XI of 'Bleak House', published in 1853, contains an impressively similar story.

Nearly thirty years ago, the late Mr Justice Cassels told a tale about a girl of twelve who had been excessively well drilled in her evidence before the case reached court. Having been sworn, she gave evidence something like this:

'On the 1st April last I entered the premises of the defendant. I there asked the assistant behind the counter, "Are you in the employment of the owner of this shop?" He replied, "Yes". I then said, "Are you duly authorized as his agent to enter into a contract on his behalf?" He replied "Yes," so I said, "Is the supplying of hot water bottles in the normal course of your principal's business?" He agreed that it was, so I informed him that I was the agent of my mummy and that on her behalf I was duly authorized to enter into a binding contract for the purchase of a rubber hot water bottle. I specially pointed out to him the particular use for which this article was required, namely, to warm my mummy's bed, and I was specially careful to say: "My mummy relies on the judgment and skill of your principal that the goods supplied are reasonably fit for the purpose of which they are required within the meaning of section 14 of the Sale of Goods Act 1893." Being satisfied that he understood me, I purchased the bottle, took it home, filled it with hot water, and inserted it in my mummy's bed. Almost immediately it burst and scalded her, as a result of which she has suffered damage.'

And the pert little miss then immediately turned to the solicitor's clerk who had primed her and asked, 'Is that all right?'

Perjury has many faces. After being caught in a lie, one witness coolly confessed that he had (as he thought) avoided giving evidence on oath and, hence, (as he thought) had avoided perjury, by promising, when he was sworn, that he would tell 'the *tooth*, the whole *tooth*, and nothing but the *tooth*!'

Thus, some witnesses seek to salve their conscience. Others lie coolly, calculatingly, blatantly. Others still are overcome by an irresistible vanity.

Thus, as I have already mentioned, in the first of the three major trials in which Oscar Wilde was involved he gave his age in his evidence-in-chief as thirty-nine. But that superb advocate, Edward Carson, Q.C., by his very first question in cross-examination, elicited the fact that Wilde's age was over forty. And spurred on by the uncovering of this utterly stupid lie about an entirely unimportant fact, Carson pursued 'as brilliant and damaging a cross-examination . . . as was ever administered to a prosecutor in a criminal case.'

Other liars are actuated by different motives. Lord Justice Humphreys was invariably mistrustful of female testimony in sexual charges. The rule that corroboration of the complainant's evidence was invariably essential, he said, 'should never be relaxed merely because the prosecuterix in the witness-box behaves like an angel and looks like a Madonna.' And, again, he claimed that an insanely jealous woman, 'will lie with equal readiness whether she is or is not on oath . . . I believe that it not infrequently happens that a woman's idea of the truth is that which will support the side upon which she happens to be.' In the same breath with which he admitted that he has 'many close friends among members of that sex,' he averred that he 'found it very difficult to imagine the case of a man who from envy, hatred or malice deliberately charged another with crime knowing him to be innocent, and supported the charge with his own evidence.'

Of course, some witnesses are inarticulate and so cannot be relied upon. Indeed, many departures from the truth are due to the fallibility of human senses. When I was a novice in my profession I had the good fortune to know a member of the English bar who, in many 'running-down' actions, most expertly cast ridicule upon evidence about estimates of speed. He would ask a witness, 'How fast do *you* think the car was travelling?' And, being well armed with data about the position of skid-marks and other facts *ex post facto*, as well as with a table which reduced miles per hour to feet per second, he could instantly upset an opponent's case.

In the days when a running-down case was never tried earlier than some two years after the accident (and, surely, things are no better today!), he once suggested the following exercise to me. 'If you witness an accident,' he said, 'try to put down on paper as accurately as you can what you *thought* you saw within five minutes of its happening. Put your written account away. Do the same after a couple of hours. After twenty-four hours. After three days. After a week. After a month. After twelve months. And then compare the seven separate accounts of what you saw.' I faithfully followed these instructions and at the end of the year I read seven vastly differing accounts of seven radically different accidents, with scarcely a common denominator between them. Of such stuff are some kinds of perjury made. Even those wonderful mechanical lie detectors for which modern science makes such extraordinary claims would fall down here! The sad fact is that not one of us mortals is humanly capable of speaking the exact truth.

Burn'd Shor's Alphabet

We talk about a problem being as simple as A.B.C., but is our alphabet as simple as we pretend? The late Bernard Shaw didn't think so – or said he didn't think so. He wanted an alphabet of 44 letters instead of 26, so that by the use of a phonetic spelling one letter should represent one sound, not two or three as at present.

Spel ass u lyke (I take it) wos hiss ruf and reddie lor (or, laugh?)

But, of course, BURN'D SHOR, besides being, quite deliberately, a bit bogus at times, was the most outrageous contradictory, iconoclastic, revolutionary and provocative writer of the past hundred years of more. When, in 1950, at the ridiculously early age – for him – of 94, he passed peacefully away, they posted a notice on the gates of his house: 'From the coffers of his genius he enriched the world.' Next day, *The Times* described him as 'a sort of intellectual Father Christmas, delightedly pulling important legs and pricking portentous bubbles . . . .' Even on his deathbed, G.B.S., ignoring the ancient hieroglyphic origin of our alphabet, and forgetting (or fallaciously assuming) that spoken and written words perform fundamentally different functions (one in time, the other in space), wanted to turn our language upside down.

Throughout his long life Shaw was an exponent of extreme left views, yet he amassed a fortune and often and clamorously ranted against the burdensome impact of taxation. Shortly after his death his estate was said to amount to £367,233. But it took five and a half years of negotiations to assess the true figure, for he was unique in the literary world, and the value of his copyrights could not be fixed by normal standards. Later on, it appeared that his estate was worth some £600,000 on which death duties would be levied at the rate of about 70 *per cent.*

Clauses 35 *et seq* of Shaw's will, which, inevitably, was disputed in the Courts, were concerned with his proposed 'British alphabet' and he wanted to finance enquiries into the advantages which might accrue to mankind from its use. In particular, he wished the following points (which I paraphrase freely) to be determined:–

(1) How many people write by the established alphabet of 26 letters?

(2) How much time would be saved if each of these persons used 44 letters?

(3) How many writers or printers of English are there at a given moment?

(4) On these factors, how much time and labour do we waste by our lack of unequivocal symbols?

(5) What is the loss or gain (in terms of British and American currency) because people follow Dr Johnson's alphabet rather than the Shavian one?

Incidentally Shaw wished one of his plays, *Androcles and the Lion,* to be transliterated into his British alphabet. His idea was to advertise and publish the new spelling in a page-by-page version with the proposed alphabet on one side and our normal alphabet on the other, and by the dissemination of copies, and by suitable propaganda, to persuade the government, or the public, or the English-speaking world to adopt it. This was described by the Attorney-General (who appeared on behalf of Shaw's executor, the Public Trustee) as a useful piece of research, beneficial to the public because it would facilitate the education of the young and show a way to save time, and thus money. And it would indeed be interesting, as one silk remarked, to see how the passage, 'Didums get an awful thorn in ums' tootsums-wootsums' (from *Androcles*), would come out.

Pause for one moment and think – in the age before computerised type-setting – what would have been involved had Shaw's alphabet be adopted. Every printer's case and keyboard would inevitably have been thrown on the scrapheap. Standing matter of years would have been reduced to a molten mass. Standard books, text books, and school books of all kinds would have needed to be reprinted. Staffs would have had to be trained afresh. Printers' readers would have aged prematurely. The output of publishers would have ground to a standstill. For years to come, the cost of corrections would have been prohibitive. We should all have returned almost to the age of Caxton – or to that of Mr Squeers of Dotheboys Hall!

Under Shaw's will the ultimate residuary legatees were the British Museum, the Royal Academy of Dramatic Art, and the Irish National Gallery. The first two of these bodies claimed that the alphabet trusts were void and that in consequence they were entitled to come into their inheritance at once. Their grounds were, first, that the trusts, being for an object and not for a person, were void, and secondly, that they were void for uncertainty. The Attorney-General appeared as *parens patriae* to uphold the trusts as charitable, and he also supported the proposition that, even if not charitable, these trusts, not being tainted with the vice of perpetuity, were a valid exercise of a man's power of disposing of his own money as he thought fit.

In this country reserved judgments are the exception rather than the rule, but in this instance, Mr Justice Harman, reading his judgment, said that throughout his life Shaw had been an indefatigable reformer. He was a kind of 'itching powder' to the British public, to the English-speaking peoples and, indeed, to an even wider audience, reminding them of their follies, their foibles, and their fallacies, and bombarding them with such a combination of paradox and wit that before his death he became a kind of oracle. It was natural that he should be interested in English orthography and pronunciation for they were obvious targets for the reformer. It was as difficult for the native to defend the one as for the foreigner to compass the other.

His Lordship thought that the research and propaganda enjoined by Shaw's will merely tended to the increase of public knowledge in a certain respect, namely, the saving of time and money by the use of the British alphabet. There was no element of teaching or education combined with this, nor did the propaganda element in the trusts tend to do more than to persuade the public that the adoption of the new script would be a good thing, and this is not education.

Who was to say whether this project was beneficial? On the face of it, that was a most controversial question. The learned judge felt unable to say that the research to be done was a task of general utility. Shaw himself was convinced, and set out to convince the world. But the fact that he considered his proposed reforms beneficial did not make them so, any more than the fact that he described the trust as charitable convinced the Court that it was. The objects of the alphabet trusts were like trusts for political purposes in that they would involve a change in the law of the land, but such objects had never been considered charitable. As to uncertainty, once an object was charitable the law would provide the means of carrying it into effect but the question of certainty became far more difficult if there was no charitable intent. The objection here was that Shaw's executor would not know how to direct his appointed statistical and phonetic experts to work.

The learned judge went on to observe that whatever his other qualifications, Shaw was a master of a pellucid style and the reader embarked on Shaw's will confident that he would at least find no difficulty in understanding the objects of the testator, especially as it was evident that this document was originally the work of a skilled equity draftsman. Unfortunately the will bore ample internal evidence of being in part the testator's own work. The two styles, as ever, made an unfortunate mixture. It was always a marriage of incompatibles, for the delicate testamentary machinery devised by the convey-ancer could but suffer when subjected to the *cacoethes scribendi* of the author, even though the language of the latter, if it stood alone, might be a literary masterpiece. The will was a long and complicated document, made when the testator was already 94-years-old, and it was youthful exuberance rather than the hesitations of old age that marred its symmetry.

In fact (although, of course, his lordship did not say so) it is now well known that two days before Shaw died, Lady Astor begged him in vain to alter his ridiculous will.

Thus Shaw's alphabet trusts failed. He probably thought they might do so for his will contained a typical jibe about their being rendered invalid by judicial decision. The truth, of course, is that Shaw monkeyed about with a professionally prepared will and failed to grasp the legal niceties involved. In the result he will be unable to monkey about with our alphabet.

Mr Justice Harman remarked that it was curious that *Pygmalion*, Shaw's play that dealt with orthography and pronunciation, which was first produced in 1914, 'has recently been tagged with versicles which I suppose Shaw would have detested, and tricked out with music, which he would have eschewed and is now charming huge audiences on the other side of the Atlantic and has given birth to the present proceedings. I am told that the receipts from this source have enabled the executor to get on terms with the enormous death duties payable on the estate, thus bringing the intepretation of the will into the realm of practical politics'.

Shaw himself once wrote: 'Nothing is ever done in this world until men are prepared to kill one another if it is not done.' Bloodshed for a new-fangled A.B.C.? Not Pygmalion likely! It looks as if Shaw from his grave has been impishly pulling our legs again.

My Doppelgänger and Mr Beck's Alter Ego

Something like thirty years ago I was accosted by a gentleman in the Bayswater Road, in London, who greeted me with, 'Hullo, my dear Mr Castle . . .'. I disclaimed his acquaintance, I hope not unkindly, but he persisted in asserting that I was one Bob Castle whom he had met at a club in Bayswater, which he named, a few weeks previously. When I reiterated, perhaps with a little asperity this time, that my name was *not* Castle and that I had never heard of his club, he went off in a huff, muttering that if I was ashamed to recognize my friends . . . etc., etc. A simple case of mistaken identity, you will say. Let me tell you another little story.

For about fourteen years, regularly every two to three weeks I had faithfully gone to the same barber's, sat in the identical chair, and had my hair cut by the same man. At a conservative estimate he had some 250 opportunities of studying, at close quarters, my appearance, my mannerisms and my gait. He knew me uncommonly well. On one particular occasion, as he was tucking the cloth around my neck and padding in the little bits of cotton wool, he remarked, 'I saw you in Oxford Street last night, Mr Ruoff, but I just couldn't catch your eye.'

Now at that time I lived and worked and spent most of my life within four miles of Oxford Street (and, indeed, Bayswater Road) and I passed through it most days of the working week. But it so happened that, by reason of quite exceptional circumstances, I was 250 miles away when 'seen' by my barber. He was a reasonable and reliable man and when I cross-examined him he was unshakeable about when and where and the circumstances in which he had noticed me. Even when I told him the facts I could see from his expression that he was reluctant to disbelieve the evidence – the very recent evidence – of his own eyes.

Perhaps it will not surprise you that, against this backcloth, my thoughts turned a little uncomfortably to the facts of Adolf Beck's sad history. They are well known but the following summary may serve to underline some aspects of the vast incompetence and foul injustice with which it was super-saturated.

1877: A brown-eyed, circumcised German Jew, aged 27, rejoicing in the undistinguished name of John Smith, was imprisoned at Portland after being convicted of jewel frauds on women. On his record he was described as a Protestant.

1877: Adolf Beck, a blue-eyed, uncircumcised Norwegian, aged 36, was then in Peru.

1879: Smith, still in prison, applied to change his religion, disclosing that he was a circumcised Jew. The facts were not entered on his record.

1895: Smith was at large. Further jewel frauds on women, similar in pattern to Smith's, occurred.

1896: Beck was positively identified by ten out of twenty-two women as the culprit and positively identified as being Smith by an ex-policeman who had arrested Smith nearly twenty years earlier, and his handwriting was identified as Smith's by an 'expert'.

Of the twenty-two ladies who had been defrauded of money and jewellery by John Smith, with his previous convictions for this very thing, no less than ten came to court and asserted that poor Beck was the culprit. Lamentably, Mr Justice Forrest Fulton failed to point out to the jury that one witness, a Miss Ottilie Meissonnier, testified: 'He had a scar on the right side of his neck, under his ear. It's a small scar, like a mole,' whereas, under cross-examination, she admitted: 'I don't see it now.'

Beck's indictment had fourteen counts, four of which referred to Smith's previous convictions. When Beck sought to prove his presence in Peru in 1877, by a piece of vicious and calculated cleverness on the part of that utterly ruthless man, Horace Avory, these four counts were not proceeded with by the prosecution, so that his alibi was ruled to be a collateral and irrelevant issue. Beck was sentenced to seven years' penal servitude and he was sent to the treadmill – at Portland. He was given a prisoner's number which indicated that he was John Smith, and previously convicted.

1898: After a number of fruitless petitions, Beck's solicitor discovered, from a Home office file, that Smith was circumcised, whereas Beck was not. That, of course, was absolutely conclusive evidence that Beck had not previously been convicted of defrauding women, and it at least suggested that he might well not be guilty of the more recent crimes. Yet the governor of Portland Prison reported the facts to the Home Office and, by an incredible piece of irony, gave Beck a new number indicating that he had no previous convictions.

1901: Beck was released on licence.

1903: Smith, greatly changed in appearance and under another name, passed through the hands of the police but was discharged.

1904: (June 27th): Beck was convicted of five more offences of obtaining jewellery from women, found guilty and, apparently, because of some misgivings in the mind of the judge, remanded for sentence.

1904 (July 7th): John Smith, now bearing the equally innocuous name of William Thomas, was arrested for a similar fraud. From now on the cat began slowly and painfully to emerge from the bag.

1906: After a departmental committee had enquired exhaustively into the circumstances of his convictions, Beck was given a free pardon and £5,000.

Unfortunately, in Beck's day there was no Court of Criminal appeal. Certain errors of law could be corrected by writ of error if a convicted person succeeded in obtaining the *fiat* of the Attorney-General, and most rulings of law could be reviewed by the Court for Crown Cases Reserved if – but only if – the trial judge, in exercise of his absolute discretion, was willing to state a case. And, at the time of Beck's first conviction, an accused person could not enter the witness box and there demonstrate his innocence by his words and his demeanour, particularly under the stress of cross-examination. And – the most significant lack of all – police records were rudimentary in character and the finger-print department at Scotland Yard, which today holds millions of records, was still unborn. Just five weeks after Beck's release the brilliant exponent of them took office. The existence of such records could have saved Beck from all trouble. Even so, cases of mistaken identity occasionally occur today, although not with such devastating consequences as in Beck's case.

From time to time *ex gratia* payments of small sums of money are made to men who, through a genuine mistake in identification, have served sentences of imprisonment for offences they did not commit. I don't know which factor outrages public opinion the more, the stinginess of these sums, or the crude anomaly of granting a 'free pardon' to an innocent person – an anomaly, incidentally, which was pointed out in Beck's case. Obviously, the feeling of the man in the street is that the measure of compensation which the State ought to pay to persons wrongly imprisoned should bear a relation to the amount of damages which would be recovered in a civil action for false imprisonment.

Over the years, as a result of mistakes in identification parades, one Home Secretary stated: 'In our law a person is presumed to be innocent until he is found guilty by a competent court. It unfortunately happens from time to time that there appears to be evidence sufficient to justify the prosecution and even committal for trial of a person against whom the prosecution, on whom the onus lies, fail in the event to prove the charge. The law imposes no obligation on the Executive to pay compensation in such cases. It would be out of the question to pay compensation in all cases. On the other hand, it would be wrong for the Executive to attempt to usurp judicial functions and to make *ex gratia* payments in selected cases on the basis of views formed by the Executive as to the moral guilt, or innocence of the accused person. Moreover, although it is recognised that anxiety and hardship may have been caused to the person concerned, it does not follow that anyone acted wrongly in bringing him to trial. Accordingly, in such cases it has never been the policy to make *ex gratia* payments.

Different considerations arise where the prosecution or committal for trial of an innocent person arises from negligence or misconduct on the part of the police or other public officials. Where in such cases hardship has been caused, although Her Majesty's government do not accept legal liability, the practice is to make an *ex gratia* payment in recognition of the hardship that the individual has suffered as the result of some failure on the part of a public official. Quite apart from any question of an *ex gratia* payment, the courts have power to award the defendant who is acquitted the cost of his defence in suitable cases.

All of which sounds a trifle on the mean side to me. Be all that as it may, whether compensation in any of these cases is a free gift or not, and whether it is generous or niggardly, I still find the knowledge that I have a real live *doppelgänger* amongst London's teeming millions a trifle disconcerting. I do so hope he behaves himself!

The Tolpuddle Martyrs

Do you happen to know, off your undoubtedly well-informed cuff, which of all the vast harbours in this world, is the one with the greatest perimeter?

Arkhangel'sk? Buenos Aires? Freetown? Sydney? Wellington? Any other? I don't pretend to know the answer but I suspect that it is one in the beautiful, secluded and largely unspoilt English county of Dorset that I often pass. I refer to Poole Harbour, with its scores of meandering inlets, many, if not most, of which are – as I imagine – navigable only by a rowing boat. I believe this harbour to have a perimeter exceeding seventy miles, give or take a couple of miles, having painstakingly tried to measure its extent on the map.

Running into this harbour from the town of Wareham is the River Piddle. Now the word 'piddle' or 'puddle' – it's all the same – does not, as you might imagine, and indeed, as I myself once thought, refer to something trifling and insignificant. It means a marshland stream. Hence, Piddlehinton is the monk's farm beside such a waterway, whilst Piddletrenthide is the land lying along some rivulet which embraces thirty hides, or households. And Tolpuddle is the manor of the fenland brook.

Wareham is an ancient town, surrounded not only by the most beautiful water meadows, but also by pre-Roman earth-works. In the eleventh-century church of St Martin, Lawrence of Arabia, who died in a motor-cycle accident in the vicinity, is buried. This is a focal point in the Thomas Hardy country. At the south end of the town there is a delightful old inn, called 'The Black Bear'. I recall the occasion, when passing this way during World War II, and stopping off at tea-time, how I and my companions were each served with two eggs on toast, that being double the prescribed weekly ration at that time – always assuming that you could actually get it – and so typical of Dorset hospitality.

Be all that as it may, only gradually, I fear, am I coming round to my theme. In the lounge of this bountiful hostelry is prominently displayed a cautionary notice, dated in 1834, in which the phrases ILLEGAL SOCIETIES and GUILTY OF FELONY and LIABLE TO BE TRANSPORTED can easily be read from several feet away. On a closer inspection, it is evident that the reader is solemnly warned that 'certain mischievous and designing persons have been for some time past endeavouring to induce and have induced many Labourers in various Parishes in this County to attend Meetings and to enter into ILLEGAL SOCIETIES . . . ' and more to the same effect, all of which was contrary to the Act of 31 Edward I, which became law in the year 1303 A.D.

That statute law had the astonishingly diminutive short title for that age in our history of 'Who be Conspirators and Who be Champertors'. It was directed towards the prevention of combinations of workers who sought to advance or fix their wages or to lessen or in any way alter the duration of their working hours.

Over the ensuing 500 years or so, more than three dozen additional anti-combination laws came on to the statute book and, all the time, they tended to become ever-increasingly severe in character.

The lengthy preamble to one of them recited that 'great Numbers of Journeymen, Manufacturers and Workmen in various parts of this Kingdom have, by unlawful Meetings and Combinations, endeavoured to obtain Advance of their Wages, and to effectuate other illegal Purposes . . . . Whereby it had become necessary that more effectual Provision should be made . . . for bringing such Offenders to more speedy and exemplary justice'.

To this end magistrates were empowered to summon witnesses; and any of them who declined to give away their friends and workmates were liable to be committed to gaol, 'there to remain without Bail or Mainprize'[28] until, eventually, they caved in. The use of *certiorari* was forbidden, whilst those who did 'wilfully and maliciously decoy, persuade, intimidate, influence, or prevail, or attempt or endeavour to prevail on any workman . . . to quit or leave his work' had, at the best, a period of confinement in the dreaded House of Correction, or, at worst, transportation to Botany Bay.

The tiny village of Tolpuddle, with its simple, gentle, rustic population, lies in the incomparably beautiful Dorset countryside. It was here, in 1834, that six brave farm labourers dared to unite in an unlawful combination, swearing, as God-fearing Christians, to stick to one another in their simple aims.

Following the warning notice in The Black Bear which was dated the 20th February 1834, these six decent agricultural labourers, whose names must forever be enshrined in letters of gold – namely, JAMES LOVELESS, GEORGE LOVELESS, THOMAS STANFIELD, JOHN STANFIELD, JAMES HAMMETT and JAMES BRINE – were tried at Dorchester Assizes.

When they were indicted for administering unlawful oaths (under the Act 37 Geo. III cap. 123 of 1796), at Dorchester Assizes – the scene of some of Bloody Judge Jeffreys' most disgraceful trials – the principal evidence against them was to the effect that they had made a somewhat pathetic attempt to copy the then newly-created Grand National Consolidated Trades Union, with its membership of some 500,000 workers.

In initiating some fellow-workers, they had blindfolded them and required them faithfully to swear upon the *Bible* that they would not blab about their proceedings. Their objects were quite simple, namely, to maintain a fair rate of wages and they most expressly and strictly forbade any kind of resort to violence.

A few months earlier than the time of the trial there had been an agreement between the farmers and the farmworkers in Dorset, based upon the rate subsisting in the nextdoor county of Hampshire, to pay a weekly wage of 10s. 0d. and, although the normal labourer lived in a mud hut and could never afford to buy a loaf of bread, this sum assuredly enabled him to grow potatoes and raise his own pig for pork.

Then, without warning, the mean employers reduced the rate of pay to 7s. 0d. Out of this most meagre sum the accused, and many of their fellow labourers, paid one penny entrance fee to their union and another one penny a week towards a common fund. These minimal disbursements provoked the trial judge who, today, would be crucified for his wicked and perverse views, to refer to the cruelty of forcing men to contribute these exorbitant sums out of their scanty earnings. And, as everyone today knows, these six Tolpuddle martyrs were all sentenced to transportation to Australia for seven years so that on the 15th April, 1834, they all set sail for Botany Bay.

According to *The Times* of the 19th March 1834, having been convicted, two days earlier, of administering unlawful oaths, their learned counsel objected, by means of a procedure that is quite unknown to me, that they had committed no offence. Mr Baron Williams, the trial judge, took two days to consider the validity and weight of this objection.

Having done so, he refused to uphold it, and observed that the accused meant no harm against any persons and that their intention was altogether without offence. He went on to add something that, in today's climate, is about as ridiculous as stating that the Earth is flat – as, indeed, the members of the Flat Earth Society still claim today!

'There are cases', said Mr Baron Williams, 'in which, whatever may be the intention of the parties, the necessary effect of the act done upon the public security is of such a nature that the safety of that public does require a penal example to be made. And if ever there be any case in which that observation applies, it is surely in a case where it is the object of men to withdraw themselves from the authority of the law, to submit themselves to no examination, and to have their conduct kept private and secret from the knowledge and observation of the rest of the world. . . .'

This pompous old Ass went on to refer to a crime upon 'which the security of the country and the maintenance of the law depends'.

Of course, the Baron cannot possibly have foreseen that all the many heinous crimes that pervade and beset our society today, and which truly deserve his kind of strictures, are punishable far less condignly than were the Tolpuddle defendants.

Be that as it may: can any of you name a harbour with a greater perimeter than Poole Harbour?

Oliver Cromwell's Head

Soccer is a game that appeals to millions of undiscriminating people in these islands. Rugby football is a superior sport but not so greatly favoured as soccer. But cricket, which is undoubtedly the most magnificent outdoor game of all time, does not enjoy quite the same following as those played during the winter months.

I was reminded of this by reading how Oliver (warts and all) Cromwell proscribed 'Krickett' throughout all Ireland which, at that time, he was bent on destroying. All 'sticks' and balls, he declared, were to be burned at the stake by the common hangman. However, seeing that during the course of the Long Parliament he and his brother fanatics purported to abolish the celebration of Christmas, the abrogation of our incomparable national game was but a further relatively insignificant step towards puritanical idiocy.

All the foregoing serves to lead me up to the point where, many years ago, I failed by a whisker to see the head of Oliver Cromwell. I mean, his actual head!

I had a dentist, a great antiquarian, who to some extent mitigated and assuaged the pains of extraction or drilling by recounting, in the most thoroughgoing manner, some of the thrilling things he had seen in the course of his holiday travels throughout the United Kingdom over many years, when he customarily unearthed a multitude of interesting facts in our island story. On one occasion he related how he had seen the actual head of Oliver Cromwell, red beard, sagging whiskers, warts, *et al*, which was ensconced in an oak casket lined with scarlet silk.

Either my friend was a little imprecise about the location of this phenomenon – which I doubt – or, more probably, my discomfiture in the dental chair distracted my thoughts, because I had formed the impression that the preserved head was kept at Huntingdon, a little to the north of Cambridge, where Cromwell's family had their roots and where, I believe, he himself was born. Certainly that constituency sent him to Parliament.

My brother, who then worked abroad, and who is well-versed in English history, was on furlough and together we spent some days seeking, in vain, for the Cromwellian cranium in Huntingdon until, eventually, we discovered in the local museum that the head, in its container, lay under the bed of a parson in the little Suffolk town of Woodbridge.

We then and there decided that during my brother's next leave we would visit Woodbridge, but a perverse Fate arranged that, before we could do so, the parson died, having appointed one of our major banks as his executor. The bank immediately disclaimed the head so that it was returned to Sidney Sussex College, Cambridge, where Cromwell was educated, and there decently interred. Thus, we missed seeing this relic by little more than a few weeks.

At this point in my story you may well ask how this head ever came into the possession of an East Anglican clergyman and that is just what I shall now tell you.

When Oliver Cromwell died in 1658 at the age of only fifty-nine, his body was embalmed and thereafter buried in

Westminster Abbey. You can well imagine the utter abhorrence with which some Royalists regarded him at the Restoration of the Monarchy, so that some of them were constrained to exhume his body which was thereafter publicly beheaded at Tyburn. His trunk was buried beneath the gallows whilst his well-preserved head was impaled upon a spike over the entrance to Westminster Hall for all the world to behold. There it remained until, at the earliest, 1684.

At about that time, on an exceedingly stormy night the spike, which had rusted and rotted, gave way so that the dead head of the late Lord Protector rolled into the gutter whence it was retrieved by an astute sentry who had the insight to recognise its historical value. He felt sure that some member of Cromwell's family would be willing to pay a fancy price for the restoration of the head. Therefore, when his spell of duty ceased, he carried this grim relic home under his cloak and stuffed it into a crevice up his chimney, not even telling his wife about his prize. On his death-bed he informed her about the dead head which she later retrieved, the face being somewhat blackened by the soot in the chimney and the nose a trifle deformed from long lying in the niche.

Thereafter, the inspissated mists of history envelope Cromwell's head although, indeed, it seems to have been restored to his family early in the eighteenth century. This heirloom – for so it was regarded – was closely protected and bequeathed from one generation to another until one profligate member of the family, who purported to be a minor poet, but whose principal interest lay in debauchery, pawned his fore-bear's pate for the price of a few drinks. At some later date it was sold to a private museum in London's Tottenham Court Road and, eventually, I know not quite how, it was bequeathed to an ancestor of Canon Wilkinson, the rector of Woodbridge in the county of Suffolk, the parson whom I mentioned earlier.

Was the head authentically that of the so-called Protector? Admittedly, the external evidence is on the narrow side. Contrariwise, the work of the embalmer has endured over more than three and one quarter centuries and the pike-head is still embedded in the poll. Surely it is not beyond the pale of normal possibility that this is, indeed, the veritable head of the dead Oliver Cromwell? Indeed, when in 1911, the members of The Royal Archaeological Society examined the remains, and compared them with Cromwell's death mask, they had no possible hesitation in stating their conviction that the head was, indeed, that of the late Oliver Cromwell who was admitted as a fellow commoner to Sidney Sussex College in 1616 but who apparently left in 1617, when his father died.

Whatever happened to the rest of Oliver Cromwell's remains? It is said that there is a sarcophagus in a brick vault in Newburgh Priory in Yorkshire that contains such as is left of his body, rescued from Tyburn. I really don't know.

There is a pungent sequel to this little story in which my brother and I are both so deeply interested. It is simply this. Had we both lived in 1642, it is unquestionable that we should have been bitterly fighting one another, the one a Royalist, and the other a Roundhead. No doubt there were many such conflicts within families from 1642 onwards.

Philistinism

Am I being unrealistic when I asseverate that future generations will regard the present time as the Great Age of Philistinism?

Incidentally, although I have known, from a tender age, about the depredations of the Israelites by the Philistines, I did not realize, until I looked the point up, two minutes ago, why this opprobrious term has been applied to persons who are deficient in liberal culture and hanker after material things.

The word 'philister' was apparently first used of the local people by students at Jena University after what we should now call a town-and-gown row, in 1689, in which a number of people were killed, because, on the Sunday following, the university preacher (possibly a little out of context) took as his text: 'The Philistines be upon thee'.[29]

Nearly 200 years later Matthew Arnold wrote of Luther, Cromwell and Bunyan respectively as the Philistine geniuses in religion, politics and literature. Quite apart from this jumbled balderdash, I think he must have invented the word because he also stated: 'Philistinism! – We have not the expression in English. Perhaps we have not the word because we have so much of the thing.' Was that really so, even then?

My opening sentence is not primarily directed to the fact that there are, perhaps, half a million acres of derelict land in England and Wales, to which nothing less than 5,000 acres are added every year. Abandoned opencast mines; the litter of discarded machinery; tall banks of debris; smouldering, suffocating slag heaps; chemically polluted waterways; deep pits that are a hazard to young children; scrap heaps that breed vermin and disease – all these would cost scores of millions of pounds to redeem and restore to a healthy, useful and aesthetic state. Nevertheless, I have other kinds of philistinism in mind.

For many years the planners and the estate developers, who are all to often as oblivious of beauty as they are insensitive to the feel of history, have been busily tearing down handsome and sound buildings in our towns and cities in order to erect some banal monolith to house more of their kidney. The destruction, in 1964, – it is but one example amongst many – of rows of elegant and habitable 17th century town houses in Mayfair, caused Mr John Osborne (that original angry young man) to publish the following denunciation. 'Greed, paralysed imaginations, and a dotty lust for some vague, shabby modernity will go on destroying. Rich influential pigs *do* behave in this way and will go on destroying so that they can put up hideous pens for other hopeful, happy pigs to work in . . . You can't have your free-for-all enterprise, your shareholders and chairmen of money grubbers *and* decency, taste, comfort and honour as well.' Obviously, at that time, Mr Osborne was still angry, and, possibly, also still young.

At the time of my writing these words, back in 1964, there was a tremendous indignation in this country because the Central Electricity Generating Board was about to desecrate one of the most delectable and unspoiled areas of our downlands in West Sussex. In years past they had then already built 44,000 of their hideous, towering pylons across some 8,000 miles of our countryside.

Our poets have written about this very county. Thus, a modern Hilaire Belloc:

'If I ever become a rich man,
Or if I ever grow to be old,
I will build a house with deep thatch
To shelter me from the cold,
And there shall the Sussex songs be sung
And there the story of Sussex told . . .
I will hold my house in the high wood
Within a walk of the sea,
And the men that were boys when I was a boy
Shall sit and drink with me.'

In these affluent times, as industries spread and as more and more people are able to afford greater comfort and warmth in our damp, bitter winters, the demands for extra power and current often threaten to outstrip the Board's ability to produce them. Clearly the Board must maintain an efficient grid system. Yet, in regard to the continuing despoliation of the countryside, the nub of their argument is that, whereas overhead lines cost at that time (1964), perhaps, a mere £120,000 a mile, they publicly stated that they have to pay their contractors something approaching £3 million for putting the cables underground. This is unadulterated nonsense. It cannot bamboozle everybody. For example, the building of our great M1 motorway, the buying of wide areas of land, the compensation for easements, the building work, the employment of a mass of men and machinery, the provision of verges and embankments and the wide-spanned bridges over the road – all these have cost, perhaps, no more than about 2 million a mile. Anyhow, a few people still believe that some of our remaining landscapes are worth far more than that sum.

People are possibly more incensed by the methods used than by the results for, after months or years of costly public enquiries, the Board invariably gets its way. It is unyielding.

The enquiries do little more than lend the colour of a democratic procedure to the Board's bureaucratic ambitions, so that even *The Times* recently carried the headline: 'Democracy stung in the face', whilst the ugly word 'wayleavemanship' was invented to describe an ugly practice.

These are by no means outstanding examples of current Philistinism. Perhaps I am putting words on the rack when I suggest that, today, some people are philistines in their mincing misuse of language. By contrast, Lord Denning once declared, in an address to The English Association, 'Judges do not speak, as do actors, to please. They do not speak, as do historians, to recount the past. They speak to give judgment, and in their judgments you will find passages which are worthy to rank with the greatest literature which England holds.' He quoted passages from Magna Carta and declared that its effect on succeeding generations had been not so much due to the particular remedies it provided, as to the language it used.

Not many statutes can match the language of Magna Carta, however. In 1964 the Scrap Metal Dealers Act received the Royal Assent. Over 100 years have gone by since there was an Act aimed against the stealing and, especially, the receiving, of stolen metal. Now it seems that about one third of the aluminium and zinc, and about one half of the copper, lead and steel produced in the U.K. is derived from scrap metal, the saving over the use of virgin metal running into more than £8 million a year. Obviously this is a field of great temptation for unscrupulous people (although the Act was not aimed at honest tots, such as Steptoe and Son) and especially for the scrap metal dealer to whom the thief will seek to dispose of his wares. The Act required dealers to register themselves with local authorities and keep full records of scrap metals passing through their hands, and also conferred rights of entry and inspection upon the police.

In speaking, in the House of Lords, on the second reading of the Bill, one noble lord remarked that those of his hearers who were connoisseurs of legal jumbles would give 'the prize to cl. 17 of the ill-fated Shops Bill of 1958, which took 34 lines of the draftsman's fearless prose to establish the principle that only a Mohammedan or a practising Jew could operate as a barber in Scotland on a Sunday.'

He thought the law that the Bill sought to amend was in a similar class for, he said: 'If one looks carefully, one sees that it is a criminal offence to sell a second-hand anchor to anyone under the age of sixteen, before 8 o'clock in the morning, and after 6 o'clock at night. The penalty is £20. But if you do it from premises over which your name is not written in letters six inches long (not six inches high, mark you) the penalty is £10 more.' He went on to point out that the bill dealt, not only with big men in the trade, but humble people such as tinkers, gypsies and rag-and-bone men. Then the noble lord corrected himself for, as he pointed out, the Act is aimed against an 'itinerant collector', which is defined as meaning 'a person regularly engaged in collecting waste materials, and old, broken, worn out or defaced articles, by means of visits from house to house.' Clearly this definition refers to my own hoarse-voiced local rag-and-bone merchant, with his battered cart and broken-down nag!

I have previously complained about such mealy-mouthed obscurities as calling a ratcatcher a rodent operative; a charwoman, a domestic cleansing executive; a dustman, a refuse operator; and (in the United States) a mere 'cop', a community relations officer.[30] The noble lord, in reporting that, at a recent trial at assizes, a nightwatchman described his profession as that of 'noctician', went on to recall the Act which changed sanitary engineers into public health officers. 'I suppose,' he said, 'we ought to consider ourselves lucky that they did not go further and ask to be known as privy councillors'.

If I could bring myself to succumb to a philistine idiom, I would add that 'I couldn't agree more.'

The Lord Chancellor's Breakfast

When is a breakfast not a breakfast? Before I retired, on several occasions, I had the honour of attending the Lord Chancellor's annual breakfast. No one seems to know much about the origins of this function but it is certain that at least four centuries ago, when the law courts were situated in the Great Hall of the Palace of Westminster and the lawyers of that day occupied the very same Inns of Court within the city of London as they now do, there was a grand procession at the beginning of every term from London to Westminster, a distance of about a mile and a half by road.

Until Tudor times the Lord Chancellor, with all the judges, serjeants-at-law and members of the Inns travelled in state on mule-back and, in an age when strict sumptuary laws regulated, with meticulous care, the proper dress (as well as the diet) of all classes in the community from the poor ploughman's blanket and linen girdle to the magnificent apparel of the Lord Chancellor himself, the procession must have been a gay sight.

In Cromwell's period carriages were used, but some years after the Restoration Lord Chancellor Shaftesbury sought to restore some of its ancient pomp to the procession, by ordering the judges to travel on horse-back. Many of the nobility took part and the route was lined with guardsmen in their splendid uniforms. However the experiment was not a happy one, for on the one hand, some of the animals, hired for the occasion, resented their unwonted riders whilst, on the other hand, not a few of the riders were accustomed neither to the particular beasts they rode nor to any other. A certain Judge Twisden, 'to his great affright and the consternations of his grave brethren, was laid along in the dirt', but although no one actually broke any bones, coaches were used for ever afterwards.

But to return to the breakfast, it seems that before the Reformation the lawyers would customarily hear Mass and receive Holy Communion in the chapels of their Inns on the first day of every term, so that they were certainly ready to break their fast at the invitation of the head of the legal profession before setting out for Westminster. The fare in Restoration times included cakes and macaroons and brewed and burnt wine which was served in a gallon-sized loving cup.

Nowadays the Lord Chancellor's official residence is within the House of Lords so that the modern reception, which marks the opening of the Michaelmas Sittings, is held in the Royal Gallery there. But first, there is a special service at Westminster Abbey and, for the Catholics, a Votive Mass of the Holy Ghost at Westminster Cathedral. After the day's service at the Abbey, the bells ring out and Her Majesty's judges walk slowly in single file from an exit near the Chapter House across the wide stretch of roadway, past the statue of Richard Coeur de Lion, astride his charger with drawn sword aloft, to the entrance of the House of Lords. At the head of the procession is the Lord High Chancellor of Great Britain, preceded only by the Tipstaff (his little ebony and silver staff of office in his gloved right hand), his Lordship's Permanent Secretary, the Macebearer, and the Pursebearer. The purse is square, not less than sixteen inches each way, with the royal arms worked in heavy gold braid, and it carries seven elaborate gold and red tassels. The Lord Chancellor looks unbelievably dignified in his black damask robes, heavily ornamented with bars of skilfully worked gold thread, having a train borne behind him, and his full-bottomed wig, lace *jabot* and ruffs, kneebreeches, silk hose and silver buckled slippers. He is followed by the Lord Chief Justice of England resplendent in scarlet and ermine, wearing his golden collar of office which is made up of thirty-six large S's separated by tasselled cords with a Tudor rose between two portcullises in front. For 150 years the collar worn by Sir Matthew Hale was handed down in turn to each new Chief Justice who paid one hundred guineas for it. However, Lord Ellenborough, who retired in 1818, broke the custom so that his successor had to have a new collar made. The collar worn by the present Lord Chief was made for Lord Chief Justice Cockburn (1859–1880) and it has descended with the chief justiceship ever since.

After the Lord Chief Justice walks the Master of the Rolls, whose dress, to the uninitiated, is barely distinguishable from that of the Chancellor himself. It was Lord Evershed who, in an after dinner speech in Washington, once complained that trying to interpret British parliamentary language was like attempting to solve a difficult crossword puzzle for, he said, 'We somewhat suffer in England by over-elaboration in detail, including details of procedure in modern statutes'. And he added: 'The final result, I have sometimes thought, might have been more speedily – certainly, more cheaply – obtained by the spinning of a coin.'

This calls to mind Lord Enniskillen who, on his father's death, inherited a potential Chancery suit in the days when they were liable to last a lifetime. The dispute was between the estate and an old lady as to the ownership of a piece of waste land. Seeking an amicable solution, Lord Enniskillen called upon his opponent, who received him so starchily that it was some time before he could ease the conversation round to the question of the land. At length he took a sovereign out of his pocket and suggested that they should settle their differences by spinning the coin. The lady called 'Tails' and the land was hers. A few days later, having had the land valued, she donated a handsome sum representing this value to a charity in which Lord Enniskillen was interested.

But I have wandered away from the procession. The Master of the Rolls is followed by the President of the Family Division and then come a dozen or more Lords Justices in black and gold, not less than sixty judges of the three divisions of the High Court, all attired in scarlet and ermine and full-bottomed wigs, the Attorney-General, the Solicitor General, upwards of thirty county court judges in their black and purple robes, a sprinkling of chaplains and other officials, and numerous silks, all formally attired. Last of all, surprisingly enough, are the Law Lords, in morning clothes.

This long procession is joined by the solicitors present and they all file into the House of Lords and move slowly up the staircase. Then each guest is received by the Lord Chancellor before passing into the Royal Gallery, where rum punch, so steaming hot as almost to scald the lips, is served. The hall is crowded and the faces of Her Majesty's judges appear ruddier and those of counsel, of a healthier tan, than when the courts rose for the long vacation two months earlier. The occasion is often a mild October day and the judges in their heavy cloaks of ermine, not to mention their flowing wigs, inevitably feel uncomfortably warm. The rum punch, too, like the brewed and burnt-wine of former days, engenders a heat of its own.

Incidentally, it is extraordinarily difficult to recognize anyone other than a near neighbour when the room is packed with upwards of 200 people wearing full-bottomed wigs. Few faces are visible in the cloud of horsehair. The fact that lawyers today have wigs at all – Lord Chief Justice Denman (1832–1850) called them 'the silliest thing in England' – may be blamed upon

Louis XIV and the quirks of fashion although, of course, periwigs were in use before his reign. On becoming bald he ordered a peruke, Queen Anne was pleased to adopt the idea, and before long every wealthy old and middle-aged man in England was wearing this artificial contrivance in preference to having his own hair dressed.

In time the habit spread to younger and poorer people. By the middle of the eighteenth century there were dozens of named varieties from the 'artichoke' to the 'spinach seed', the 'pigeon's wing' to the 'she-dragon', and the 'staircase' to the 'judge's ladder', the last-mentioned being the prototype of the modern full-bottomed style. All fashionable wigs were made of human hair and had to be overlaid with an incredible mess of pomatum to keep the curls and the ringlets in place and this, in turn, was heavily coated with white powder. This elaborate *coiffure* needed constant re-dressing by an expert to remain even tidy. Gradually, the wearing of wigs was dropped until finally the army and the church gave them up, leaving them solely to the legal profession.

Then when Pitt, in spite of a passion of protest from bench and bar, put a prohibitive tax on wig-powder, an ingenious wigmaker named Humphrey Ravenscroft conceived the idea of manufacturing wigs from horsehair in such a way that they would retain their shape permanently and thus get rid of the need for the pomatum, the powder, and the constant dressing. (Incidentally, a firm, bearing his name, still make wigs today.) However, when horsehair wigs were first introduced, the more conservative judges disliked the invention and Mr Justice Allan Park even refused to recognize his own son when he appeared before him in the new-fangled headgear.

But to return to my original question: when is a breakfast not a breakfast? And the answer must be: when you don't sit down to break your fast as at the first meal of the day. In fact the Lord Chancellor's invitation is to an afternoon 'reception', colloquially known as a breakfast, at which (besides sipping hot rum punch) the cream of the legal profession meet and enjoy a standing buffet whilst recounting their experiences during the long vacation.

The First Commonwealth Conference of Lawyers

Just twenty years after his Norman father had conquered all England, William Rufus boldly forsook the safety of his fortress in the Tower of London and began to build himself a palace two miles further up the Thames at Westminster. He boastfully referred to its Great Hall (which was much improved and beautified in the reign of Richard II) as 'a mere bedchamber.' This vast hall is all that now survives of that palace and it forms part of the curtilage that contains the Mother of Parliaments, with Big Ben – whose wartime strokes told anxious ears abroad of Britain's continuing survival – looming like a giant above it. In this very hall, in July 1955, more than eight and a half centuries later, the first Commonwealth and Empire Law conference ever to be held was opened by the Lord High Chancellor of Great Britain, Lord Kilmuir.

The scene of pageantry was both impressive and moving. At the beginning and, again, at the end of the ceremony, the great audience, drawn from the ends of the world, rose silently to its feet as the puisne judges in their scarlet robes and full-bottomed wigs went in slow procession, followed by the Lord

Justices and the Master of the Rolls, solemn in their sombre black gowns enriched with gold and finally, preceded by the Macebearer, the Lord Chancellor himself, attired with the unbelievable splendour that belongs to this office.

The fact that her Majesty graciously allowed Westminster Hall to be used as a setting for this brilliant scene was peculiarly fitting because of the long association of the building with English law. For if, today, the Australian in the city or the outback claims that he can get the best kind of justice in the world he can do so because that very justice was evolved through many centuries in this 'spacious nursery of the English common law.' Within its venerable walls at first the King dispensed his own justice in person, although sometimes suppliants and litigants in quest of it had to follow their sovereign all over the Kingdom when he was on his travels. But Magna Carta required justice to be available *'in certo loco'*; and the certain and only permissible place was this same great hall. Here, from the thirteenth century onwards, the courts of Common Pleas and King's Bench and (a little later) the Court of Chancery were held. Here for some days, the martyred King Charles I bravely faced his accusers and judges and, with a skill and knowledge and patience far greater than that evinced by any of them, argued cogently that the Court lacked jurisdiction to try him. Here Oliver Cromwell got himself installed as Protector. Here too, Guy Fawkes was condemned to death for his gunpowder plot. Here the seven bishops who defied the illegal dispensing powers of James II rejoiced in their acquittal. And the seven weary years of the trial of Warren Hastings for corruption dragged to an end here.

When vacation time came round the courtrooms were entirely dismantled and the great hall was cleared in order to be used for banquets and other royal purposes. Indeed, Henry VIII played tennis there and, only thirty or so years ago, an old tennis ball was found jammed in the oak beams of the roof – it may well have been struck there in anger by the royal hand. In consequence of these usages the structure and furnishings of the courts were of a rudimentary and temporary nature, each room being bounded by a low wooden partition which did nothing to keep out the icy blasts from the east door and which could not muffle the ceaseless din in the place. For such space in the Hall as was not occupied by the actual courts was filled with bookshops and the stalls of milliners and other pedlars and a noisy surging crowd of eager sightseers. Beneath the Hall were three drinking dens (like modern dives) known locally as 'Paradise,' 'Purgatory' and 'Hell,' wherein, no doubt, waiting litigants braced themselves for their ordeal and disappointed suitors sought a temporary consolation.

Nevertheless it is remarkable that it was in this inauspicious and distracting atmosphere that English history was in part moulded and the mighty fundamental principles of liberty and justice and probity and fairness that are to be found wherever English is spoken were hammered out. These facts were referred to by the Lord Chancellor as he welcomed delegates to the conference from Australia, Canada, New Zealand, South Africa, the Indian sub-continent, and many smaller dominions and colonies throughout the world.

Here in Westminster Hall (he said) our forebears developed the fundamental concept of rationalism in the application of legal forms and principles. 'How long soever it hath continued', says Sir Edward Coke, 'if it be against reason, it is of no force in law.' What a debt do we owe to this concept, and what a burden, too, have we lawyers laid upon the shoulders of that ever resilient figure, the reasonable man, whether he be sitting on a Clapham omnibus, or at the controls of some jet-propelled rider of the skies. Long may he reign, to the comfort of my brother judges throughout the Commonwealth.

The Lord Chancellor pointed out that above all else it is fair to claim that it was within these walls that the long battle for

95

freedom was fought and won, for it is by the law that our liberty is assured. The painful lessons of recent history have emphasized once more that justice and liberty cannot be isolated from each other because there can be no real justice without liberty, and no real liberty without justice. Through the history of our law's development there runs what the late Lord Tomlin described as 'a romantic thread of passionate attachment' to freedom of thought and speech, and only when that freedom is accorded, and in the atmosphere created by it, can the mind of man develop and display its finest flowers.

After the opening ceremony the delegates began a most strenuous week of deliberations and, in the intervals between them, of the enjoyment of almost unceasing hospitality and entertainment. Whatever may be the upshot of the discussions upon our many common problems as lawyers, I find it impossible to doubt that during this week in London many new bonds were forged in the minds of peoples whose homes are widely scattered over the surface of our earth. Indeed, it is surprising that a gathering of such potential importance to us all as this conference should have been postponed so long. We live in an age when some allegiances within the Commonwealth are being weakened and our mighty association of peoples is not as vigorous and united as it was some years ago. Nevertheless *The Times* made this heartening comment:

'The common law is the inherited way of life of the English, so far as it can be systematically expressed as a nexus of rights and duties. In so far as this way of life has come to be regarded by other peoples as worth importing or imitating, so that the common law remains voluntarily accepted in whole or in part by nations who have been gladly released from any duty of obedience to the British Parliament, Empire stands justified at the bar of history. It is the proudest achievement of imperial Rome that to this day, in lands where the eagles never flew, judges still turn to the Digests and the Institutes as sources of living law. In that sense the Roman Empire has not fallen, has scarcely declined; and this week's gathering encourages the British Empire to look forward to a comparable diuturnity.'

I would add simply this. Although the system of Roman law was wide in its scope and both rational and reasonable in its concepts, it lacked some of the finer qualities of British jurisprudence. The Roman citizen had no *habeas corpus*. He enjoyed no trial by a jury of his fellows. And he could not, as we can, freely sue great departments of the State in the courts of our homeland for civil injury.

TAILPIECE

It was not until 1882, after succeeding generations of lawyers had clamoured for the abolition of the inconvenient site at Westminster, that the Royal Courts of Justice in the Strand were opened. For many years one government after another had adamantly refused to spend any money on this project because they were bent upon abolishing income tax entirely!

Deplorable, but Inevitable Tax

Mr Justice Danckwerts (as he then was) once said:[31] 'It is always rather a discouraging pursuit to endeavour to find consistent principles in the statutes relating to income tax . . . The only clearly discernible principle may be that of enabling the tax to be charged on the largest numbers of persons with the least exertion on the part of the officials entrusted with the duty of collecting the tax'.

On the very same day, Mr Justice Davies, in another court, in dealing with a company formed with the legitimate object of avoiding the payment of unnecessary tax, and aptly named Noble Enterprises (1953) Limited, was heard to utter the judicially explosive opinion that 'All tax is unnecessary'. This, surely, was said, *obiter*, although an English Chancellor of the Exchequer, not long afterwards, remarked: 'There is a jolly good case against any tax in this country'. Then, perhaps a little repentant, he added: 'I cannot think of one that I could not riddle with criticisms'.

Then, when Lord Evershed was Master of the Rolls he had some scathing remarks to make about the fact that when a man goes to a hospital to develop films, he is assessed under a different head of tax, with vastly different liabilities, according to whether he is developing them for a private patient or for a hospital patient. 'When income tax becomes a game like that', he said, 'it loses a certain amount of its virtue'.

For my own part, the tax people often remind me of the French lady who consulted her fowls as to whether they would rather be boiled or roasted . . . .

My story today concerns a gentleman to whom the mysteries touching the distinction between tax avoidance and tax evasion had never been adequately unfolded. His parents gave him the sound, sober English forenames of 'George Frederick' and he inherited from them the improbable and entirely non-materialistic surname of 'Soul'. Hereafter, for the sake of brevity, I shall call him simply 'S'.

S. was, of course, a man. He was aged 49, by occupation a garage proprietor. He was also a landlord in a large way. He was described by counsel – without specifying his sex – as 'a cunning and calculating spider who spun a web of lies and deceit to deprive the Inland Revenue of enormous sums of money'. To his pawns in the game of money-making he called himself variously, 'a fairy godmother', 'a well-wisher', and 'your patron, an elderly lady who delights in doing good works secretly'.

His methods were simple in their conception – though complex to unravel – and they were, no doubt, suggested to his mind by the fact that he himself was a married man with seven children, for all the people he used for his schemes had enormous families. One of them had fifteen children and another, eighteen. He used to watch the local papers for news of the birth of triplets.

In addition to his activities in his garage, S. bought a large number of properties over the years, many of them consisting of the fag ends of long leasehold terms, let to weekly tenants, in Bethnal Green, or Battersea, or Paddington, or some other slum area of London.

Now when, some twenty years ago, we in this island were invaded by a multitude of unsophisticated Irish building labourers, S. began to haunt the pubs on a Friday night, where some of these delightful immigrants were striving to wash away the dust and the cement from their parched throats. Approaching Spud Murphy (the name is fictitious), a labourer with a dozen children, S. would buy him a beer and tell him about a fairy godmother who would not live long and certainly would not die happy unless she could give Spud a property from which he would receive 10s. a week rent and a bonus at Christmas as well. Such is human cupidity that Spud speedily accepted this generous offer and, in fairness, it must be put on record that he did thereafter receive his weekly sum. Eventually, promised S., the property would be transferred into Spud's very own name and become his absolutely.

Many an agreement, many a power of attorney, were signed with the scrawl of an illiterate Irish working man bending over the flat top of a piano in the local. On the other hand, some of S.'s 'nominees', as he called them, had properties registered in their names without being aware of the existence of their most generous patron and it was suggested that S. 'committed wholesale forgery of any document that was necessary for the carrying through of his scheme'.

Why, you may well ask, should anyone be so generous as S. was? According to the records of the Inland Revenue authorities S. owned no property. According to those records Spud (with his twelve children), rather more than twenty years ago, earned about £400 a year as a casual labourer and collected, perhaps, £1,000 as landlord and, of course, the tax allowances attributable to his large family swamped the schedule A tax so that he was not liable to any. (The child allowance alone for a father of twelve was, at that time, £1,325.) The same was true of many other men with large families and in no less humble circumstances than Spud. Meanwhile S., who drew the actual rents, amounting to some £19,000 a year, paid a few sums of 10s. a week over to Spud and his like, without paying any tax whatever.

And so, over the course of a few years, S. bought 1,000 properties in the names of 37 of his 'nominees'. In all, he evaded well over £50,000 in taxes.

An eighteenth-century English wit[32] might have had S. in mind when he wrote:

'O that there might in England be
A duty on Hypocrisy,
A tax on humbug, an excise
On solemn plausibilities'.

Clearly Spud and his friends knew even less about income tax returns than any educated man in this country sixty years ago who, unless, indeed, he was in the very top income bracket, probably died peacefully in his bed without ever having been made aware of the existence of the dreaded Commissioners of Inland Revenue. Thus when Spud received an assessment form he added to it a complete list of his children with their ages and signed on the dotted line. This he did on the most careful and explicit instructions from S., probably having no notion of what was involved. He thereafter posted the form to S. who most thoughtfully, and in advance, provided Spud with a stamped, addressed envelope for the purpose. Thenceforth, out of the goodness of his heart, S. ensured that Spud was bothered no more with the technicalities of taxes.

Yet, although the Inland Revenue authorities travel leisurely, they advance inexorably. After a tedious and extensive investigation by them and by Scotland Yard, S. was eventually charged with making false returns of income (for which he was sentenced to fifteen months' imprisonment), and forgery and uttering forged documents (two years' imprisonment). His appeal to the Court of Criminal Appeal inevitably failed.

Even that was not the end of this story, for the Revenue

people don't like being outwitted. They therefore sued S. as landlord[33] for the full amount of tax on all his properties without the benefit of children's allowances. Inevitably S.'s defence that he was merely an agent for his 'customers' failed. Undeterred, he went to the Court of Appeal which closely investigated the character of the investments by these same customers, none of whom at any time laid out any money. In support of his contentions, S. actually started an action against one customer who claimed to own the properties standing in his name and the court held that there was no resulting trust in favour of S. That decision did not, however, avail S. in the Court of Appeal because the whole scheme was so utterly bogus and, in the cases they had to consider, S. had been personally entitled to and received the rent and profits.[34] Leave to appeal to the House of Lords was refused.

The moral (if moral there be) is that you cannot beat the Inland Revenue people at their own game for long, if at all. They are, indeed, like the French lady who consulted her fowls about whether they would rather be boiled or roasted.

Bold Chanticleer protested; 'But, madam, we do not desire to be either boiled or roasted'.

'My dear fowls, you are wandering from the point!'

Profits and Commons Sense

Although, being learned in the law, you will be aware that a *profit à prendre* is a right to enter upon the land of another person and take something from it (as distinct from an easement, where the right is simply one of using the servient tenement), I question whether many of you have ever had much occasion to deal with profits (other than highly productive ones – I hope) in your daily practice, despite the fact that, in England and Wales, profits are common (indeed, they are often called 'commons'). The commonest of them all today is that of pasture which is, clearly, the right to graze cattle on another person's property.

In 1980 there was a lot of fuss and bother about rights of pasture in the tiny hamlet of Pundle Green Bartley, which pasture is entirely surrounded by the New Forest, because a certain farmer, by the name of Alfred Newman, could only graze his cattle there by passing through the royal domain, into which his wholly illiterate cows sometimes strayed when he was not on the spot to guide and advise them.

That the New Forest, lying roughly to the north and west of Southampton Water, is the property of the Crown, will be evident to all of you who cast your minds back to your very first child's history book. William Rufus, you will remember, was hunting there when he was struck by an arrow from the bow of Sir Walter Tyrrel, who was in attendance on the King, which (so he said) he had aimed at a stag. Tyrrel fled to the Holy Land whilst, today, the bones of Rufus lie in Winchester Cathedral with the arrowhead still embedded in them.

Even today judicial officers known as verderers administer the forest laws. The name, 'verderer', is derived from the Latin *viridis* (green) and the duty of these agisters is to preserve the 'vert' (or venison) from poachers and generally to deal with trespassers.

All of which brings me back to Alfred Newman and his cattle which had to pass through the unfenced New Forest in order to graze lawfully at Pundle Green Bartley. The verderers found out that some of Alfred's cattle did not bear, on their flanks, the appropriate mark to indicate that he had paid them the annual 'marking fee' to enable him to put them to graze on the property of the Crown although, of course, it was other land, entirely surrounded by the royal property, where the grazing – or, certainly, the substantial part of it, took place. So Alfred was attached and fined by the verderers at their Swainmote Court. This riled him because, he argued, his cattle were wholly unable to comprehend these legal niceties. Moreover, he and his forebears had enjoyed rights of grazing without molestation for centuries. He was all the more outraged because, every breeding season, wild stallions from the New Forest (for which, obviously, the verderers were directly responsible) invaded his farm, rounded up his pedigree mares, and decoyed them miles away into the wilds of the forest.

Therefore Alfred sought the prerogative writ of *certiorari* in the Supreme Court. Alas, it turned out that his undoubtedly ancient rights had, in recent years, been so hedged about by an ungenerous legislature, that he was left without remedy. This made him angrier than ever, and the publicity which his sad case received locally united the many farmers who enjoyed rights of pasture in the vicinity, causing them to declare war on the wicked verderers and their randy stallions.

Of course, the right of pasturage is only one of a number of extant *profits à prendre*. Some years ago, when I was still Chief Land Registrar, a team under the leadership of my friend, Bryan Parker, was preparing the Land Charges project for searching by computer, under which more than five million charges were recorded against the names of some four million landowners with a prodigious retrieval rate of well over four million searches a year.

My friend had joined the Land Charges Registry shortly after he had completed a computerised system of logistics for the Polaris submarine on behalf of the United States Navy Department. (For example, where is the nearest point at which a submarine commander can acquire a new rudder, or, even obtain a few spare cocoa mugs?)

It is scarcely surprising that he and a few of his lay colleagues were flummoxed when they discovered the existence of rights of estover, which entitle the dominant owner to pick up faggots, or even to cut live timber, usually for use as fuel. Their utter puzzlement cannot have been in any way eased by the fact that there was a little village called Estover, just outside Plymouth, where they were working at the time.

I thought that the best way of opening up this esoteric subject was to write an explanatory rhyme for them, which I entitled 'Profits & Commons Sense', and here it is:

'You said you don't know about *profits à prendre*
Or any such commons which might correspond
To this lawful, subsisting and valuable right
Rightly called 'common', it's not recondite.

I strolled through the fields one morning at six
And saw an old woman a-picking up sticks:
So I said to myself, as I thought the thing over,
'I'm blessed if she hasn't a right of *estover*'.

All cattle levant and couchant as well
Graze on the waste of the manor. They dwell
By common of *pasture*, their owner's true right,
By sunlight, by moonlight, by day and by night.

By *piscary*, fisher, let none say you poach
As you cast for a salmon, a perch or a roach.
This right which you hold to fish other men's streams
May yield a good catch – or just piscator's dreams.

This evening I spotted an ancient bent serf,
Huffing and puffing, he cut the peat turf.
Tonight, in his settle, he'll warm his cold bones
By *turbary*, burnt in his old chimney stones.

Esoteric and ancient, these laws seem to you,
But why do you make such a hullabaloo?
Your systems are modern, your A.D. P. bold
But the laws you compute are a thousand years old!'

Gibberish

Mr Samuel Langhorne Clemens, who was born in the United States of America two years before Queen Victoria came to the throne and who left our worldly scene during the year when George V became sovereign of our commonwealth, was a humourist of the very first water and no mean novelist besides.

This American gentleman, coming out of church one Sunday morning, congratulated the parson, a learned Doctor of Divinity, for his memorable and enjoyable sermon, in words to the following effect:

'I welcomed your dissertation as an old friend. I have a book at home that contains every single word of it.'

This so greatly upset the divine that his hackles rose just as a dog's do.

'I'm certain you've no such book', he angrily asserverated.

Said Mr Clemens, 'I assuredly have'.

The Doctor: 'I'd like to have a look at it. Please send me a copy.'

Whereupon Mark Twain – for such was Mr Clemens' pseudonym – sent the doubting parson his complete set of the *Oxford English Dictionary*.

I wonder – did you ever realise that the name 'Mark Twain' was derived from the cries of the pilots on the Mississippi River – whilst they were making their soundings.

All of which tempts me to talk, as I have done before, about words. As one who has, over many years, been deeply in love with the English language and who truly adores it for its mellifluous elegance, its virile succinctness, no less than for its pellucid precision, I constantly deplore the bastard origins of much babblative prattle or, if you prefer it, gobbledegook.

As a schoolboy I was taught Latin grammar, but never English grammar so that, almost inevitably, in the many millions of words which, over the years, kind publishers have disseminated in print on my behalf, I have probably made one or two horrid syntactical errors from time to time, whilst purporting to enunciate my native tongue. Nevertheless, as I well know, purity and simplicity and, above all, comprehensibility, comprise the *sine qua non* of a complete understanding between writer and reader. Which, of course, is the sole – I repeat, the sole – object of the exercise – simply, communication between you and me.

When recently I was in Australia, I read, in their daily press, many examples of a bastard tongue derived, for the most part, from the U.S.A. Words such as 'lubritorium' which was supposed to mean a garage; 'retiree' for an old age pensioner; 'people movers', a phrase used by a Senator in the Federal Parliament in Canberra which, when reduced to comprehensibility, is apparently meant to refer to the transportation of people, rather than sheep.

Then another Senator – no less – declared that some project had 'plateaued out'. Seemingly, what he had intended – but failed – to state was that it had attained a common denominator. But I am not sure, simply because I am no expert at translating garbage talk.

All this is quite insignificant compared with some of the

ludicrous phrases that, all too frequently, bastardise our language in the U.K. I am thinking of such rubbish as the *soi-disant* 'junior sphere removal officers' at Wimbledon who, in real life, are just little ball boys. Two other revolting and meaningless neologisms that emanate from local government are an 'after outreach worker' which is supposed to indicate a community worker, and a 'patch team clerk' which, beyond every bound of probability or possibility, is said to mean a clerical asssistant. What verbicide!

A crematorium in Nottinghamshire has recently advertised its memorialisation facilities. In plain English, it is seeking to sell gravestones.

This kind of horrid error and garbling of language, is something that I have sought to destroy over the past forty years, if not for far longer. Even the law is not blameless. The other day an earnest young police detective who was giving evidence repeatedly referred to 'custody suites' in the Crown Court at Oxford. 'Surely you mean cells', snapped the judge.

Then there are irrelevancies. Surely lawyers, of all people in this world, are the greatest hunters of them. Non sequiturs are, quite simply, an anathema to all of us. As Gordon Hewitt, sometime Lord Chief Justice of England in my youth, once said: 'If you add four pounds of butter to four o'clock, what is the result to the nearest square shilling?'

TAILPIECE

Since the above was written, I have read in *The Times* about an American pilot who announced over the intercom: 'Please fasten your seat-belts. We'll be destinationalized in twenty minutes.'!

Lady Chatterley's Lover

Although, in this ultra-permissive age, the famous Lady Chatterley Case represents no more than a rumbling of neo-permissive apprehension, it seems to me that some historical interest may yet be squeezed from the then-existing state of the public conscience.

Therefore, I am passing on to you, in no true sort of chronological order, some of the comments that were made before, during and after the trial. But first, to recapitulate. The story is a slightly ludicrous one about the sex-starved wife of a baronet, paralysed by war wounds, who satisfied her desires, mainly with her husband's gamekeeper in a forest. Thirteen episodes are amply described and the book is generously bespattered with four-lettered Anglo-Saxon names for parts of the body and its functions.

The Obscene Publications Act of 1959, under which the prosecution for obscenity was brought, introduced the revolutionary idea that no offence is committed if publication is justified as being for the public good, because it is in the interests of science, literature, art or learning, and it allows experts to give their opinions 'to establish or negative literary, artistic, scientific, or other merits'. The defence called thirty-five so-called experts, all of whom, in their ignorance of normal standards of morality, spoke of the book's extraordinary literary merits, and they proferred thirty-six more witnesses. The jury had four days to read the book for themselves.

Still recapitulating: between 1925 and 1928 the late D. H. Lawrence, who had by then already suffered convictions for the obscenity of his paintings as well as his writings, completed three separate versions of *Lady Chatterley's Lover* and, whereas an unexpurgated edition was published on the Continent, the English version was thoroughly bowdlerized. Then, in the mid-1950s, Penguin, whose boast it is that they have never yet published a shortened version of any book, announced that they would put 200,000 copies of the full work on the market on the 25th August, 1960. Voluntarily they handed copies to Scotland Yard and this test case, the first under the then new Act (apart from a minor prosecution of the author of a directory of prostitutes), was launched.

Mr Mervyn Griffith-Jones (prosecuting counsel, opening to the jury): Do not approach this matter in any priggish, high-minded, super-correct, mid-Victorian manner . . . This book sets on a pedestal promiscuous intercourse and it commends sensuality as a virtue . . . Sex is dragged in at every conceivable opportunity – this, mark you, from the mouth of prosecuting counsel! The plot is little more than a padding until we can reach the hut again, or the undergrowth in the forest . . . The characters . . . were little more than bodies which continually had sexual intercourse.

Mr Gerald Gardiner Q. C. (defending): The book must be taken as a whole . . . If a book is obscene merely because of an extra-marital relationship then I would suggest that nineteen out of twenty novels which are written are obscene . . . The author was clearly a strong supporter of marriage and the book, so far from encouraging promiscuity, made it very plain that the author hated it.

Lawrence himself: This story is . . . one of 'phallic tenderness' and is never, in any sense of the word, pornographic . . . It will bring me only abuse and hatred.

The Bishop of Woolwich (defence witness): I think Lawrence tried to portray the [sexual] relation as, in a real sense, an act of Holy Communion. For him, flesh was sacramental of the spirit . . . (In re-examination): This is a book which, in my view, Christians ought to read. (Questioned by the judge): This book portrays the love of a woman in an immoral relationship, so far as adultery is an immoral relationship . . .

Me: Obviously this un-Christian priest had never read the seventh commandment. Is the bishop ignorant of his own Prayer book, or merely being a buffoon?

The Archbishop of Canterbury (commenting): The Bishop of Woolwich . . . was mistaken to think that he could take part in this trial without becoming a stumbling-block and a cause of offence to many ordinary Christians.

Me: A masterly understatement!

Mr Cecil Day-Lewis (poet and author, defence witness): Although Lady Chatterley committed adultery, I would not call her an immoral woman.

Mr Griffith-Jones (of a purple passage in the book): You would have to go some way in the Charing Cross Road, the back streets of Paris, and even Port Said, to find a description of sexual intercourse as lurid as that.

Lawrence himself: We are today, as human beings, evolved and cultured far beyond the taboos which are inherent in our culture.

Mr St John-Stevas (author and barrister, defence witness): I have no hesitation in saying that every Catholic priest and moralist would profit by reading this book because they have the aim, in common with Lawrence, to rid the sexual act of any claim of false shame . . . As a Roman Catholic, it is quite consistent with my own faith.

Rev A. S. Hopkinson (Anglican adviser to Associated Television, defence witness): I would like my children to read the book and I like to think they would discuss it with me or with their mother.

Dr Roger Pilkington (geneticist, a marriage guidance counsellor): I, and at least five of my acquaintances, including three marriage guidance workers, refused to testify for the defence.

Mr Richard Hoggart (Senior lecturer in English literature at Leicester University, defence witness): This novel is highly virtuous and puritanical in some aspects . . . It is a highly educative book in the most proper sense, doing the job of all good art.

Dr Hemming (educational psychologist, defence witness): *Lady Chatterley's Lover* is a positive antidote to the shallow, superficial values about sex which . . . are corrupting the attitude of young people towards sex.

Rev. D. A. Tytler (director of religious education, defence witness): This book makes clear that Lawrence was against irresponsibility in matters of sex and therefore by reading it, young people, even those who are potentially promiscuous, are likely to be pulled up short.

Miss Dilys Powell (film critic, defence witness): A great deal of contemporary cinema seems to degrade the whole sanctity of sex by treating it as trivial, whereas in this book sex becomes something to be taken seriously and a kind of holy basis for life.

Miss Helen Gardner (fellow of an Oxford college, defence witness): By the time one has read the last page [a four letter word beginning with the letter F] has assumed great depth of feeling in relation to natural processes.

Mr Gardiner: The author . . . thought that if he used words which have been part of our spoken speech for about 600 years, he could purify them from the shame which rested on them . . . If these words can deprave or corrupt, then 95 per cent of the Army, Navy and Air Force are past redemption.

Mr Stephen Potter (author and critic, defence witness): Lawrence was trying to take the four letter words out of the context of the lavatory wall so as to give them back dignity and meaning, away from the context of obscenity and swear words.

Me: Alexander Cruden, 18th century author of the famous Concordance, used to tramp the streets of London with a wet sponge in his pocket with which to rub out rude words scribbled on blank walls.

Miss Sarah Jones (Classics mistress at a girls' school, defence witness): I have inquired from a number of girls after they have left school and most of them have been acquainted with these words by the time they were ten.

A journalist who knew Lawrence: When Lawrence's wife began to use, in company, the four-letter words she had to type so often for him, the most embarrassed person present was Lawrence.

Lawrence himself: The words that shock so much at first don't shock at all after a while . . . The words merely shocked the eye, they never shocked the mind at all.

Me: I remember a boy of four or five who, in order to impress his parents with his defiance, announced, with arms akimbo, 'I'm going to say a rude word now – Bum!'

Mr Gardiner (in his final speech): The witnesses . . . included professors of English literature, readers, lecturers, authors, critics, reviewers, teachers, editors, representatives of the Church, and students of literature from all classes of the community . . . Then, when [the prosecution's] turn came to call evidence, they called none at all.

The Times (after the verdict): In spite of the impressive parade of witnesses for the defence, well nigh all affirming that the publication of *Lady Chatterley's Lover* could do nothing but good, it would not have been difficult to match them, bishop for bishop and don for don, with a similar parade, taking exactly the opposite view.

Mr Gardiner: Is Lawrence always to be confined to the dirty book-shops? That would be the greatest irony in literary history. We are a country known throughout the world for our literature and our democratic institutions and it is strange indeed that this is the only country where this Englishman's work cannot be read.

Mr Griffith-Jones (in his final speech): I do not question the absolute integrity of all these witnesses but I suggest that they have got a bee in their bonnet. . . You, members of the jury, will judge the case as ordinary men and women, with your feet planted firmly on the ground . . . It is for you to decide the case and not the so-called experts.

Mr Gardiner: The whole attitude which Penguin books was formed to fight against . . . is that it is all right to publish a special edition at five or ten guineas but quite wrong to let people who are less well off read what those other people read.

A Soho bookseller: Erotica have always been a part of a rich man's library.

A correspondent of The Observer: How would you like this book to fall into the hands of *your* gamekeeper?

Hilaire Belloc (Obiter Dicta):
Your Lordship is sound to the core.
It is nearly a quarter to four.
We've had quite enough of this horrible stuff
And we don't want to hear any more.

Mr Justice Byrne (who summed up to the jury for 2 hours and 10 minutes): This book is to be put on the market at 3s. 6d. (at today's prices, say, something under £10), a copy. In these days when there are not only high wages but high pocket money, 3s. 6d. will be putting the book within the grasp of the vast mass of the population . . . In considering whether the merits of the book are so high as to out-balance its obscenity, so that its publication is justified as being for the public good, you must consider the public, not so much the student of literature, who may read the book under the guidance of a tutor at a university, as the person who knows nothing about literature or the author, but who buys it for 3s. 6d., or borrows it from a library and reads it during the lunch break at a factory and takes it home in the evening to finish it.

The Jury (of nine men and three women, after a three hours' absence): 'Not Guilty'.

The Press: as a whole, welcomed the verdict and many claimed that the prosecution should not have been brought.

The Times: It is hard to make the major premise of the book other than that Constance Chatterley was behaving naturally in being unchaste both before and throughout marriage and was justified in lying with one man after another until she found one to her satisfaction . . . What makes *Lady Chatterley's Lover* unique is that all the details, circumstances, and sensations of copulation are made explicit . . . A decent reticence has been the practice in all classes of society and much will be lost by the destruction of it.

A lady witness (after the case): In the twenties it was considered smart to be promiscuous – that's why Lawrence was revolutionary then. Nowadays it's smart to be faithful and I'm certain he had something to do with it.

A correspondent of the Times: I am 62-years-old . . . I am just an ordinary man, horrified and a little frightened . . . all this last week, to read in your columns, from the lips of prominent men and women, that the simple virtues of modesty, decency, reticence and clean living, which our parents taught us, were wrong.

Another: If [the verdict] . . . brings sex out of the cupboard where it has hidden far too long, and makes it a normal and unveiled facet of our everyday existence, then the jury's verdict will have been a most admirable and progressive milestone in our civilisation.

Another: Whether to indulge in pre- or extra-marital sexual relations is entirely an individual choice and does not concern society collectively at all.

Another: I may have a somewhat naive idea of what constitutes literature but I cannot see how anything which would deprave and corrupt could be for the public good or could be called literature.

Another: The spectacle of lawyers, experts and laymen probing D. H. Lawrence's rather dated passion is almost ludicrous when we think how the time might have been spent in examining the violence, sadism and horror of so many current cinema and television films, or the sex-angled, scandalous features of some of our popular newspapers.

The Times: It is possible to imagine a society so austere that nothing could corrupt it. It is easy to envisage one so depraved that corruption could go no further.

Me: After the trial, the 200,000 available copies of *Lady Chatterley* sold within a few minutes on the day of publication. I was told I must wait six weeks before I could even *order* a copy of the second imprint of 300,000. Nevertheless, I got the book and ploughed through it and, despite all the literary giants, I found it to be totally humourless, leaden (or should I say, wooden?), utterly tiresome and boring. Most teenagers would not have the patience to read even ten pages of it.

The Ashes of a Destroyed Marriage

Since 1st January 1971 the *sole* ground upon which a petition for dissolution of marriage may be presented by either party is that the marriage has broken down irretrievably. The 'breakdown' may be proved through specified facts such as adultery, that the petitioner finds it intolerable to live with the respondent, desertion for at least two years, and so forth.

But before 1971 there were a number of grounds for divorce which included those now embraced by the 'specified facts'. What follows was originally written in 1963.

Our old friend Anon., who has straddled the centuries with his prolific output of literature and music, once wrote this epitaph:

Here lies a poor woman who was always tired,
She lived in a house where help wasn't hired:
Her last words on earth were: 'Dear friends, I am going
To where there's no cooking, or washing, or sewing . . .
Don't mourn for me now, don't mourn for me, never,
I'm going to do nothing for ever and ever'.

Had this poor woman lived today it is possible that she would not have died as prematurely as she undoubtedly did for, even in an age when several million Joneses have cars to save their poor feet, washing machines to save their poor hands, and 'tellys' to save their poor brains, she might have been able to obtain a release from her agony of drudgery through divorce. In this country, it is possible for a down-trodden wife to get a decree upon the ground of cruelty because her husband is so utterly bone idle that he is always in debt, whilst she battles continually with his creditors and the bailiffs, and bears the brunt of supporting the family.[35]

Lord Justice Denning (as he then was) once said that 'if the door of cruelty were opened too wide we should find ourselves granting divorce for incompatibility of temperament'.[36]

We have not yet quite come to the point where a wife can allege incompatibility – which, I gather, is a diluted form of cruelty – on the ground that her husband wears a tie that she dislikes. It would be a sad day for England if ever wives could choose their husbands' neckwear! I would utterly refuse to abandon my bacon and egg MCC tie. Yet cruelty takes odd forms.

A South Australian lady, a friend of mine, when visiting London, was put into a bedroom exhibiting an urn which contained the ashes of her landlady's husband, a fact which shook her to the core. Yet, according to an unreported case, it is not legally cruel if, upon remarriage, a widow insists upon keeping the ashes of her late husband in a sideboard where is stored some of the food that her new husband is expected to eat. As a matter of fact the later husband dumped the ashes of his predecessor in title in the coal cellar, so opening to speculation whether that very fact might not amount to cruelty on his part. I should have thought that it well might do so.

The law has no foot-rule (not even the length of the Lord Chancellor's foot, as Dr Johnson once seemed to suggest) for measuring the personalities of people who happen to be married,[37] and many marriages are ship-wrecked 'solely because two people of inflexible will [are] daily pitting themselves against each other in every small rub of married life, without any particle of the softening influence of mutual affection and esteem'.[38] For example, some fifteen years ago a girl of eighteen married a manikin of twenty-one. Within a week of the ceremony he took off his shoes and socks one evening and demanded that she should tickle his feet, not just for ten minutes or so (which might have been a matey thing to do in the first flush of connubial ecstasy), but for three and four hours on end, even when both of them were watching a television programme, and his peculiar requirement was repeated, night after night, week after week, for nearly six months. If she failed to tickle, he sulked into silence. In one case the plethora of tickling caused him to fidget so much that she could not keep her fingers still. He was held guilty of cruelty.[39]

Yet cruelty usually takes more humdrum forms as the five following unreported cases, taken at random, tend to show. A wife who smites her husband upon the head with firetongs, knifes him, throws boiling water over him, and stubs her cigarettes out on his arm, is cruel. Too b—y right! Yet if she merely clouts him, albeit in the essentially critical presence of his step-mother, hides the family store of tea and sugar (surely, in itself, an heinous offence?) and hurls a potted plant at him in front of so-called friends, she is not legally cruel. But a husband who habitually insists upon driving his wife to and from parties when drunk ('For God's sake, give me the wheel!') is cruel, although drunkenness alone seldom amounts to cruelty.[40] Then there is the elementary question which gives rise to numerous quarrels. Which programme? A wife has been told by the courts that a dispute about which television programme she and her man should watch is not cruelty, yet a husband has succeeded in proving that his wife was cruel because (inter alia) of her threatened violence if he would not bring himself to look at the television programme of her choice. Perhaps this subtle distinction exemplifies the superiority of visual over merely aural perception. Yet do not all such commonplace factors amount to no more than what Lord Justice Asquith once called 'the reasonable wear and tear of married life, and, if [they] were a ground for divorce, a heavy toll would be levied on the institution of matrimony'?[41]

When it was alleged to be cruelty for a man to gamble and get into debt, Lord Goddard caustically remarked: 'Next it will be said that if a man with a highly neurotic wife goes and plays golf every weekend, it is conduct conducing to her insanity'.[42] In parenthesis; whilst it might be possible to find a few golfers, off the course, who in an unguarded moment might admit that the game sometimes has a corroding influence upon matrimony, and whilst – I suspect – they might not be *good* golfers, nevertheless it is necessary to remember that Stephen Leacock once described it as 'not being a game . . . but being a form of moral effort'. But to continue: the late Mr Commissioner Blanco-White, whom I knew well, once said in an unreported case where a husband, a respectable public servant, conducted a dance band at night: 'Wives must put up with their husband's hobbies'. Thus a husband, though a rotter, is not legally cruel if he goes to watch a football match instead of taking his wife to the nursing home to have her first baby, but he is cruel if he shares his wife, in a small flat, with a python, a boa-constrictor and an alligator. To these unreported decisions may be added those in which Mr Justice Sachs observed that 'to drink in public houses is not yet of itself a matrimonial offence, any more than it is to be a vegetarian or go fishing', whilst Mr Justice Wilmer surmised that 'you may marry a keen fisherman or a golf addict . . . These come within the phrase, "for better or worse" '.

The case in which a wife persistently pulled her husband's hair, seized him by the ears, shook his head violently and called him horrible names far into the night looks, at first sight, a commonplace one. In fact, it was quite otherwise. The wife's object was to pester her mate into having a reluctant intercourse with her so that, by the time he was thoroughly exhausted by her importunities, his sole means of getting any rest at all was to comply with her demands. Thereafter, of course, the fact that he did so condoned her previous cruelty.[43] But a wife who refused intercourse to her husband, invariably wore men's clothes, smoked a pipe, and rode a man's bicycle, *was* guilty of cruelty.[44] So, too, was a husband who habitually flaunted his desire to dress as a woman in front of his wife,[45] although when a husband powdered himself, dressed as a woman in private and still went to great pains to hide his feminine clothing from his wife, he was held not to be cruel, though she was alleged to have had a nervous breakdown through his transvestism.[46]

These reflections on the vagaries of human behaviour were, in part, prompted by what was then a revolutionary decision of the House of Lords. Henceforth, a husband whose insanity caused suffering to his wife would have no defence to a charge of cruelty under the M'Naghten rules for, whatever his state of mind, and although his conduct was not aimed against his wife, she was enabled to divorce him simply because the character and gravity of his acts amounted to cruelty.[47]

I was also prompted by the abortive attempt by Mr Leo Abse, M.P., in a private member's bill, to make seven years' separation a ground for divorce at the instance of either the deserted or the deserter. Doubtless, many of our adversaries gloated over the Vassall-Profumo-Ward-'Lucky' Gordon-Rachmann-Etcetera scandals, and may have concluded that we English are a decadent nation. Yet Mr Justice Marshall, in his address to the jury in the Ward trial, whilst warning them not to adopt a Pecksniffian attitude, remarked: 'One would have thought from what we have all been faced with in the national newspapers that this country has become a sort of sink of iniquity. But you and I know that the even tenor of family life over the overwhelming majority of our population goes quietly and decently on'. Perhaps the essential truth of the learned judge's words accounts for the fact that such strange bedfellows as the Church of England, the Roman Catholic Church and the Free Church Federal Council all agreed that Mr Abse's proposals introduced a 'dangerous new principle'. Their views supported by Sir Jocelyn Simon, President of the Probate, Divorce and Admiralty Division. Stating that the importance of the stability of family life to general human happiness is axiomatic, he went on to point out that the children who may be affected by a divorce cannot petition the legislature with their grievances or plead their injuries. 'It is at the moment of break up of the home that one finds a sudden and alarming deterioration of the child – bad behaviour, speech disorders, and plummeting down in class'. He told a story with a 'macabre verity' about a woman who, in seeking guidance, wrote: 'My husband keeps telling me to go to hell: can I take the children?' Sir Jocelyn also pointed out that wives are sometimes brought under 'a quite cruel and relentless pressure' to divorce husbands who wish to re-marry and that divorce by consent would increase the scope of these situations.

To such arguments Mr Abse and his followers retort that the majority of the 33,818 divorce petitions in 1962 were undefended. What else (they say) is this but divorce by consent, save that the law, somewhat hypocritically, likes adultery to help it along?

The real question, it seems to me, is who suffers most from a cruel situation? The deserter? The deserted? Or the children? (God forbid that a millstone should be put around their young necks!) If you seek an objective judgment on this question, ask yourself what our friend Anon's comments might be in 100 or 500 years' time.

Babblative and Scribblative Lawyers

We lawyers ought at all times to have a special regard for words for they are the tools of our trade and, properly used, they are mordant, and full of power.

'But words are things; and a small drop of ink
Falling, like dew, upon a thought, produces
That which makes thousands, perhaps millions, think.'

By habit we are usually careful how we choose and use these tools, for whoever heard of an inarticulate but yet successful lawyer? There is scarcely one of us who would not put his hand upon his heart and identify himself with Confucius, who is reported to have said that if language is not correct, then what is said is not what is meant; if what is said is not what is meant, then what ought to be done remains undone; if this remains undone, morals and arts will deteriorate; if morals and arts deteriorate, then justice will go astray; if justice goes astray, the people will stand about in hopeless confusion.

A number of things can blunt and spoil our tools of trade as, for example, verbosity, or obscurity, or euphemism. Over 400 years ago one of our judges declared that 'the law hath appointed in what words [the judgment] shall be given, and if other words should be suffered, great uncertainty and confusion would ensue, and needless Verbosity is the Mother of Difficulty'[48] And even in our own hustling, bustling age when time is worth gold we sometimes meet what Robert Southey (had he been holding my pen) might well have called babblative barristers and scribblative solicitors.

As to obscurity, there is the story of Mr Justice Maule, and the floundering advocate. 'Mr Smith,' said the learned judge, 'Do you not think that by introducing a little order into your narrative you might possibly render yourself a trifle more intelligible? It may be my fault that I cannot follow you. I know that my brain is getting old and dilapidated. But I should like to stipulate for some sort of order. There are plenty of them. There is the chronological, the botanical, the metaphysical, the geographical; even the alphabetical order would be better than no order at all.'

Believe it or not, on one occasion some lessees – hard-headed business men – who were clear in their own minds that they wanted an existing seven years' lease to be renewed for a further term of fourteen years, wrote to their lessors asking merely for a new tenancy 'upon the terms of the current tenancy' and then, later on, expressed themselves aggrieved at getting no more that the seven years they had really asked for.

'What a man has written, he has written,' ruled the Court of Appeal. Of the plea that the writer should not be taken to mean what he wrote because in his inmost (although unexpressed) thoughts he intended something different, the Court said: 'If that were accepted, a state of chaos in regard to all documents would soon be produced.'[49]

There is a proverb that trouts are tickled best in muddy waters, but how often does it pay the lawyer to sully the stream! Rather more than thirty years ago, in an important document prepared by counsel, I came across that inconclusive phrase 'and/or' which was once scornfully described in the House of Lords as a 'bastard conjunction'.[50] On a still lower plane, some then current regulations about rear lights on cars explained that 'the expression "illuminated area" means, in relation to a lamp, the area of the orthogonal projection on a vertical plane at right angles to the longitudinal axis of the vehicle of that part of the lamp through which light is emitted.' (My word! at what angle are we now travelling?) I am tempted to offer a prize, consisting of a copy of this book, for the clearest and most concise exposition of what this definition was designed to mean. Would-be competitors may regale themselves with the thought that in a certain case bristling with technical difficulties Baron Martin once asked:

'Is not the judge bound to know the meaning of all words in the English language? Or if any are used technically or scientifically, to inform his own mind by evidence and then to determine the meaning?[51]

On the other hand they would do well to remember that Lord Justice Scrutton once remarked: 'I can only endeavour to construe this section by the words used in it, but if I am asked whether I have arrived at the meaning of the words which parliament intended I say frankly I have not the slightest idea.'[52]

No doubt mealy-mouthed speech is harmless enough on the lips of immature people but to anyone who admires the strength of plain words it is poor stuff. We talk of calling a spade a spade. So did the Greeks 2,000 years ago. (But why a spade, of all things?) When today a burning question of public importance rears its excited head, a Royal Commission or a select committee is usually set up to consider it. A number of exceedingly busy, learned people spend a long time, perhaps three or four years, or fifty, or even more, considering all aspects of the problem and eventually they make recommendations, quite often unanimously. The work they do is of great worth and yet the pigeon-holes of Whitehall overflow with their unheeded reports. There is no prospect that the results of their valuable researches will be converted into law for many years to come and the invariable excuse for this lack of parliamentary time. Yet it is against this background of vital legislation constantly neglected that both Houses of Parliament found time to debate a bill calling itself the Sanitary Inspectors (Change of Designation) Bill some thirty years ago.

Obviously, at that point in time, we were producing a new breed of sanitary inspectors who were too squeamish to call themselves such. They wished to be known as 'public health inspectors.' Oh! Dan, Dan, the sanitary man, what will our children's children make of you? 'The word 'sanitation', it is said, though as a matter of etymology it means the same as health, has in popular parlance come to be connected with drains, sewers, water closets and the like: and this, it is argued, leads to a quite inadequate and partial view of the wide scope of the work of these officers' – embracing, as it does, anything from the sampling of ice cream to the abatement of a smoke nuisance. It was seriously argued in the House of Lords that the proposed change of name would materially assist recruitment to the under-staffed public service. In opposition one of their Lordships argued that 'though the word "sanitary" does in fact mean exactly what is required, an increasingly ignorant public thinks that it means something else, namely, concerned with drains . . . Being increasingly ignorant both of Latin and of English, people think, when they hear the word "sanitary", not of health but of sewers. It would be a melancholy thought if years of compulsory education had resulted in our people becoming more and more ignorant of the meaning of words, and if every few years Parliament had to pass an Act to deal with, or pander to, their increasing illiteracy'.

The speaker pointed out not only that the title 'sanitary inspector' was right but that the proposed title 'public health inspector, but, whatever it is that these admirable men inspect, it is not public health.
inspector, but whatever it is that these admirable men inspect, it is not public health.

In the House of Commons where it was said, 'This is

fundamentally a silly Bill and a foolish proposal', one member thought that 'it would be a great pity if people got the idea that environmental health was now a rather delicate affair, which could be done by going along with a penicillin spray without having to tackle the basic problems of bad smells, bad drains, bad refuse collection and all the kinds of things that, at the back of our urban civilisation, are the real dangers of the spread of infectious diseases.' And one speaker after another testified to the honour that attached to the title of sanitary inspector which the bill proposed to abolish – honour that had been gained in the past in fighting powerful slum landlords. Others saw in the change of name a lever for an increase in salaries. However, it is a melancholy reflection that this foolish trifle ultimately became law.

As I write I have at my elbow an antipodean friend, a Melbournian, who assures me that the people of that city still call ratcatchers 'ratcatchers', although perhaps charwomen and domestic servants have turned themselves into cleaners and household workers. By contrast, an English friend of mine, a man with some old-fashioned ideas, who has young children at home, being plagued with rats, sought expert assistance in destroying them. He telephoned to his local town hall and asked for the aid of a ratcatcher. 'Ratcatcher?' questioned a slightly shocked voice. 'Surely you must want our Rodent Operative!' (He would, of course, have sounded a little less stupid if he had spoken of a rodent extinction operative.) But at least these gentlemen never sought the help of parliament in order to assume their high-falutin' title.

But perhaps my whole attitude to this question is ill-founded. Perhaps (as one of our legal writers here has suggested) we solicitors ought to do something about changing our name! After all, we must respect words, and the very last thing we are allowed to do as professional men is to solicit.

The Bums Invade Smout's Castle

The late Lord Justice Harman, with his tall, upright figure and high silk hat, was almost to be compared with Saul, the son of Kish who, from his shoulders and upwards was higher than any of the people. Metaphorically, too, he towered above many of his brethren and, besides that, he expressed himself in his judgments pellucidly and mellifluously with many classical and other allusions.

Having myself often quoted Lewis Carroll, I take comfort from the fact that Lord Justice Harman did that very thing about a quarter of a century ago. He said that 'during this extremely interesting case, I was reminded irresistibly of a poem by an eminent mathematician:

"And when I found the door was locked
I pulled and pushed and kicked and knocked
And when I found the door was shut
I tried to turn the handle but."

"Is that all?" said Alice.

"That is all" '.

That, he considered, described the situation in the case before him which in effect, and to a limited extent, decided whether or not an Englishman's house remained his castle in the year 1963 (let alone, today), for, of course, it always used to be such. For example, writing about us little more than a hundred years ago, Ralph Waldo Emerson said, in reference to our passion for independence: 'The laws are framed to give property the securest possible basis, and the provisions to lock and transmit it have exercised the cunningest heads in a profession which never admits a fool . . . The house is a castle which the King cannot enter'. Then again Pitt once told parliament that 'the poorest man may in his cottage bid defiance to all the forces of the Crown. It may be frail, its roof may shake, the wind may blow through it, the storms may enter, the rain may enter – but the King of England cannot enter; all his forces dare not cross the threshhold of the ruined tenement!'

I myself was suckled upon the truism that an Englishman's home is his castle but it is some years now since I was weaned away from it. To take a simple though, by modern standards perhaps, an extreme example. Having suffered a housebreaking in this most burglarious of all neighbourhoods in London during the past year I have no less than twice recently feared (though not physically) to tackle two other intruders, in an uninhibited fashion, lest the court punish me more severely than it punishes them, for such things do happen. The fact that they turned out, despite their furtiveness and their curious choice of hours, to have had no provable felonious intent is neither here nor there.

In considering our state of castlelessness (just in case there might be such a word) I am not thinking seriously about the officials who are allowed to demand entrance to my castle in order to satisfy themselves that I am not fiddling with their gas and electric light meters installed on my property, for today their legal rights are reasonably circumscribed. Perhaps I can even bring myself to tolerate – but not, of course, on my own premises – those whose business it is to see that a house is not insanitary, dangerous or in conflict with some building law. But I would stifle at birth the multitude of miserable, soulless, meddlesome little men whom the law of England allows to poke and pry, unwanted and uninvited, within the portals of my home, in order to satisfy their morbid curiosity as to whether I have an excess of weeds in my garden (which I have never had), or some forged trade mark (hidden under my bed), or a machine for producing artificial cream (somewhere or other), or the apparatus of illegal gambling (obviously up the chimney) or even an obscene book by my bedside (where it would be if I had one). Thank goodness that if a policeman comes to the house to inquire about some road accident and I request him to go away I can treat him as a trespasser if he refuses to do so.

Yet, a London magistrate granted the police a warrant to search for and seize any documents suspected of having been forged in the offices of a firm of London solicitors![53] When the problem came before the Divisional Court it was not determined because the search warrant proved to be bad on its face. Yet how can a reputable firm of solicitors hope to carry on their essentially confidential business if it is even remotely possible that some busybody may at some later date be permitted to peer into their private papers?

In short, as someone (I know not whom) remarked in the House of Lords a year or two ago: 'An Englishman's home is no longer his castle, any more than your lordships' castles are any longer your homes'.

Of course, in these days, only a handful of peers – and perhaps, a thimbleful of commoners – actually live in castles in Scotland and England. There are not that number of castles left to go round. But today, as I write, there is a report in the daily papers about a member of the House of Commons who actually lives in a castle in the West Country. A member of the council of the local authority was passing this fortress when he heard the unaccustomed roar of a pneumatic drill. There happened to be, as he knew, a wartime blockhouse in the castle grounds and this fervent servant of the public, on the evidence of his ears, feared that it was being demolished without official permission under our town planning laws. The outcome of this squabble – which involves no less a person than a member of parliament – matters nothing. But really, I ask you . . .

But to return to Lord Justice Harman's case.[54] It concerned, he said, a plumber with the Shakespearian name of Smout, whom I regret I have been unable to identify. Perhaps his lordship had in mind the tinker Snout in *A Midsummer-Night's Dream*? At all events the living present-day plumber, Smout, had come into collision with two essentially live bailiffs named Southam and Bland. Pause and just try to imagine a remorseless chap like a bum with the genial name of Bland! He is calculated to make Fang and Snare, the sheriff's officers in *King Henry IV, Part II*, look unabashed rotters.

At all events in the foggy month of November 1962, in the heavily industrialized Lancastrian town of Barrow-in-Furness, Messrs Bland and Southam knocked at the front door of the house of a certain Mrs McGuire in connexion with a judgment debt against her of twenty-five shillings. They knocked in vain for she was out but, with the prescience of most county court bailiffs, they straightaway went to the home of her son-in-law, the redoubtable plumber Smout, where, with typical foresight, Bland hammered on the front door whilst Southam took up a strategic position at the rear of the premises. The door was not locked but merely stuck so that Bland's repeated rappings caused it to open and, as you may well have anticipated, he immediately went through the house and admitted his pal Southam. Now at that moment it seems that Mrs McGuire could not, like the eighteenth-century wit, Isaac Browne, claim of the delights of tobacco –

By thee protected, and thy sister beer,
Poets rejoice, nor think the bailiff near.

– and that, for at least three reasons. First, because so far as I know, she is not a poet. Secondly, because the bailiffs were not merely near, but in. And thirdly, because at that particular moment she was busy giving her grandchildren their dinner.

But Smout the plumber was there. And for some reason not known to me he recognized that Southam was a bailiff. Furthermore, evincing a fair and restrained knowledge of his legal position, instead of knocking Southam down in a blunt Lancastrian manner, he contented himself with saying, with apparent politeness, 'You are not asked into this house. Go out and ask to come in'. (Those, at any rate, are the words used in the report.)

Unfortunately history has been deprived of the knowledge of what Smout would have done had Southam complied with his eminently reasonable request for, in fact, the bailiffs failed to take themselves off so that Smout, although he did not smite Southam, removed him with no more force than was necessary to eject a trespasser. Meanwhile Mrs Smout borrowed twenty-five shillings from a neighbour – for the Lancastrians are an essentially kindly people – and paid off the bailiffs on her mother's behalf, so that they departed without arresting Mrs McGuire. Why they should have been resentful after such a successful operation, I cannot tell but Southam later complained to the county court judge that he had been assaulted in the course of his duty and Smout was fined £10.

Smout felt sore and appealed to the court of Appeal where Lord Denning, Master of the Rolls, observed that as this was a criminal case the prosecution had to prove beyond reasonable doubt that the bailiff was not a trespasser. Lord Denning has often dealt some hard blows against old laws that he regards as incompatible with present day conditions and a modern outlook. In this he is as scornful as Lord Macmillan who, in one case,[55] referred to 'a legal system which for so long admitted as suitors in its courts those wholly fictitious persons,

John Doe and Richard Roe'. In the present instance Lord Denning considered that the question depended upon an early 17th century proposition 'that the house of everyone is to him as a castle and a fortress'.[56] A sheriff is not allowed to break in. What, then, is to happen when a door is shut, but not locked, bolted or barred, but may be opened by lifting a latch, turning a knob, or just by pushing? A distraining landlord may open a door that is simply closed[57] and his lordship was unable to see a distinction in principle between a landlord entering under lawful process to make a distress and sheriff's officer entering under a warrant to effect an arrest under civil process.

However, the bums had chosen to invade Smout's castle, not that of his mother-in-law and Lord Denning, having asked what right he had to do so, answered his own question by stating that the law on this subject was well settled. If a bailiff enters a stranger's house to execute process, he does so at his peril. If the defendant's goods or the defendant himself are not there, the bailiff's intrusion is unlawful. If they happen to be there, he is justified by the event. Lord Justice Harman concurred, although he considered it extraordinary that a bailiff who entered a house which was not the debtor's castle was justified in doing so only if he happened to find the debtor within its walls. It was, he said, a case of justification, not by faith, but by works. The court dismissed Smout's appeal but reduced his fine from £10 to £2.

Thus, with the passing of time, status symbols change. Jones may vie with Jones over the size of his washing machine, the quality of the tube in his 'telly', or the number and (especially) the performance of his cars, although he cannot get into Debrett merely by owning a *felis onca*. Yet he no longer seeks to surround his stronghold with a moat, a drawbridge or a portcullis and, I suspect, it would avail him little if he did.

Smout evinced the normal healthy independence of a typical Englishman but he had neither the money nor the truculent obstinacy of a financier for whom the late Frank

Lockwood Q.C. acted in a series of appeals right up to the House of Lords. Having lost there the financier demanded, 'Well, where do we go to now?' 'You know, they ought to breed from you', replied his counsel.

Singapore

From time to time Marjorie, my wife, and I have stopped off on our way to Australia at the fascinating equatorial city of Singapore.

Fortunately, on most of our visits, the monsoon cloud-bursts have kept us indoors no longer than the odd half hour, so that we were able to see many strange sights and observe much of interest, not only to laymen, but to lawyers also.

For example, immediately after our arrival, on being driven from the airport to our hotel, our chauffeur told us that the speed limits were 60 kilometres per hour on ordinary roads and 80 kilometres per hour on highways – a tell-tale light flashes on the roof of your car if you go over the top. More importantly, no one is permitted to drive with any alcohol whatever in his system. I am no wowser, but surely by anyone's standards that cannot be otherwise than a sane and wise precaution.

In England, where tens of thousands of people – many of them innocent people – are killed or maimed beyond recovery every year, a number of top-ranking police officers would like to introduce a total ban on driving on the part of anyone who has taken any alcohol whatever, but the pressures on members of

Parliament against supporting legislation to this end would be quite intolerable. I believe that the opposition is based upon a wrong-headed interpretation of the word 'liberty'.

You do see and hear some peculiar things as you walk around the main streets of Singapore. Waiting at traffic lights, I saw a Chinese on a bicycle with a medical thermometer in his mouth. I should love to have your best guess: what *was* he supposed to be doing? Another odd thing. We had just visited a sacred site. Outside were two young Australians. From long experience I should have known how dangerous it is to bet with anyone from that great betting country. However, I felt constrained to say:

'I've just done something I'll wager neither of you blokes has ever done.'

'What's that?'

'Gone to the loo in a Buddhist temple.'

'We've just done the same, mate!"

Vast tracts of the Republic of Singapore have been reclaimed from the sea, and here some 2,500,000 people live, made up of 75 per cent Chinese, 13 per cent Malay and 9 per cent Indian, whilst most of the rest are of British origin. One thought is uppermost in my mind and recurs constantly. It is simply this. At a time when we in Britain were running wild in the ancient rain forests, clad in the skins of native wolves and tigers, and, beneath, coloured with woad stains, these people of China were as civilised as we are today. No wonder so many of them exude courtesy and culture in every walk of life.

Incidentally, when, in the famous Raffles Hotel, I bade goodbye to our delightful Chinese head waiter – a true gentleman if ever I met one – two or three guests at a nearby table looked down their long superior, toffee-covered, colonial noses, just as if I had shaken hands with Apollyon himself.

Whilst in Singapore, amongst a multitude of interesting experiences, we sailed in a junk round the island and visited a crocodile farm. The belly of one of these revolting creatures, when the skin has been polished with milk and white of egg, produces the material for a lady's handbag or a man's wallet that fetches $S32 (call it very roughly £11) per square inch!

Incidentally, on our travels we passed one superb-looking golfcourse – rather a tiger one, I thought – where, we were told, playing members are required by the rules of their club to wear two pairs of stockings when wearing shorts. Surely, this is carrying decency a trifle far? Or, perhaps, there were venomous snakes about the place!

We also visited Changi Prison where many of my and, doubtless, your friends and relatives were incarcerated during the Japanese war of 1941 to 1945. There we saw the chapel which was formerly a hospital for wounded Allied prisoners of war. On the walls there were plaques bearing the regimental badges and names of many famous fighting units, but I scanned the entire place in vain for any mention of the East Surrey Regiment in which my younger brother fought all the way down the Malay Peninsular from the Thailand border to Singapore before being captured there. As a prisoner of war he worked on the infamous Thailand-Burma Railway, running alongside the River Kwai Noi northwards from Kanchanaburi, later to be transported to Japan. Not only did he survive but, today, at the age of sixty-eight, he is still playing cricket as the skipper in charge of a bunch of schoolboys. I dare say a good many wrinkles about our national game, and other things beside, rub off on to these youngsters.

When visiting Changi Gaol we were all required, somewhat reluctantly, to surrender to the warders on duty, not only our precious passports, but also our wallets containing all our money. That was something that I would *never* agree to do, so that I concealed all my money, as well as all the jewellery that my wife was carrying in her handbag – and the prison warders never searched me!

One remarkable fact about life in Singapore is that no less than 81 per cent of the population live in publicly-provided housing. Also, we saw many 'factory flats' where people live above their place of work – that wouldn't suit me. Women are apparently debarred from bearing more than two children, although I must confess I fail fully to understand how this prohibition is enforced in the ordinary course of daily life. Nevertheless, all women who have graduated from university are permitted to breed as many offspring as they like. Perhaps that's merely a novel way of rearing a race of elite youngsters!

One thing that struck me most forcibly about Singapore is that Lee Kuan Yew keeps his people on a fairly tight rein. Strict speed limits on the road. Population control. And no litter on the streets. Especially, no litter! London, which used to be one of the most impeccably clean cities in the world is now one of the filthiest. But here, in Singapore, should you be so unwise as to drop one single bus ticket on the pavement, you become liable to a maximum fine of $S500 – which, I believe, cannot be less than about £170.

Coincidence in the Dead Heart
of Australia

'The Ghan' is the name of a train that carries passengers to the dead heart of Australia. It now runs directly from Adelaide to The Alice (as Alice Springs is universally known), whereas when I went there 37 years ago, you had to travel from the South Australian capital to Port Pirie on a train having a gauge of 5 feet 3 inches; afterwards you changed to a gauge of 4 feet 8½ inches towards Port Augusta (known locally as 'Port Disgusta'); before you finally embarked upon the exciting 700 or so miles trip to The Alice on the Ghan's gauge of 3 feet 6 inches, which constantly rocked you from side to side and up and down as you sat in your carriage, but mercifully lulled you to sleep as you lay down for the night.

During the first hot summer week of January 1951 when I made the trip to The Alice in the old Ghan, my companions were a crocodile hunter from Darwin, a truck driver from Adelaide and a bank inspector from Sydney. We wore only shorts plus plimsoles, the latter to safeguard our feet when we jumped down on to the burning sand at some station. And what fun we had! Whenever, after every forty, or fifty, or sixty miles we stopped at some town marked upon the map, which sometimes consisted of no more than an hotel, a store, and a telegraph office, we first plunged into the bore water tank (containing water for cattle), and then, dripping, slowly made our way towards the pub where we quenched our undoubted thirst until the engine driver tootled a warning of his imminent departure, whereupon we collected a few bottles of cold beer before boarding the slowly moving train.

When, finally, after passing through a throat-parching red dust storm, with the temperature well above the ton, the old Ghan arrived at The Alice, I was guided by an Australian gentleman, who worked there and who is still a dear friend of mine, to one of the two pubs that then existed in the city. Jackeroos (workers at a sheep or cattle station) by the score, in spurred high-heeled boots and ten-gallon hats, were sitting on the concrete floor, quaffing their beers whilst their horses were tethered outside. I and my travelling companions and my new-found friend were soon doing likewise when, to my astonishment, a chap with a drooping moustache in a twenty-or-more gallon hat, and with hands about seven or eight inches wide, advanced upon me and announced, 'I'm the Mayor of The Alice. My name's Bob Buck.'

'How d'ye do, Mr Mayor', said I, gripping his punishing palm, 'I didn't even know that The Alice had a mayor'.

Now Lassiter was a gold prospector who was sponsored by the Government after he had declared that he had discovered rich seams in the desert to the far west of Alice Springs. He disappeared, possibly killed by the aborigines.

So I said: 'But I know you, Bob Buck. I know that you found Lassiter's body.'

Do you know, the fellow took several steps backwards on his heels. He was so astonished by the fact that a mere Pom knew about Lassiter. As you can imagine, we celebrated his ignorance by putting down one or two cool beers. So, after well over thirty years these wonderful and vivid memories flow back.

But earlier, as we had chugged and jolted and sweated at about an average of seventeen miles an hour through red desert, red soil, red mountains, reddish sky, red dust everywhere, and, emphatically, red heat, we came eventually to Oodnadatta, a township containing just three buildings. As we were putting down one or two cool drinks, I was astonished to see an English girl serving behind the bar because, in those distant days, no decent lady ever appeared in a pub anywhere in Australia.

I asked her where she came from.

'Near London'.

'I know London well. Whereabouts?'

'Well actually it's in Hertfordshire.'

'I've lived in Herts much of my life. Just whereabouts?

You wouldn't know it. A little place called Broxbourne.'

'I know Broxbourne well. Whereabouts in Broxbourne do you live?'

'Do you know Broxbourne railway station?'

'Very well.'

'There's a lane leads from there up to the main London-to-Hertford Road.'

'I know it.'

'Where the lane meets the main road there is a Queen Anne house.'

'Yes' (said I) 'and on the London side of it lies a paddock with ten loose boxes for horses.'

She was astonished. 'I was born in that house', she said.

'In which room?' I asked.

'If you go up the stairs from the front door, turn right, and take the first door on the left – that was where I was born.'

'Let me tell you', said I, to this casual acquaintance in Oodnadatta, 'that long before you were born, I often slept in that very room.'

TAILPIECE

Bob Buck asked me to play cricket for The Alice but, unfortunately, my travel arrangements would not allow me to do so. Pity! It would have been a wonderful story to brag about at Lords or the Oval. Or in an after dinner speech.

Fog, Clean Air, and Chimney Sweeps

Occasionally, very occasionally, I yearn to be a benevolent dictator. I should like to compel other people to enjoy a few of the things that I myself enjoy. For example I should like to make them read, towards the end of every December, *A Christmas Carol* by Charles Dickens.

Dickens' descriptions of the holiday vary like our December climate. In *The Pickwick Papers* the hero and his friends, when they were not thawing themselves with hot punch round a roaring fire, spent a freezing morning, their hands blue with frost, skating on the ice. In *Bleak House* there is a contrasting scene in which Esther Summerson artlessly asked the law clerk whether there was a fire, because the streets were so full of dense brown smoke. 'Oh dear no, miss', he said, 'This is a London particular. A fog, miss,' he added by way of explanation. At the opening of *A Christmas Carol* it was a cold, bleak, biting Christmas Eve with the fog pouring in at every chink and keyhole. The miserable Scrooge, the miser, in his counting-house could hear the passers-by wheezing, beating their hands on their chests, and stamping their feet on the pavement. The city clocks had just gone three, but it was quite dark already.

All this, of course, would chill you physically and (I imagine) metaphorically also. And that the passing of the 'pea-soupers' of my boyhood days should give me a feeling of nostaglia is, I realize, quite beyond reason. Often I have seen 'the yellow fog' as T. S. Eliot calls it 'that rubs its back upon the window panes.' Today we have far fewer coal fires but far more motor cars with their insidious and carcinogenic fumes. In consequence, our fogs are now grey rather than yellow in colour but they still make your throat sore and your eyes smart and they are deadly. In 1952 4,000 Londoners choked and gasped in sudden death in a mere four days of smog. Another 8,000 men and women died soon after from the same cause. And, of course, smog is now blamed for much carcinoma of the lungs. That is not surprising because in 1952 over 600 tons of smoke came from Londoners' domestic fires each day and a further 400 tons were produced by London's industries. Over seventeen tons of solid sulphur fell to the square mile in central London in one month. Indeed, throughout Great Britain eighty per cent of the population is urban and 12,000,000 men with their families then lived in grossly polluted areas. And, thirty and more years ago, the cost of this pollution (in addition to the waste of fuel) exceeded 150,000,000 each year.

Death on this unprecedented scale shook us all out of our lethargy. Local authorities up and down the country started to fight the menace with by-laws and private Acts although, at first, in some industrial areas, this meant little more than that they compelled people with smokey chimneys to raise their chimney stacks higher.

The citizens of Manchester, however, were pioneers in setting aside an experimental area of 400 acres within which they imposed an absolute ban upon all smoke. Just after they had done so I myself visited the city and saw something that no one within living memory had every seen regularly there – blue skies above me. Nevertheless, just after this remarkable change, the densest brown blanket in living memory smothered Manchester and this 'ocean of filth' (as the local M.O. calls it) caused a sharp and sudden rise in the death-rate. Even so, the city's 'smokeless zone' is far cleaner than the surrounding areas. The Mancunians were proud of their achievement and they claimed that it is only when a man is aware that clean air is more than a remote ideal and that he is determined, and knows that the local authority is also determined, that his neighbour shall not get away with an offence which he himself has been required to refrain from, he will be ready to play his part with a good grace.

Then, in the early part of 1955 one of the London boroughs created a tiny 'smokeless zone' in a new housing estate, making it a condition of tenancy that no smoke whatever should be emitted.

This word 'smokeless' is an euphemism for 'less smoky' because of course, the local authority is powerless to raise barriers to stop heavy smoke from drifting across from ten thousand factories in adjoining areas.

A week or two later the ancient city of London itself became a smokeless zone. For some days there were reports (although I myself saw nothing) of hidden policemen spying from behind chimney stacks on rooftops in order to catch offenders. Even so there were then still twenty-seven boroughs who were polluting their two cleaner neighbours as well as themselves. And, of course, even the partial abatement of smog takes time and vast sums of money.

A far more ambitious scheme for purifying, in not less than fifteen years, the whole of England, Wales and Scotland was contained in the Clean Air Act, 1956 which aimed to cleanse our atmosphere in a number of ways. Thus it declares that 'dark smoke shall not be emitted from a chimney of any building.' Penalties are fines of £10 on householders and £100 on others for each offence. And in case those of you who are advocates immediately speculate how you might succeed in a defence

146

which sought to quibble about the density of the smoke, I may tell you that both 'smoke' and 'dark smoke' were carefully defined. Dark smoke, in fact, 'means smoke which, if compared in the appropriate manner with a chart of the type known . . . as the Ringelmann Chart would appear to be as dark as, or darker than shade 2 on the chart'. This talk of 'appropriate manner' and technical charts makes me think that prosecutions under the Act will involve the calling of smog inspectors and experts as witnesses so that I wonder whether the Mancunian remedy of watching my neighbour and being watched by him is not a more effective and cheaper one.

Next, the installation of new industrial furnaces were prohibited unless they could be operated without emitting smoke. The owners of existing furnaces had to find ways of eliminating soot, ash and gritty particles, but a number of defences are provided under the bill to ensure fairness. For example it is open to an industrialist to show that his pollution of the neighbourhood was due to his lighting up a coal furnace. Even a householder may successfully plead that his local coal merchants had run out of smokeless fuel.

Local authorities were encouraged to declare 'smoke control areas' in which the emission of *mere* smoke – as distinct from *dark* smoke – was punishable. The fabulous cost of converting some ten million fireplaces in private homes, to say nothing of assistance given to industry, was borne by grants both by the Exchequer and by local authorities. Thus on the conversion of domestic fires the owner was required to bear thirty per cent of the cost, the local authority thirty per cent, and the National taxpayer forty per cent. Perhaps, therefore, you begin to realize why I referred to this clean air scheme as ambitious – indeed, so ambitious was it that, inevitably, it had to be modified in its application to dirty London where, ever since the birth of the Industrial Age, the stones of many famous public buildings have been rotted continuously before our eyes by sulphurous fumes.

147

Of course, pollution began much earlier than that era. There is a report of an action in 1628, written in the crude bastard language that lawyers then used, in which a landowner complained that only sixteen feet away from his premises the defendant 'ad erect la un brewhouse . . . et en le use de ceo arde sea-cole [inferior coal, as you can imagine] en grand quantity; et que horribles vapores et insalubres surge del brewhouse' so that all the plaintiff's 'biens et utensils fueront spoil per le smoke.' Even the judges conceded that 'sea-cole n'est cy sweet come wood,' although they sought to distinguish these happenings in the provincial city of Gloucester from 'un common nusans pres at Withal, ou le Roy inhabita' because, as everyone knew, le Roy 'est cy tender nosed que ne poit indurer sea-cole.'

Whilst strolling last week in a quiet and little known London square (where, incidentally, in 1784 Lord Chancellor Thurlow had the Great Seal of England stolen from him) I looked in at a church which is known (or used to be known) locally as 'The Sweeps' Church'. In 1834, as a protest against the cruelties of child labour, a testator bequeathed £1,000 to the rector and churchwardens upon trust to provide 100 poor chimney sweeps' apprentices with a good fat Christmas dinner each year. This recalls the days when the method – and, indeed, the only recognised method – of sweeping chimneys was, first, to set fire to the soot, and, then, as the blaze died down, to drive up the flue a miserable hungry wizened child of tender years, armed with a broom, where he spluttered and choked even if he escaped being scorched and blistered.

Today, these barbarous practices seem to us to belong to a remote past but it was not until 1840 that Parliament took any successful steps 'to prevent various complicated Miseries to which Boys employed in climbing and cleaning Chimneys are liable.' Perhaps, in a decade or two, there will be no more chimneys to sweep and then, perhaps, public opinion will deem it monstrous that I am now at liberty to belch domestic smoke over my neighbours and, equally, that I am bound to tolerate their showering their smuts upon me.

But to return to the sweeps' apprentices; under the express terms of their gift these wretched little creatures each received on Christmas Day half a pound of roast or boiled beef, half a threepenny loaf of bread, half a pound of potatoes, half a pint of ale or porter, half a pound of plum pudding and – when thoroughly replete – a bright new shilling. Can you imagine a more genuinely Dickensian Christmas scene than this conjures up?

Juries

It must surely be a fundamental principle of English law that a jury cannot err. The very word 'vere-dict' means a true answer. Yet Mr Dooley,[58] you may remember, had no flattering opinion of jurymen. A man was being tried before twelve indignant grocers, dragged from their stores and protesting that they would be made bankrupt through serving their country, when Mr Dooley observed: 'About noon his honor is woke be a note fr'm th' jury askin' how long they ar-re goin' to be kept fr'm their dinner. He hauls th' black cap out iv th' bandbox an' puttin' it on over his wig, says: "Pris'ner at th' bar, it is now me awful jooty to lave ye'er fate to a British jury. I will not attimpt to infloonce thim in anny way. I will not take th' time to brush away th' foolish ividence put in in ye'er definse. Ye'er lawyers have done as well as they cud with nowthin' to go on. If anny iv th' jury believe ye innocent let thim retire to their room an' discuss th' mather over a meal iv bread an' wather while th' chops burn on th' kitchen stove an' their clerks ar-re distributin' groceries free to th' neighbourhood.'

This theme of the juror caring enormously for his stomach recurs in English literature. Dickens brought it into his account of the trial of *Bardell* v *Pickwick*, and Pope went so far as to complain:

'The hungry judges soon the sentence sign and wretches hang that jurymen may dine.'

Nevertheless, although it was once the practice, for the sake of keeping jurors safe from outside influence, to incarcerate them almost like the criminals whose cases they tried. I cannot find much evidence in the law reports that they were allowed to become unduly ravenous in the interests of justice. It has been known for a jury to get supplies of food and beer by means of a string let down from the window of their retiring room. Thereafter they awarded excessively large damages![59] There has been talk of drinks and cigars with the plaintiff's solicitor.[60] And in the reign of Elizabeth I a jury took figs and pippins with them (which were not, however, supplied by either party to the action) when they retired to consider their verdict. For this impropriety the eaters were fined the crippling sum of £5 and the non-eaters, 40s. 0d.[61] But these cases must be regarded as exceptional.

On the other hand, lawyers sometimes complain that a jury is perverse because its findings upset the rigid pattern of the laws to which we have become accustomed. Yet the jury is always right. So it was that in the days when the stealing of something worth more than a shilling was a capital felony, many a jury deliberately disregarded the true value of the stolen property and grasped at some fiction in order to save a wretch's neck. They were right. And when a jury refused to convict William Penn the Quaker of unlawful assembly in the teeth of an unequivocal direction by the judge to do so, they were right – although they had to go to prison first in order to prove it![62]

The late Lord Justice MacKinnon once gave this picturesque description of what it means, in the age-old phrase, to put oneself upon one's country.[63] 'The clerk of assize for centuries said: "Culprit, how wilt thou be tried?" But he did not by "culprit" mean "You who are in fact guilty." For on the culprit saying in the time-honoured ritual "By God and my Country" the clerk rejoined "God send thee a good deliverance" .' And so today when an accused person puts himself upon his country, it is, in the words of Blackstone, 'The most transcendent privilege, which any subject can enjoy or wish for, that he cannot be affected either in his property, his liberty or his person but by the unanimous consent of twelve of his negihbours and equals.'

Of course, I am not saying that juries and jurors never misbehave. I have read of an unreported action in which one of the jurymen turned out to be the plaintiff in the case, although this did not become apparent until his counsel called on him to give evidence, whereupon he was seen to leave the jury box and make towards the witness box. When asked by Mr Justice Shearman, to explain his conduct, he answered: 'Well, my lord, I thought I was rather lucky!'

Then there were the jurors who, weary with having sat up all night, agreed in the morning to put two papers in a hat, marked P. and D. and to draw lots. P. came out and so they found for the plaintiff.[64] Again, a juror once confessed that after thirty hours' deliberation he and his fellows decided their verdict by tossing a coin.[65] However, so long as they truly make up their minds 'the highminded and intelligent dozen of men whom he saw in the box before him' – as Serjeant Buzfuz called them – are always at liberty to do so in their own ways. I am constrained to quote Mr Dooley again:[66]

'Whin the case is all over, the jury'll pitch th' tistimony out iv th' window, an' consider three questions: Did Lootgert look as though he's kilt his wife? Did his wife look as though she ought to be kilt? Isn't it time we wint to supper?'

The late Lord Goddard, when he was the Lord Chief Justice, appeared not to have quite the same unquestioning faith in the British jury as some of his contemporaries. In 1949, when speaking on the Juries Bill in the House of Lords, he said: 'I have often wondered whether the lip service that we all pay to the great palladium of British justice, the jury, is well justified, because it is a fact that many criminals want to be tried by the magistrate and not by a jury if they can possibly persuade the magistrate to take that course, and the same applies nowadays very much to civil cases.'

Then, in 1955, when swearing in a new Lord Mayor of London, he commented that failures of juries to agree had then of late been more frequent than formerly. A disagreement, he said, was always a great misfortune and often a calamity. The cost of successive trials might be very heavy and the inconvenience to witnesses perhaps incalculable. He asked whether the time had not come for an alteration in the law so that a majority verdict might be returned both in civil and criminal cases. If the dissentients were not more than one or two would there be any real risk of injustice?[67]

In Scotland majority verdicts are, and for centuries, have been, allowed. If in that country the verdict could be returned by eight votes to seven, of a jury of fifteen, he did not believe that any injustice would result if the law of England allowed a verdict by a majority of, say, nine to three. (However, in parenthesis, let me remind you that Scotland is also the home of that unhappy, inconclusive and almost accusing verdict of 'Not proven'.)

Lord Goddard went on to speak of the possibility of reducing the number of jurors from twelve to seven, as was done during the war, except in capital cases. Yet he doubted whether a majority verdict could be taken from so small a number, though the saving in manpower would be considerable.

Lord Goddard's pronouncement provoked an immediate reply from Sir Travers Humphreys, who wrote out of his vast experience to *The Times* next day: 'I was brought up in the school of the first Lord Halsbury and the late Sir Harry Poland,

K.C. Both those great criminal lawyers regarded the right of a person accused of serious crime not to be deprived of his liberty until he had been convicted by the unanimous verdict of a jury as part of the unwritten constitution of our country – and they were both in the habit of adding, *"and a jury is always right".'* (author's italics).

'There are men of business', he continued, 'who regard any trial of any issue of fact by a jury as a waste of time. They may be right, but, after all, it is the English way and has lasted for over a thousand years. Abolish unanimity and you abolish the jury system.' As to reduction of numbers, Sir Travers' view was that seven was 'a dangerously low number.'

I imagine that many advocates prefer a jury, if only for the reasons that juries can be persuaded and that by persistence it is occasionally possible to change their minds even after they have given some indication of what their views are. It is said that whenever the great Carson was briefed in any case before a jury it was his practice to study the panel of jurors because a knowledge of their occupations might enable him to make the most of a technical point involving one of those very occupations.

TAILPIECE
After this chapter was originally written the Juries Act 1974 permitted majority verdicts – ten out of eleven jurors in the Crown Court and the High Court, and seven out of eight in the County court.

A Spanish Water Court

My first sight of the south-eastern corner of Spain, precisely due south from Greenwich and a thousand miles away, reminded me with a pang of parts of Australia. I saw a sunburnt country, often arid and bare, with an intensely cultivated coastal belt whose fertile soil bore, in different districts, rice, maize, bananas, citrus fruit, olives, almonds and vines, so that sometimes, without any effort of imagination, I thought that I was indeed in Queensland. In much of Spain, as in much of Australia, the presence of water spells life; its absence, death, destruction and ruin. There the likeness ceased, for Spain is stricken with poverty and her sons must toil (subject to a needed siesta in the afternoon) for long hours in the day, and sometimes at night too, in order to live. The Spaniard's way of life is in many ways quaintly mediaeval. Bullocks often draw his wooden plough, donkeys and mules provide transport, and amongst this hard-working, proud, abstemious, poor, but smiling people, woman is in many ways still subservient to the male. When each morning, she carries her pitcher on her hip to the fountain for water, she is using a vessel identical with those which Homer described some 800 years or more before the birth of Christ.

The peasants who live in the fertile coastal belt of the province of Valencia have inherited, unchanged, an ancient system of irrigation from the Moors. Precious water is stored in dams and from these, water channels (*aséquia*) a foot or so wide and equally deep and built of concrete, lead in an intricate pattern all over the countryside. Crops are planted on small plateaux (or *tabla*) which vary in size from a few square feet to about half an acre and the soil of the *tabla* is subdivided by shallow ditches, shaped with a mattock. The flow of water is controlled by tiny wooden gates (*puerta*) and in each locality one or more well-trusted members of the community decide the day and hour upon which the *puerta* shall open. If my allotted time happens to fall on the seventeenth day in the small hours of the morning, then I must leave my bed, ready, by lamplight, to alter the course of my own soil ditches by the deft use of my mattock, so as to ensure that all my land is evenly flooded. The customs governing the use of water are, of necessity, elaborate and stringently enforced.

If, on a Thursday mid-morning, you happen to be in the neighbourhood of the cathedral at Valencia, you may see, beside the Apostles' Porch, and only a stone's throw from the busy city traffic, the most ancient tribunal in Europe in session – the Tribunal of the *Aguas*, or Water Court. There are eight judges, honest and trusted laymen, who have been elected by their fellows, each of whom represents a principal *aséquia* and is intimate with the needs, perils, vagaries and usages of his own locality. They are bronzed and weather-beaten countrymen, dressed in black smocks with white, rope-soled sandals and they sit, railed off from the crowd, upon a green sofa brought from a nearby house. Their function – their entirely unofficial function – is to determine water disputes and abuses of custom. Directly they have assembled they remove their caps and their *alguacil* (or constable), acting as clerk of the court, opens the proceedings, speaking in the Valenciano patois. There is absolute silence. The parties, caps in hand, are deferential, for they know that it is in the court's power to deprive them of water. They may appear only in person. The decision of the court is swift, rough and ready, but essentially just, and, inevitably obeyed. There are no written records and the ruling or the penalty in each case has usually been carefully meditated upon beforehand and remains only to be formally pronounced.

Normally no one would contemplate defying the court so that fines are paid immediately on the spot. But if, for example, some wretch in a moment of greed or passion has stolen his neighbour's water or burned his crops, his sentence may well bring him utter ruin. On the other hand any attempts at an official investigation of larceny or arson by the State's Civil Guard would be futile, for not a soul would admit to any knowledge of the matter. Indeed, it is said that a betrayal of the secrets of the *Aguas* might be met with death. Unlawful private vengeance? Crude mediaevalism? Taking the law into one's own hands? Yet there can scarcely be a more truly democratic institution than the Tribunal of the *Aguas* which safeguards, by full and free common consent, the rights both of the community and of the individual and harms no one but the wrong-doer.

On arriving back in London from sunny Spain I found that precious water was leaking fast from sombre summer skies and did not cease from doing so for days on end.

Leprechauns and the Law

This particular piece (written in 1968) ought to be named 'Gossip column from Baile Atha Cliath', because I have just returned from the twelfth Conference of the International Bar Association, held in Dublin's fair city where the girls are so pretty, together (*inter alia*) with 203 Australian men and women.

First, may I express my commiserations with those Australians who, whilst travelling by air from Sydney, were compelled to make an unscheduled stop at Darwin because there was an insufficient supply of spirits aboard (both aviation fuel and whisky) to carry them and their plane across the ensuing seas. Never before did I realize that the jurisdiction of the Little People extended 12,500 miles from Ireland. But I am anticipating events.

By contrast, you could not possibly convince me that on my own journey from London any leprechaun crept aboard. Although, a day or two after flying over the green, grassy countryside of Ireland, I visited the Glen of the Downs and saw the famous 'forty shades of green' in trees, meadows, valleys and mountains, my very first impression of the Emerald Isle was that post-boxes everywhere were sage green instead of red. But I am bound to confess that at the beginning of this, my very first visit to the Republic, I did not believe in the real existence of these elfin sprites. That, of course, may have upset them.

I found myself in a country, clearly a foreign one, which my forbears had despoiled for many centuries. Despite this, our Irish hosts took us to a brilliant performance, in the Abbey Theatre, of Brendan Behan's *Borstal Boy*, the story of a teenage boy, cruelly treated by us English, but whose innocence we could not destroy. Indeed, I could recount one or two true histories of sadness, brutality and suffering under the Black and Tans about real people whom I met last week, and I saw with my own eyes many piteous relics of 'the Troubles'[68] in the Dublin museum. Yet our Irish hosts welcomed us with an unrivalled warmth of heart so that on that score the Little People ought not to have been against any of us. However, a number of apparently odd and unaccountable things began to happen.

First let me tell you how President de Valera, eighty-five years old, almost blind and led by the hand, straight as a ramrod but, it is said, much mellowed, attended the opening ceremony. With him were the Taoiseath, the Minister for Justice, and the Chief Justice who explained that the Irish word for 'welcome' (fáilte) has a double meaning for it implies both a salutation to a guest and a feeling of pleasure on the part of the host. Indeed, for centuries before 'the Troubles' came upon this gentle island, its kind-hearted inhabitants were always renowned because they regarded all strangers as their 'neighbour's children'.

Perhaps my first faint feelings of something odd going on were instilled by a letter to the editor of the *Irish Times* which my eye fell upon just as I sat down to breakfast on the first morning. 'Dear sir [said the writer], J. B. has got it all wrong. His cure is far too mild. One has to eat a feed of very salty bacon to induce a good thirst, not to drink afterwards for several hours, until the thirst becomes unbearable, then to hold one's open mouth over a bason of porter. Then the reptile will come out to drink. This old tale is known all over Ireland . . . '

Only one hour later an Australian V.I.P. told me that, on arriving at her hotel, and confessing to a real thirst, she asked for a Familiar Expensive English Long Drink. (I must not, of course, advertise.) 'I'm sorry, madam,' said the Irish waiter, 'but we don't serve FEELDs on Sunday.' My friend, with typical judicial caution, abandoned her quest for whatever this Irishman thought these Feelds she wanted were. This was one of the first things which began to lead me to believe that the Little People were trying to assume control.

Despite my then being a fairly hard-boiled sceptic, I began to have further doubts on the first morning of the conference because, in a printed paper about codes for ensuring fair trials and a free press, the unequivocal Irish view was given thus: 'It is essential in the interests of justice that . . . the previous bad character of a person accused of crime should be known to the jury.' Obviously, the leprechauns had got to work in the printers' shop. But did their influence go deeper? In answer to the question whether codes of conduct to ensure a fair trial should, in principle, be objective, one Australian representative answered that: 'Objectivity is a pure fantasy of the mind, there is no such thing.' Right or wrong, I cannot help feeling that this somewhat bald, harsh statement may have offended the Little People.

There was an evening reception at The Four Courts and the Honourable Society of King's Inns. The latter was founded by that evil English oppressor, Thomas Cromwell and, seeing that our ancient customs like dining in hall, and the wearing of wigs and gowns in court, still subsist, it is scarcely credible to me that there has ever been a rebellion. Irish barristers do not do their homework in chambers, but in the library of The Four Courts. Thence, as necessary, they are summoned by their clients for conferences.

Traffic conditions in Dublin are as bad as in most other capital cities and when one or two guests arrived at The Four Courts about half an hour before starting time, the police began to be worried about a parked car. A constable consulted his sergeant, the sergeant went up to his inspector, and this inspector to his superintendent. Eventually it was decided to tow away and impound the offending vehicle but . . . Just as the removal gang were opening up its doors, the Chief Justice himself walked out of the Four Courts and demanded to know why the gardia were tampering with *his* car. Clearly the leprechauns do not confine themselves to mere visitors.

So far as I myself was concerned the Little People were slow to react. At the lunch break on the first day, a lady barrister from South Australia accused me of having 'save-the-world' eyes. 'Do I look so lugubrious?' I asked. 'No' she answered, 'it is their humourous twinkle, and humour is the only salvation of this world.'

Thereafter, a number of people recognized me as a writer for the *Australian Law Journal*, rather than as the Chief Land Registrar for England and Wales, as I then was. One man from Perth told me that his young son was thinking of giving up the law and taking to reading this learned journal. Yet a prophet is without honour in his own country. One English solicitor who has had lunch under the same roof as me two or three times a week for about twenty-five years confessed, on thrice being introduced, to not knowing me. All this was a trifle odd, but no more.

However, just before another of these evening functions I dropped into a restaurant for a snack to serve me by way of blotting paper. The place was brim full. One local chap would not let me sit at his table because, as he bluntly asseverated, he wanted to read his paper. A gentleman nearby, seeing my predicament, immediately invited me to sit with him and his wife but, alas, until after they had both left – and he had, incidentally, and unknown to me, paid my bill – I did not realize that he was the judicial head of this hospitable country. The Little People had blinded my eyes and so I had to don a white sheet. And, to make me even more miserable, on arriving at the party, innocuously described as 'an Irish evening', I was immediately sat at a table and offered a four-course cold buffet. I avoided trouble in part by posing as a vegetarian. Clearly, however, the leprechauns were on my tail. Yet I never once saw a single wizened little chap, dressed in a green-dyed lamb's wool coat, with breeches of white bog cotton and a cap of dried mushroom.

One session of the conference was devoted to the discussion of a centralized computer system for storing legal knowledge. The idea is that reports of decided cases and the relevant statutes should be fed into a memory bank and then classified so that a lawyer would be able to retrieve relevant information and, in consequence, avoid long hours of research. This would not involve the replacement of lawyers, but merely divert their energies from hours of possibly fruitless reading to devising effectual remedies.

Accuracy is, of course, a *sine qua non* of legal work. But those were the days when many people were ignorant of the potentialities of computing techniques. Uninitiated people loved to relate computer horror stories, overlooking the fact that all computers are merely logical slaves and that such ludicrous mistakes as do occur, usually arise from bad programming. Of course, if one of the Little People were to distract the mind of your program writer, he might produce the sort of result that one of his kind did with the hippy whose hypodermic needle was filled with alphabet soup, so that when the poor fellow injected himself he came out in a four-letter word rash.

Another session dealt with a most informative and important paper on the support and custody of children, both illegitimate and belonging to divorced parents. Three short playlets, not written by Brendan Behan, were enacted by some lawyers there present, with the use of a real live baby, and happily the theme from most countries of the world seemed to be that the best interests of a child must override all other considerations. To what age should a child be supported?

The Irish claim that their world-renowned stout, produced in the famous brewery beside the banks of the River Liffey, is the best that a pregnant woman can take because, they say, 'when a child is born, he is almost fit for work'. The majority of delegates somehow found time to visit this brewery. Nearby is a public hospital which looks exactly like an army establishment. And well it might do because when, under British rule, the authorities in Whitehall designed, simultaneously, a barracks for somewhere in India and a hospital for the Irish, the Little People swopped the plans, and so frustrated both ideas.

Of course many of the delegates at this conference played hookey in order to go sightseeing. Thus I and some of my Australian friends saw a number of the ancient castles which the British built to last for ever – as well they may do, although not quite for their original purpose. We passed through villages where, it is claimed, the gulls fly upside down in order to keep the houses clean. Others went to Killarney to kiss the Blarney stone – a feat in bending backwards that must have presented formidable difficulties to one exceedingly stout Australian gentleman whom I met. I and one or two of my companions heard that there were diggings in County Louth near the River Boyne, the scene of the battle at which William of Orange defeated James II. At this, we all had visions of unearthing gold crocks, hidden by the leprechauns, but, in fact, alas, these were archaeological excavations. Of course, we went to Tara where St Patrick dwelt, so ridding Ireland of all snakes.

The harp that once through Tara's halls
Its soul of music shed,

Now hangs as mute on Tara's walls
    As if that soul were fled.

And, of course, today there are no walls. Only grass-lands, blown by the breezes, with vast vistas over the country-side in every direction.

Thus Freedom now so seldom wakes;
    The only throb she gives
Is when some heart indignant breaks
    To show that still she lives.

We also saw the thousand-year-old Celtic crosses at Monasterboyce, carved in a granite-like stone and depicting dozens of well-recognizable biblical scenes. An even there, at the foot of one pillar were the figures of two of the Little People.

On the last day of the conference, seeing that 1968 is the International Year for Human Rights, we were most fortunate in having U Thant address us. He explained how, both nationally and internationally, lawyers can strengthen the understanding by the public of the essential importance of our respecting the intrinsic dignity of the human being, regardless of creed, colour or sex. I nearly missed the chance of hearing him. My hotel was the best part of two miles from the site. He was to speak at 9.30 am. I arranged, as usual, to be called at 7.00 am with a pot of tea and the daily newspapers. Alas! Some leprechaun must have overpowered the night porter in my hotel with that delightful liqueur known as Irish mist and then obliterated my name from the call list. I was *not* awakened. I woke suddenly at 9.10 am and, with only twenty minutes to go, by a considerable effort, and some good fortune, I was there in time, unshaven and breakfastless, and damning all leprechauns, to hear U Thant speak.

During the final evening we were lavishly entertained in a former stately home at Castletown, in County Kildare, built in 1722. There were Irish pipers to greet us and from the very first moment everyone had enormous fun. One of my Australian friends was wearing a trendy button inscribed, 'Keep the Irish off the moon.' Of course, he cannot have heard the story about the Russian who bragged that they would be there in 1973, capped by the Americans who put their date in 1972. An Irishman, not to be outdone, claimed that his people would land on the sun before then. When some well-wisher explained that their astronauts would be burnt up, this Irishman explained: 'Not a'tall, a'tall. Shure, we'll do it be noight!'

So our work and our revels ended. My airplane gained height, the shy, darting, leprechauns disappeared from sight and eventually even the emerald mantle of this island dissolved in an Irish mist.

In view of some of the things I have written above, I decided that it might be unsafe to drop this piece into one of those green letter-boxes. Instead I have smuggled it home and dropped it into a familiar red one, which, I can assure you, is not under the influence of the Little People!

Danger in Sports

Gone are the days when a Victor Trumper could score a century before lunch! That happened in 1902 at Old Trafford, yet England lost by three simple runs.

Nevertheless I have often wondered at what stage a potential century maker feels in his bones that he will achieve the rounded perfection of 100 runs. Does he set his mind upon it whilst padding-up? Does he see it as a fair chance, perhaps when his 50 goes up on the score board? Or does he simply hope for the best when he reaches the eighties or nineties?

Only a few months ago I was having a drink in one of the 11,387 licensed premises in London's Metropolitan Police area when I chanced to overhear a man say that he was a lawyer from Victoria. His English companion seemed to be a little vague as to which continent Victoria was in! I approached and interrupted the conversation. 'What city do you come from?' 'Melbourne'. 'Do you ever read the A.L.J. (i.e., The Australian Law Journal)?' He did; and he proved to be one of my regular readers.

For thirty-six years I wrote a monthly letter for that learned journal; but subjects don't always come easily and I was scratching around, looking for that loose ball which would put my 100 up (i.e., my hundredth contribution), when I came across a fantastic letter written to an English provincial newspaper which gave me what I wanted.

I would mention, in passing, that over the then past year there had been a considerable correspondence in papers all over the country about cruelty to animals, with particular reference to stag hunting and other blood sports. The letter I have mentioned, however, included the following astonishing paragraph:

'It is because of unnecessary cruelty to worms that I would also suggest the prohibition of all games on grass. I once saw a beautiful worm unnecessarily killed by a rugby player's boot, and no doubt death by violence must be caused to millions of these useful creatures by the pursuit of balls.'

I began by referring to cricket; after reading this absurd letter, which no one outside England could have written, it was obvious to me that ball games must be my subject, particularly as in a recent case, by an odd concatenation of events, some little boys killed a man with a football. The case[69] does not appear to have evoked any novel principles and it has not been officially reported. For six years or so the defendants, an important manufacturing company, had allowed little boys up to the age of ten to play on a stretch of their grassland adjoining a busy highway. Football was the favourite game and the lads improvised goal posts by using a tree on one side and their jackets on the other. Sometimes, after a good kick, the ball rolled into the road and one day when this happened, the ball caused a motor cyclist to skid and fall off his machine, fracture his skull and die. His widow claimed damages for negligence.

Inevitably, the famous cricket ball which ten years earlier crashed into the House of Lords[70] was cited in this case. You will recall that in that case a batsman hit a straight drive just over 100 yards right over a fence at the top of a slope outside the boundary, the total height of bank and fence being seventeen feet above the wicket. Unfortunately, on landing the ball struck a lady standing in the roadway outside her house. It was a prodigious stroke but, as counsel observed, balls are not hit out of the ground accidentally for there is a reward of six runs for accomplishing the feat and it was urged on the lady's behalf that the cricket club was liable in negligence and nuisance.

In case you consider 'prodigious' too strong a word I would mention that the striker was merely a Saturday afternoon cricketer so that his accomplishment is not to be compared with what Alletson of Nottinghamshire did against Sussex at the seaside town of Hove in the spring of 1911. Played primarily for his bowling, he went in ninth and made 189 in 90 minutes. Inevitably his score was rich in fours and sixes but that is not all. He sent one ball through a window of the pavilion and more or less destroyed the bar. He wrecked the clock face. He drove no less than five balls clean out of the ground and one of them, possibly helped by the wind and a mild slope, finished up on the sands of the sea shore, a mile away. It is true that since that feat certain sceptics have suggested that a small boy (happily unharmed) helped the ball on its way, but if there is one person I dislike more than another it is the rather soured, ungenerous, unimaginative chap who is always ready and eager to label a good story as apocryphal.

But to continue with the cricket ball case: in evidence, members of the club of twenty years' or more standing agreed that the hit was altogether exceptional in comparison with anything previously seen on that ground and it was said that only six balls had been hit into the roadway in 28 years – all without accident. Indeed, in nearly 90 years of cricket no one outside the ground had been injured. The action failed because the learned law lords held that the findings of fact showed that the number of balls driven straight out of the ground was so small as to be almost negligible and the probability of a ball so struck hitting anybody in the roadway was very slight. An ordinary careful man does not take precautions against every conceivable risk, only against those reasonably likely to happen. There was no negligence and, that being so, it was conceded that there could be no nuisance.

One grand slam does not necessarily make a rubber. The cricket ball case is distinguishable from that in which the unfortunate Mr Castle lost an eye when a golf ball (driven, incidentally, from the thirteenth tee by a gentleman who was not represented at the hearing because he had decamped to Australia!) struck the wind-screen of the taxi which Mr Castle was driving.[71] He was travelling along a busy thoroughfare which ran parallel with and close to the thirteenth fairway and it appears that the absent defendant sliced badly when driving. The distinguishing feature of this case was that balls driven from the thirteenth tee all too frequently landed on the road or flew over it and a number of vehicles had actually been struck. As Mr Justice Sankey remarked, 'Everybody who plays golf slices at times and I suspect that the very best of players occasionally slice the ball. A bad player does not slice at all because he does not hit the ball.' He held the directors of the golf club to be liable because they knew (or ought to have known) that, without any carelessness or bungling on the part of the players, many balls struck from the thirteenth tee landed on the road so that the tee was a public nuisance.

In the football case Mr Justice Ashworth said that the proximity of the road, the amount of traffic, the age of the children, the nature of their amusements, and the frequency with which the grassland was used were matters which a reasonable man in the position of the defendants must have considered. In addition, he had to consider first, whether there was any risk of damage to persons using the road as a result of the children's activities, and, secondly, whether that risk was so small that he could rightly refrain from taking steps to prevent the danger. Although in the cricket ball case Lord Reid had said that the difficulty of remedial measures was irrelevant on the issue of liability, in the present case it would have been a simple matter to fix wire netting, or for the defendants to have told the boys to kick in the opposite direction. A reasonable man would have concluded that there was a risk which was not so small that it could be safely disregarded so that the claim in negligence succeeded.

I can tell you one thing. On the single occasion when I was invited to play cricket for Alice Springs – unfortunately an injured back and the exigencies of travel prevented me from accepting – no consideration of what might have happened when I carted the ball over the boundary – if I had been lucky enough to do so – would have entered my head.

A Sale of Ancient Manors

There was a time when I could scarcely work in my office in Lincoln's Inn Fields in London because of the din. The mechanical drills were at work, day in, day out, preparing beds for new telephone cables to be laid. The workmen, incidentally, unearthed an old system of wooden water pipes. In my lunch hour I had a chat with the foreman of the gang, a knowledgeable man, who told me that these pipes were laid down in 1621 by the New River Company which had been formed a year or two earlier for the purpose of providing London which, even then, was expanding, with extra supplies of water from Amwell, in Hertfordshire, at the instance of Sir Hugh Middleton.

The pipes were made of elm trunks, about twenty feet long, hollowed, and well limed to purify the water. No auger could then have bored through twenty feet so that instead of the tool cutting into the wood, the wood was revolved and applied to a stationary auger. The lengths of trunk were wide at one end and champed narrow at the other and as the system was laid, the smaller 'male' ends were jammed into the wide 'female' ones. The 'married' tubes so formed led into wells but no junction pipes were made.

All this, of course, was exceedingly modern by comparison with the unique Temple of Mithras (c. 300 A.D.) which, at about the same time, was being dug out on the site of some bombed offices in which, as a youth, I bound myself by articles of clerkship to a solicitor.

But, speaking of things past, towards the end of the year 1954, I acquired a printed catalogue of an auction sale advertised to take place in a few days' time. Twenty-seven lots were to be put up for bidding and twenty-nine further lots were for disposal by private treaty. All the lots consisted of manors – incorporeal hereditaments which, in some instances, have corporeal heath and wasteland attached to them. These manors had been acquired by a country solicitor and his son over the past century in much the same way as other people collect Georgian snuffboxes or etchings by Rembrandt. Now the grandson proposed to sell them.

Never before had there been a sale like it in my lifetime and I don't suppose there will be another such. As my catalogue says: 'History is under the hammer. Titles are for sale. Honours are in the market. Feudalism, in short, is up for barter.'

Now, as you know, the ancient copyhold methods of holding and dealing with land were utterly swept away by Lord Birkenhead's famous real property statutes of 1922–1925. All land then remaining copyhold was enfranchised and became ordinary freehold to be thenceforth held free of manorial dues, and the lords of the manors throughout this country were thus deprived of many occasional perquisites of varying value, although they were entitled to receive some compensation for their loss. Their nominal title – one of the oldest in English usage – of 'Lord of the Manor' (or very occasionally, 'Lady of the Manor') remained and so did a few minor rights. This title is one of gentility but not one of nobility such as that of a duke, marquis, earl or other peer.

In addition to buying the right to be called lord of a

particular manor, some at least of the purchasers would, and did, acquire rights having a small monetary value, such as rents for rough grazing, or for allowing land to be used occasionally as a fair ground, or for electricity wayleaves, or payments for taking turf or gravel. Rights such as these remained the property of the lord even after 1925.

But one of the greatest draws of the auction were the documents that go with the sale because, besides receiving normal title deeds proving the ownership of the manor, each purchaser acquired a great number of ancient records. These commonly included the Court Rolls which, in earlier times, were usually written in contracted dog Latin and which recorded births, deaths, marriages, farm business, sales and leases of land, punishments for crime and a multitude of miscellaneous daily happenings in the locality. In some few instances, there were beautifully engraved maps of the district, or bailiff's accounts, or old survey books, which were of considerable antiquarian interest. Many Americans proposed to bid; but the Master of the Rolls has some jurisdiction to see that old deeds are kept in a safe and good condition – for they are regarded as national as well as private possessions – and I doubt very much whether any of them would ever be permitted to cross the Atlantic.

Some of the entries in these records make interesting and amusing reading. In the Manor of Wivenhoe (otherwise Wienhou, or Wyenho, or Wynenho, or Wyfenho, or Wyvenho, or Uvenha) with its Members, there is an entry of a Court held on the Wednesday after Epiphany, 1404, which shows how inchastity was frowned upon:–

'Sworn on oath of [twelve named jurors] that no widow who holds a tenement as her free bench [i.e., a life interest] after the death of her husband may keep that tenement after *visitatu vel violata fuit* [presumably, committing adultery, &c.] according to the custom of the Manor, and they say that Margery of Peter atte

173

Cleve gave birth to a son out of wedlock. Therefore she shall lose the tenement with its appurtenances in Eldebethe called le Cleveland and le Newemelleland, which she held as free bench.'

In the Manor of Earls Hall the lord had the right, which was fairly common, to all timber growing on his tenants' properties. In a Court of 1758, one James Moore was presented for having cut down and sold some 'pollard Timber Trees through inadvertency and humbly prays the Favour of the Lord of this Manor to accept a proper Satisfaction.' He was fortunate in being made to pay only 13s. 4d. for his trespass.

In the manor of Bovill Hall, in 1754, 'it was presented that William Meakins, a copyhold tenant, was accidentally killed by a Cart since the last Court, whereby the said Cart became forfeited to the Lord of the Manor as a Deodand for which, the widow being poor, the Lord compounded for 10s. 0d.' Deodand was abolished in 1846 – probably because the owners of the railways then spreading their meshes all over Britain were desperately afraid that every train that was involved in an accident would be forfeited!

Throughout these records, events little and great, familiar and unknown, are woven. Here one reads of a baron who was numbered amongst those responsible for enforcing Magna Carta upon the reluctant King John. There one learns of an earl who, being too zealous in the Lancastrian cause in the Wars of the Roses, was with others 'hade to the Toure Hylle [beside the Tower of London] where was made a scaffolde of viij fote hyzt, and ther was there hedes smyton of, that alle menne myght see; whereof the moste peple were sory.'

In another manor there is a blank period of three years (1351 – 1354) in the Court Rolls. Even now, with a little imagination, one can picture the last agonies of these people whilst more than half of England's population of four millions were dying of the dreaded Black Death.

Finally, in Wivenhoe (which I referred to above) there is

some direct evidence about the Peasants' Revolt of 1381. This, you may remember, was an uprising under the leadership of men like Jack Straw and Wat Tyler, fostered by the Lollards with their grandiloquent ideas of liberty and equality, and I regret to say that one of their aims was to kill all lawyers! Perhaps the main cause of their dissatisfaction was their bitter feeling against the tyrannical customs under which they held their homes and land, for they set out to destroy all records of ownership of land in order to do away with the evidence of these very customs. Often copyhold tenants were required to pay their lord about two years' annual value of their properties on each transfer or upon death, as well as a pourboire to the steward. They were liable to have their property forfeited if they allowed its miserable buildings to fall into disrepair. Their best beast, or their most prized chattel was liable to be seized on the death of a tenant. There was the right to timber I have mentioned. And if a tenant's daughter married a man who lived outside the Manor, her father often had to pay a heavy fine to recompense the lord for her services lost at harvest time. (I say nothing of *droit de Seigneur!*)

The records of two courts in Wivenhoe held in January and May 1381 indicate that everything was going on as usual. Then, on January 8th, 1382, appears the following statement: 'Whereas the tenants of the said Manor, holding native tenements, with other evildoers and adherents, maliciously burnt and caused to be burnt both the Rolls of this Court and the extracts of the Rolls of Account, and claim to hold the said tenements at their own will, freely, and not at the will of the Lord as they did before, to the disinheriting of the Lord, wherefore all the said lands and tenements were seized into the Lord's hands as forfeited; Now the said Lord, of his Special Grace, has regranted all the said lands and tenements to the different tenants, to be held at the will of the Lord in bondage, by the ancient services and customs, as will be evident below.'

Thus these men who might, under the system then existing, have been deprived of life, and their widows of livelihood, were restored to the very same conditions under which, to put it at its worst, they and their forebears had lived for uncounted generations.

Memoirs of a Woman of Pleasure

In the eighteenth century, as in the twentieth, there was more than one edition of *Fanny Hill* – sub-title: *The Memoirs of a Woman of Pleasure*. John Cleland, a Scot, educated at one of the better known of our English public schools, was aged 40, and had been in the consular service, had come unstuck, and was in the Fleet Prison when, in 1750, a meaty edition of his work was published. Even in that slack, sensuous, careless age, the Privy Council pulled him up fairly sharply. He was, he pleaded, a poor man. He had written the book simply in order to make money. He had been paid £50 for it; and, over a short period of time, his publisher had received some £10,000 for it.

£10,000? Perhaps you could call that, at a rough guess, some £500,000 today!

In the result the Privy Council awarded Cleland – For past services? For repentance? Out of pity? For what? At that time, a pension of about £60 per annum.

Fanny Hill reappeared during 1964 unexpurgated, and in a paper-back edition (price, 3s. 6d.) in the Charing Cross Road, in the West End of London, an area where you could sling a cricket ball at random and be almost certain that it would land on one dung heap or another of pornography.

177

Fanny Hill is an erotic book but never pornographic. It is the story of a humble orphan girl from Lancashire who comes to London to seek her fortune. A corrupt old madam causes her to be teased with lesbian practices so that she is induced, in time, to enter a brothel which, let me make it abundantly clear from the outset, was a brothel of the highest possible class. There Fanny encounters a multitude of sexual adventures and, despite her eventual professional status, still manages to enjoy 'the constitutional calls of pleasure' whilst, almost miraculously, she manages to steer, without apparent effort or care, between the Scylla of unwanted pregnancy and the Charybdis of venereal disease.

Eventually – believe it or not – she marries her true love and settles down to a happy family life. In achieving this desirable end she drags the reader through numerous and varied descriptions of the act of sexual intercourse (some of them in the presence of witnesses), one or two acts of flagellation, and a few examples of both male and female homosexuality. That is *my* summary. If you wish to know more, you really must read the book for yourself.

One other thing. The book is written in the elegant English of the eighteenth century. There is not a single vulgar four-lettered-Lady-Chatterley-like word in it.

It was in these circumstances that 171 copies of the paperback edition of *Fanny Hill* were seized by the police from a bookshop – not one of the dirty ones – in Charing Cross Road. There were three possible courses open to the prosecution. First, they could bring a common law charge, like that in the 'Ladies Directory case', on the ground that there was a conspiracy to corrupt public morals,[72] but it seems that the prosecution is often constrained to play by the rules of White Man's Cricket and they did not take this inconvenient course. Secondly, they could have brought *Fanny Hill* before a jury under s 2 of the Obscene Publications Act 1959, just like *Lady*

Chatterley, with the possibility of a fine and imprisonment for publishing an obscene work. Yet that case was bedevilled by spurious experts – by which I mean that many of the witnesses, whether hazy-minded bishop or pretentious critic, were spurious *as experts*. Their sham, eccentric values of decency and indecency reminded me, at the time, of Samuel Johnson's remarks to Boswell about a gentleman who was similarly odd. 'If he does really think (said Johnson) that there is no distinction between virtue and vice, why, Sir, when he leaves our houses, let us count our spoons.'

In the case of *Fanny Hill*, the prosecution chose a third, equally legitimate, course of confiscating a number of copies of the book and requiring the defendant to show cause, before a stipendiary magistrate, why these should not be forfeited and destroyed under the Obscene Publications Act, on the grounds that they were obscene, meaning thereby that, taken as a whole, they tended to deprave and corrupt persons who were likely, having regard to all relevant cirumstances, to read them.

A defence to this offence consists in the defendant proving (for the onus is upon him) that publication of the work was justified as being for the public good on the ground that it would be of interest to science, literature, art or learning, or some other object of general concern.

This defence, of course, opens the field to the 'experts'. One witness, an author himself, declared that 'so far as *Fanny Hill* has a moral, it is that love is the justification and crown of sexual activity . . . Fanny is an advocate of the pleasures of straightforward sex and, when she describes deviations, she makes it clear that she considers them inferior substitutes for straightforward enjoyment.' He added: 'The eighteenth century was a period of enlightenment.' And he purported to express the not insignificant historical importance of knowing how a country girl, having dressed up in London, would appear when she went back home.

Another witness observed that 'even Fanny Hill's bedroom manners are elegant'.

Another, confronted with a flagellation scene in the book, could offer no more than that the description of our heroine's dropped curls 'was interesting from the point of view of ladies' hair styles of the eighteenth century.'

Yet another spoke of the value of this 'gay little book' in which the contemporary phrases 'dumb waiter' and 'teatime' and 'well-to-do' appeared for the very first time! Still another expert witness alleged that the treatment of sex and deviations from normality corresponded, to a remarkable degree, with the public attitude today.

And so on; and so forth. Trifle after trifle. In short, there was a pathetic attempt by the 'experts' to prove that *Fanny Hill* had historical, literary and artistic merits. Yet even Cleland ratted on his own heroine, declaring her memoirs 'a book I disdain to defend and wish, from my soul, buried and forgot'. Be that as it may, the magistrate read *Fanny Hill* for himself, ruled that it was obscene, and had no hesitation in ordering the forfeiture of the seized books.

The quesiton then arose: was all this worthwhile? I ask this for a number of reasons. First, because the seized book is a paper-back edition selling at 3s. 6d., whereas other, far more expensive editions are, and always have been, available to those who want them, including an illustrated edition selling (in 1964) at about £25. Indeed, further editions priced at 9s. 6d. and 45s. were then about to be put on the market. Secondly, because only 171 copies were seized and were a subject of an order by the Bow Street magistrate. His order cannot extend beyond his own jurisdiction to the 99,000 or so other printed copies of *Fanny Hill* of which some 82,000 had been distributed to bookshops all over Britain even before the police took any action. It is true that there were seizures in Manchester and, later in Sheffield, but these acted as no more than the mildest discouragement to booksellers elsewhere. Thirdly, it is notoriously simple for anyone who seeks smut to borrow *Fanny Hill* from a number of less scrupulous London bookshops for the sum of £2, of which £1 is returnable when the book is brought back.

In short, although *Fanny Hill* is an undistinguished dirty book, the recent proceedings are unlikely seriously to hamper its dissemination.

There are, however, other factors which tend to minimize the importance of the *Fanny Hill* affair. First, the Obscene Publications Act 1959, had far too many gaps in it through which, nowadays, I suppose one should drive airplanes, if not rockets, rather than coaches and horses. For example, there is that old chestnut that obscene articles in a shop window are not offered for sale but merely there displayed to invite offers.[73] Again, by a faulty definition, the filthiest negative imaginable is untouchable even though a positive print of it could send the maker or owner to prison.[74] Finally, just because, in the nature of things, a hard-boiled policeman cannot be corrupted by a salacious book, we are faced with the farce that that particular book goes free![75]

But over and beyond all this, it is a sad and incontrovertible fact that every week, every month, every year, sordid little men in the United States of America are exporting to sordid little men in the United Kingdom, *scores of tons* of salacious books, any one of which would make *Fanny Hill* look as innocent as a scorned virgin. In 1960, our Customs officers seized 4,800 books and magazines. In 1961, the figure was 500,271; in 1962, 267,136; in 1963, about 388,300. At the same time (1963) Scotland Yard confiscated from amongst American imports, 276,187 magazines, 143,859 paper-back books, and 79,881 photographs, all of which were obscene to a degree.

Thus, during the year 1963, the Yard held so many tons of paper containing filthy writings and pictures that it was impossible for them to burn it all without flagrantly transgressing the provisions of the Clean Air Act!

181

After all this, perhaps you are wondering how I myself contrived to read *Fanny Hill*? (Do any of you picture me slinking down the back streets of Soho?) I read the book a good many years ago. A friend of mine who was acting as executor for his late father-in-law, a solicitor, discovered an original copy of the work in the firm's safe. Upon the flyleaf were inscribed, lightly in pencil, the words 'To be kept as security for costs in the matter of X v. X'. On making further inquiries my friend discovered that his father-in-law had acted for Mrs X in her divorce suit and that this being in the days when a wife, in order to succeed, was required by English law to establish some other matrimonial offence against her husband in addition to his adultery, Mrs X had sought to prove, as an act of cruelty, that her husband nightly compelled her to read portions of *Fanny Hill* aloud to him in bed!

Eventually a Charade

When I was a child and all of us were accustomed to simple ways of living we used, on dark winter's evenings, to have really rollocking fun before being sent to bed and, at the same time – no easy task – contrive to amuse our elders and betters by acting dumb charades. 'What word shall we have?' We children were assembled in the chilly passage outside the drawing-room, where a variegated mass of adult clothing on the vast hall-stand hung ready for use, and time was the essence of the affair. There would be a dozen hastily whispered suggestions. Then someone would say, 'Let's do 'deceitful'. Last time Aunt Sarah guessed that one and gave us sixpence'. 'D' called for some acting prowess. 'Seat' was easy. So was 'full'.

Then there was the word 'pigmentation' which, as we all recalled, so delighted Great Aunt Felicity (that terrifying Victorian lady with the moustache) when she got it right first time. The last syllable, 'Shun!' was easily put over in those early days of the first World War and, when we came to act the word as a whole, we all loved daubing our faces with burnt cork.

Out of the distant past these memories came back to me when, in 1964, a disappointed plaintiff, a dark gentleman – I know not whether he was a West African or a West Indian – by name, Moses Gohoho, embarrassed the Court of Appeal by stripping off his jacket, trousers and underpants and prostrating himself naked, save for his shirt, on the desks immediately beneath the learned Lord Justices. What a histrionic thing to do! The next case after his had been called on and a lady litigant, who had been sitting next to Mr Gohoho, rushed out of the swing doors. The Court inevitably, felt constrained to commit Mr Gohoho to prison for contempt but, as I think, most humanely limited the period to one week.

Quite incidentally, at about the same time, a married woman who was accused of shoplifting pleaded that 'she had never been the same' since seeing a man running about in the nude. 'I have been under sedatives from my doctor ever since then', she alleged.

A month or two later, a Pakistani, Mr Faiz Akbar Khan, was taken on as a bus conductor by one of our northern local authorities. He was a strict Muslim and, for religious reasons, had worn a beard since reaching manhood. Yet, on the second day of his training, his instructor ordered him to shave off his beard because, he said, conductors were required to report for duty properly dressed and clean in appearance, whereas Mr Khan's beard was untidy and made him look dirty. He was sacked and, with some indignation, brought an action for wrongful dismissal. Said the judge who tried his case: 'His beard is of a neat and rather distinguished variety of which many Englishmen would be delighted to be the proud possessor'. In the result, Mr Khan recovered reasonable damages.

Not long after, a tremendous row began in Halifax in the North of England because, in investigating the felonious stabbing of two people, the police interviewed a large number of Pakistanis through an interpreter and, as each alleged offender came up, the authorities stamped a number in indelible ink on his wrist, so as to save themsleves the trouble of having to explain later, to other police officers, that they had already interrogated the marked men. None of the latter were forced to have a number impressed on their wrists. None of them objected. Yet, from the protests that were made by certain gentlemen in the press, you might imagine that we were almost suffering a Nazi revival in this country.

'Rightly or wrongly, it gives the impression that you cannot tell one from another', stated the Secretary of the National Council for Civil Liberties. How right he was!

On this point a London doctor confessed, in *The Times* that he had never less than 200 Pakistanis as patients. And he asked: 'How do you get the name and address of a person who does not understand the question? And as for interpreters [he said] I have always regarded the arrival of an interpreter with a sinking of the spirits. It gives me two people to understand instead of one.' To this, one bright lady, right out of this world, asked whether the doctor could not learn one simple sentence of Urdu? But a worldy-wise correspondent of *The Times* retorted that it would be necessary to know Bengali as well as Urdu and, perhaps, Sindhi also.

All this fuss was directed to the point that the rubber-stamping of a person, articulate or inarticulate, detracted from his human dignity. Really? I well remember how, at the outbreak of the last war, thousands of English girls and boys who could read and write their native language as well as most of us, and better than some adults, were all labelled with their names and addresses and destinations as they were about to be transported to the comparative safety of the countryside, away from Hitler's bombs. And I imagine that Nino Culotta, before he became acclimatized, would have been only too glad to have had a few rubber stamps on his hands and wrists in order to explain his honest intentions to some tantalizing Sydneysiders!

We now turn to an incredibly daring charade. In order to perform it, the chief actor deceived several different people, at one and the same time, in quite different ways. It's not the sort of story that could have been presented before Great Aunt Felicity. The criminal side of it concerns a certain Mr Else, an undoubted villain, and Mr Kemp an undoubted simpleton.

Else, a married man whose wife was living in the Emerald Isle, was resident in England when he met an English girl named Mary, aged 28, who was living with her mother. As you must have guessed already, Else told Mary that he was single and proposed marriage to her. However, before they could be 'married', Mary found that she was pregnant by Else and, not knowing what we now know, she pressed him to marry her and he arranged a wedding accordingly. Two days before the ceremony – for he was no bigamist – he confessed to poor Mary that he was already married. Even so, he suggested to her that he knew of a face-saving way out of this dilemma. They would [he said] go down to Plymouth, where Drake played bowls and where, incidentally, Else had an uncle, and, on returning, they would comfort Mary's mother by pretending that they had been married there.

Down to Plymouth they went but, once there, Mary's heart failed her. She refused to deceive her mother. So back they both came. Else then purported to make a telephone call to his solicitors and, immediately afterwards, he announced, triumphantly but improbably, that his divorce from his wife (about which Mary knew nothing previously) was final, absolute, and in all ways effective. Therefore he arranged to marry her by special licence at a little country church in the hamlet of Oldberrow, some distance from her mother's home but, as he was not free to marry anyone, he deceived her, her mother, and her brother, who was to be their best man.

Yet Else was not prepared to commit bigamy, so he proceeded to hoodwink his friend Kemp, whom he had earmarked as a clergyman from London who would perform the marriage ceremony, with an entirely different set of lies. He told

186

him about Mary, *said that he had already married her* at Plymouth, but alleged that her mother was extremely distressed because she had not been present at the ceremony. However, he had [he said] got permission from the vicar at Oldbarrow to re-enact the ceremony in the village church for the benefit of Mary's mother and he had [he said] been assured that it was quite unnecessary for a priest to be present. If only Kemp would agree to dress up as a parson and read the material parts of the service, everyone would be happy. Thus, if Else's scheme came off:–

(1) Poor pregnant Mary would believe herself to be an honest woman.

(2) Mary's mother would believe that Mary was duly married to Else.

(3) Kemp, who was only too well aware that he was not a cleric, would believe that he was no more than an innocent agent in helping his friend and bringing pleasure to the old lady.

(4) Else himself would be over a difficult hurdle.

On the day, Kemp turned up at the church in a clerical collar and cassock and read the marriage service out of the Prayer Book, Mary's brother giving her away in the presence of her mother. The couple gave the customary responses and made the usual vows and Kemp place a ring on Mary's finger. Unquestionably Mary's mother believed that a genuine marriage had taken place, but, when they went into the vestry to sign the register, she thought that the book in which she put her signature looked rather too much like an ordinary notebook. She became suspicious, inquiries were made, and in due course Kemp was charged with knowingly and wilfully solemnizing a marriage according to the rites of the Church of England, falsely pretending to be a clerk in Holy Orders, contrary to s.75(1)(d) of the Marriage Act, 1949. Else, the real culprit, was charged with counselling and procuring Kemp to commit this offence.

Both were convicted. Both appealed. At the trial the learned judge had ruled that Kemp's state of mind was immaterial, but the Court of Criminal Appeal held that a man could not necessarily be said to have 'knowingly and wilfully falsely pretended' to be in Holy Orders merely because he put on a certain dress, uttered certain words and did certain acts. A pretender was one who claimed to be what he was not. An actor who dressed up on the stage as a clergyman did not 'knowingly and wilfully falsely pretend' to be a clergyman, for he believed that everyone seeing him would know that he was not one. Kemp's state of mind was therefore material and when the trial judge ruled otherwise, he prevented Kemp from putting forward a defence. His conviction was therefore quashed. Inevitably in consequence, the conviction of the real villain had to be quashed too.

But what a charade – and no dumb charade at that! I shudder to think what Great Aunt Felicity would have thought about it.

Hit a Six or Hole in One!

Surely *Gale*[76] has always said the last word about easements? I have always understood that, whereas in the nineteenth century learned judges and learned writers claimed that no further rights of a novel character would be recognized as having been annexed to land, the better view now is that no one should regard the classes of possible new easements as being absolutely closed. Even so, I was mildly surprised some years ago, when my eye caught a questioning headline in *The Times* which read: EASEMENT FOR CRICKET BALLS?

What happened was that the captain of a Surrey village cricket team, suing on his own behalf and also on behalf of all the other members of his club, sought a declaration that they had an easement to swipe cricket balls over the boundary into a garden adjoining their ground, and a further easement to enter that garden and reclaim those balls. Obviously, on each occasion it was a pre-requisite to the claiming of an easement that some batsman should hit a six and, incidentally, the plaintiff also claimed the return of thirteen balls alleged to have been wrongly seized and detained by the defendant or, in the alternative, their value.

The defendant, the owner of the garden, denied the existence of any easement and sought an injunction to restrain members of the cricket club and their opponents, firstly, from scoring sixes in the direction of his home and, secondly, when they had wilfully done so, from going into his garden to reclaim the mightily struck balls.

One remarkable feature of this case in which Mr Horton, the plaintiff, when he was not leading his team on to the field at weekends, earned his living as a taxi-cab driver, was that he conducted his and his club's action in person, with learned counsel on the other side. For several days he batted with considerable verve and ability. In opening his innings he conceded that no less than eighteen balls – five more than he had claimed – had been returned to the club and that £10 had been paid by the fielding side (the defendant) for detinue. Nevertheless what, in effect, he pleaded was that unless he and the batsmen following him had complete freedom to continue to hit sixes into the fielding side's garden as often as they could contrive to do so, it would be impossible for his team (or any other team) to play brighter cricket. He claimed that you can no more half play cricket than you can, without disgust, put half an effort into any other game.

Just imagine the scene over the years. There could scarcely be a better incentive to playing an uninhibited, exciting game than the prospect of hitting every loose ball into hostile territory. Not only would the home team, when batting, strive to reach the defendant's garden but surely, too, they would often whisper a subtle hint to their opponents in the pavilion to do likewise – probably in the knowledge that they would post their own best outfielders at deep mid-on and deep mid-off against the moment when, with their bowlers contriving an apparently innocuous on-off-drive trap, the batsman's efforts would fall short.

Anyhow, was this matter of the lost balls so important? I

well remember the story of a Welshman, a great personal friend of mine, of the attitude to rugger in a small town in Wales, that home of rugby football. The field lay alongside a river and one Saturday afternoon the ball was kicked into touch, and well into the middle of the stream. For a few seconds there was talk about who should retrieve it. Then up spoke a Welsh scrum half. 'Don't worry about the bloody ball, man! Let's get on with the game!'

But about the cricket action: at all material times, before the defendant came upon the scene, the gentleman who leased the playing ground to the club was the owner of the house and the garden into which sixes were commonly hit. It was, of course, inevitable that keen batsmen would also hit balls into adjoining gardens as well. Yet none of these neighbouring owners ever complained. They always allowed the players to recover the balls from their grounds.

The worthy captain-advocate submitted that cricket was a lawful game and was not intrinsically dangerous. Mr Justice Lyell answered that it had its hazards and indicated that there were certain protective measures which were normally taken and all of these suggested that there were some dangers.

The first witness for the plaintiff, who had been a member of the Egham Cricket Club since it was formed in 1912, spoke of the seven- and fourteen-year terms granted to the club in 1932, 1939 and 1946. The leases contained clauses by the club (the lessees) that they would not cause any nuisance or annoyance to neighbours around the ground yet, during the subsistence of the several leases, the then lessor allowed the club to recover balls from his own garden, provided its members did no damage. Another witness, who had been a member of the club for forty-two years, confirmed the local custom as to the recovery of balls. A number of other witnesses gave similar evidence, although it was referable to more recent periods of time.

The defendant, who bought his property in 1954, stated in evidence that he had played cricket at school and also for his Old Boys' team, and he claimed that he was interested in a variety of other sports. He said he had a swimming pool in his garden and it seems that the burden of his complaint was that he frequently found between eight and ten cricket balls in this pool. They caused damage to his fruit trees, vegetable beds, flowers and lawns, and there was danger to those who swam in his pool.

In a reserved judgment Mr Justice Lyell awarded the plaintiff nominal damages of forty shillings in respect of an assault, for there had been a minor collision between fieldsmen from the dominant tenement and the fieldsmen of the servient, ball-receiving tenement . . .

The learned judge did not decide whether the right to hit and reclaim cricket balls upon and from neighbouring land could or did constitute an easement. But he held that in the present case there was no implied grant of an easement of cricket ball, either hit or retrieved. What had been done in the past (he found as a fact) had been done by goodwill and courtesy. He also held that the existence of a prescriptive right had not been established. Finally, he dismissed any claim based upon a lost grant (cf. *Phillips* v *Halliday* [1891] AC 228, 231).

You can imagine some of the headlines in the popular newspapers next day: 'JUDGE BOWLS SIX-HIT BATSMAN'. 'JUDGE BOWLS OUT TEAM.' 'IT'S CLOSE OF PLAY.' And much more to the same effect. The sedate granny *Times*, having opened with 'Easement for Cricket Balls?' and continued with 'Not Cricket', was content to end with 'Cricketers's Easement Claim Fails'.

Switching to an entirely different sport, I have, since the age of fifty or so, been an indifferent performer at the exasperating game of golf. Yet I must confess that, in my conceit, whenever I am faced with a short tee shot, I invariably hope to hole in one. Not, mark you, in 0, as was done by a player in a medal competition at Northwood, in Middlesex, in 1934 who was allowed one stroke and sank his ball with an iron off the tee. The fact that certain American players have holed in one at 427 yards and 425 yards merely fills me with despondency. So, too, does the fact that in 1951, at New York, no less than 1,409 players who had previously done the ace, hit between them 7,045 shots – yet the nearest ball, finished 3½ inches from the elusive cup. So, too, does the fact that Walter Hagen, surely one of the greatest characters in golf of all time, only once holed in one. Then, there are a number of recorded instances in which a player who has, unknown to himself and his opponent holed in one, searched for an apparently lost ball, failed to find it, and in despair has conceded the hole, and so lost it.

Yet considering how many one-armed players have achieved this, the greatest of golfing accomplishments, I long to do the same. My conceit lies in the fact that I close my mind to some of the intrinsic difficulties. Last summer, at Moor Park, not many miles from my home, a certain gentleman earned £6,250 for a hole in one at the eighteenth tee. The newspapers spoke of it as a fluke, rather than a stroke of skill. Yet what do you suppose that this player intended to do? Indeed, what do you suppose that I, the merest tyro at this incredibly difficult and intrinsically unnatural game, aim to do as I address the ball at a short hole? Do I attempt to place my ball within thirty feet of the pin? Or twenty feet? Or ten? Or what?

Consider what Lord Reid stated in the House of Lords (in a case touching the relevance of intention in regard to cruelty by one spouse to another). 'In real life, either you are aiming at something, or you are not: in law, either you have proved an intention or you have not . . . In fact people often intend something quite different from what they know to be the natural and probable result of what they are doing. To take a trivial example, if I say I intend to reach the green, people will believe me although we all know that the odds are ten to one against my succeeding; and no one but a lawyer would say that I must be presumed to have intended to put my ball in the bunker because that was the natural and probable result of my shot . . .'.[77]

The truth of the matter is that in serious matters we always aim to hit a six, or hole in one, whenever the chance occurs, in all that we undertake in life.

A Trade Union Story

I understand that the very first labour strike occurred in an early Chinese dynasty. It arose because workers in the ricefields who toiled in the heat of the day thought they ought to be paid what we now call 'differentials' over and above the wages of those who laboured in the cool of the morning. They got what they wanted. Nearly 1,200 years before the birth of Christ some of the workmen who were building a necropolis at Thebes for Rameses III refused to go on because, they said, they had not received their rations, but I don't think they succeeded. Over 600 years ago, in England, the masons who were building Salisbury Cathedral struck for an extra farthing a day. This event is perpetuated in a street named Pennyfarthing Street which you may see for yourself today.

In Covent Garden, when it was still London's largest fruit and vegetable market, a merchant who had purchased a crate of Australian apples was prohibited from lifting it on to his own lorry – he had to pay a porter 3d. or 4d. a box (this was written 30 years ago) for doing what he would often prefer to do himself. Similar rules govern Smithfield, our greatest meat market. A butcher once tried to carry away the carcasses he had bought and there was an action in the City Court to determine his rights as against the meat porters (who are picturesquely clothed in blue suits and white peaked caps and named 'bummarees').

They claimed a monopoly in porterage and when the court found against them, commented thus through their union organiser: 'The judge said [the butcher] could move the meat himself. The butcher said he would. [The union] said he couldn't – and he didn't.

Thus men have always sought for better working conditions and more adequate pay. For at least sixty years past they have also tried to get for themselves greater security through permanency and certainty in employment. Jobs are created for fear of unemployment. All these aims are the very things which justify the existence of trade unions. In these circumstances I shall now tell you, without comment, the facts of a case which was never officially reported.

The plaintiff was by trade a fitter and turner who lived with his family near the shipyard where he worked. He belonged to a trade union – the second largest in the Kingdom – which exists for the protection of many and diverse kinds of engineers. In his home district, where shipbuilding was the major industry, ninety per cent of all the works were closed shops. This, of course, meant that anyone expelled from the union would forfeit the right to earn a living at his chosen trade, at all events in that neighbourhood.

On a particular occasion when the plaintiff's employers refused an increase of wages, the union ordered its members not to work for twenty-four hours. The strike was not authorised by the rules of the union, and the instruction to the plaintiff to stop work was given him only the day before that on which the strike was to begin, although under his contract of employment seven days' notice was needed. The plaintiff refused to strike, and so was summoned to attend a meeting of the district committee of the union where, in the presence of ten members of the committee and their secretary, he was charged with failing to carry out the direction to strike. He pointed out that the decision to strike was unlawful and stated that in like circumstances he would again refuse to strike. When, in consequence of a question put by the secretary as to whether the plaintiff had endeavoured to get other members of his firm to ignore the instruction to strike, the committee proposed to call a witness to give evidence to this effect, the plaintiff threw down his summons, indulged in some hearty swearing, and stamped out of the room. Behind his back the district committee resolved to recommend his expulsion from the union, putting on record their disgust, not only at his arrogant attitude, but also at his attempt to prevent his work-mates from answering the direction to strike, although no notice of a charge of coercion had been given him and although it seemed that the only evidence that could support such a charge was to the effect that he had tried to persuade a single other member to adopt the same attitude as himself.

The executive council of the union declined to approve the expulsion. Therefore, it was not effective under the union's rules. Once again the district committee met and, in the plantiff's absence and without notice to him, they purported to expel him for his 'arrogant attitude'. And once again the executive council refused to approve this resolution which accordingly was ineffective.

The plaintiff then gave up his job and left the district for two weeks but, when he sought to return to his normal work, the district committee held an emergency meeting, at which they unanimously authorised their secretary to circularise all factories in a number of districts where they had official shop stewards in an effort to ensure that the plaintiff should not be allowed to start work under any consideration. This the secretary did, instructing shop stewards to inform their employers that if they employed the plaintiff, it was the committee's intention to withdraw all labour in protest. (The district committee did not of course, possess the power to call a lawful strike.) The result of these acts was that it became impossible for the plaintiff to obtain employment at his trade anywhere in the locality.

The secretary of the district committee also took it upon himself to go still further afield and write to the union secretary in a nearby area in order to tell him of the efforts to prevent the plaintiff from getting employment in their district and suggesting that he might seek work in the neighbouring area. But the secretary did not tell his correspondent that the executive council of the union had refused to countenance the plaintiff's expulsion nor did he mention the fact that the plaintiff was still a member of the union.

The plaintiff got a job at a new place but was unable to produce his contribution card to the convener of shop stewards there and, as a result of representations by that person, he was given a week's wages and dismissed. These representations were based upon the fact of his not having his union contribution card rather than upon his trouble with the committee of the district where he was first employed. Later, the union secretary of the new district in which the plaintiff tried to get work wrote to all conveners of shop stewards in his area stating that the plaintiff was 'not desirable' until he had made peace with his own district committee.

The plaintiff then went cap in hand, seeking to make his peace with the committee of the district where he had originally worked but they refused to see him. Later on he applied to the branch secretary for his contribution card, but in vain. Eventually he was informed by the branch secretary that he had been expelled from the union because his contributions were in arrears, so that from then on he was unemployed.

In the action which he brought (*inter alia*) against the secretary and members of the committee of his original district branch of the union he claimed damages for conspiracy with intent to injure him because he refused to comply with the unlawful direction to strike. In their defence, the defendants admitted that the plaintiff was a member of their union until he was expelled, but they denied the wrongfulness of the call to strike and denied also the acts said to constitute conspiracy.

The late Mr Justice Harman, who tried the action, made some preliminary observations about closed shops. It was not, he said, for English lawyers to dislike or distrust the closed shop because they themselves lived and thrived upon the principle. No man, unless he had served his time and received his union card (namely, his call to the bar), was permitted to practise advocacy. But monopolies of this kind could only be justified if they were regulated so as to promote the public interest. The weapon of expulsion from a closed shop was a step of the most extreme gravity and one to be taken only after very careful enquiry and then only in the case of the gravest offence.

On the facts of the case his Lordship said that it was conceivably arguable that in the early days of the dispute the district committee honestly thought that nothing short of expulsion would uphold the prestige of their union, although this view was so wrongheaded that it would be hard to accept. Yet after the executive council's decision against expulsion any question of expulsion was closed, so that thenceforth the acts of those defendants were a gross abuse of their powers. They were directed towards injuring the plaintiff in his trade and not towards protecting the defendants' trade, and they had caused the plaintiff damages. Secondly, the dispute between the plaintiff and these defendants was not a trade dispute within the meaning of the relevant statute law for the defendants were not asserting a trade right and no interest of the trade was involved.

No notice was given by the committee to the plaintiff of the charge of coercing others against striking and it was entirely unsupported by evidence. If the charge was that the plaintiff insisted on questioning the validity of the call to strike this charge was a denial of the right to hold an opinion. As to the 'arrogant attitude' it was sufficient to point out that the defendants' rules provided for a penalty of 2s. 6d. for the use of bad language! In short, the defendants flouted the decision of their own executive committee and they sought to produce all the effects of expulsion both in their own district and in another district by other means.

It was ironic, commented the learned judge, that whilst pretending to visit the plaintiff with a penalty for disloyalty to the union the defendants were themselves guilty of that very offence. They thought only of their own ruffled dignity and 'they were determined to use every weapon ready to their hand to vindicate their authority and grossly abused the quite frightening powers at their command'. All the elements of civil conspiracy were present.

In the result the plaintiff was awarded £500 damages and given liberty to apply for an injunction should any further victimization take place.

I said that I would give you the facts without comment. Indeed if I were to express any opinion I should be over-egging the pudding.

Computer Conversations and Conveyancing

A few years ago it was reported that a Mr John Miller, a senior law lecturer from the Victoria University in Wellington, New Zealand, claimed to have prognosticated 'that advances in computer technology will change the practice of law forever, throwing vast numbers of the legal profession out of work and wiping out the legal publishing business'.

I don't know what Mr Miller's background is, nor where he learnt about computing but, be all that as it may, he is, for the most part, talking nonsense. He is undoubtedly right when he claims that modern technology will inevitably and considerably alter many – if not most – of the day-to-day practices in a law office – it is already happening both here and in his country – but he is considerably wide of the mark when he asseverates that massive unemployment and the obliteration of legal publishing will ensue from an ever-increasing use of the computer. On the contrary, this magnificent machine will allow every competent practitioner to deal with an ever-increasing number of clients and their never-ending problems, whilst all those law publishers who are already in the computing business envisage that their computerisation in the production of standard textbooks will in no way diminish their printed output. The manual and the computerised systems will complement one another. This is what publishers realistically believe today.

In particular, Mr Miller's assertion that the impact of expert systems 'will provide the level of advice which will make much of the legal profession redundant' is an exaggeration and, as I believe, a most dangerous one. The prime purpose of an expert legal system is to embody and produce almost exhaustive specialised information about a particular branch of the law so as to enable the ordinary practitioner to recover it and, thereafter, to exercise his true function, namely, that of judging how far what is thrown up is relevant to the needs of his clients, and thereafter to advise them expertly accordingly. Assuredly, expert systems, so far from throwing lawyers out of work, will inevitably enlarge the scope of all efficient legal practices. The inefficient and non-computerised ones will, equally inevitably, go to the wall.

However, there is one aspect of modern technology which will, beyond any peradventure, clearly revolutionise the daily working habits of the solicitors' profession. It will be an enormous step forward. I am thinking of voice recognition which, before long, will become available to all of us in a wide-ranging, efficient, and totally acceptable form. Of course, as we all know, many people of our generation, and of the generation before us, and of the generation before that, and even of a yet earlier generation, are totally unwilling and, indeed, unable, to sit in front of a visual display unit and work at its keyboard for every possible purpose connected with their daily work, whether it be consulting their diary for the day, learning thereafter what appointments they have to meet and, especially, what information or money they will need to provide for each single event of the current day.

Just in case, in this year A.D. 1988, one or two of you

may think that I am talking in Orwellian terms, you must come down to earth by realising that the legal profession will soon be flooded by young people who, in their schooldays, have totally accepted the computer as a very ordinary, albeit useful, tool in their everyday lives.

But my main purpose is to write about the most vital advancement that will affect this profession in the years ahead. I refer to voice recognition. Research on voice recognition systems has been going on, to a limited extent, for at least thirty years, but the vocabulary is still scant. The computer is able to recognise about 100 words, or perhaps, today, slightly more.

You may well ask what is inhibiting progress in this area? The answer is that the one single thing that severely blocks progress lies in the way in which we normally speak. Now when you and I write sentences, we leave spaces between each word, so that it is abundantly clear to each and every one of us precisely where each word begins and ends. However, when we talk to one another, all the sounds we make run into each other, and yet, even so, our brains are conditioned to pick out, and to divide from one another, all the variety of noises which we call words. Now, as I'm sure you will realise, it is extremely difficult to get the computer to follow suit.

That is by no means the whole problem. For example I'm totally reconciled to so-called 'strine' – the Australian accent. I am to some extent reconciled to American accents and indeed I can, to some slight degree, understand the very broadest of Liverpudlian chatter. But if you put me in a pub in county Durham, full of miners, much as I love 'em all, I don't understand one single sentence of their conversation. It's not so much the pronunciation as the use of words that have never come into my own vocabulary. How does the computer sort out this problem?

For the moment we must all of us try to forget the rich heritage of our multitudinous local brogues. This is because the only way in which it is possible to teach the computer to recognise the human voice is by instructing it to get to know the accents of one single speaker, and this is something – believe it or not – that is easily accomplished.

Optical character recognition has been a comparatively easy task for some years past. But what about voice recognition? Here you are dealing with something infinitely more difficult and complex, involving, as it does, not only pitch and timbre, but also vibration. The chief stumbling block to complete voice recognition – and it really is a tremendous one – lies in the size of the vocabulary that can be attained, simply because the more words the machine is capable of recognising, the longer will be the time it takes to pick out the particular word that has been uttered.

The essential reason for this is that the machine is required to recognise a pattern of symbols and obviously, to the extent that you increase the number of words, just so you bedevil the general pattern, and make it more complex, so that more time needs to be disbursed for allowing the machine to grasp many differing patterns.

The basic difficulty about voice recognition is that the computer just cannot comprehend where words begin and end. This, of course, is only another aspect of the first inhibition that I mentioned earlier, namely, that the computer finds it incredibly difficult to know how to separate one word from another. Now it so happens that most voice recognition systems tend to operate with the use of nouns, rather than adjectives, simply because what is really spoken is a list of discrete items, rather than a well-ordered complete sentence.

Obviously, problems arise when two or more entirely different words are pronounced identically. The example which immediately springs to mind is 'straight', meaning without a curve, and 'strait' like the narrow gate in Bunyan's *Pilgrim's Progress*. Therefore, the computer must, at all times, be told what the context is, so that, for example, when it hears the noise 'great ape' it instantly is made aware that the context is anthropoidal, rather than something to do with a lead-coloured cotton strip ('grey tape').

It may surprise you to know – and I do so hope that I am not teaching my grandmother how to suck eggs – that voice recognition is now being used daily in warehouses, factory bays and production lines through the use of the digits 0 to 9, which the computer is now well able to comprehend and instantly follow. It also needs to be taught to learn and obey one or two other elementary instructions such as 'start', 'stop', and 'mistake'.

Once the computer has absorbed these few easy notions, it can be given, for example, the task of checking the goods that are being unloaded from a lorry into a warehouse. All that is necessary is for each item to be allotted an identifying number so that, for example, instead of a lorry-driver or a checking-in clerk referring to the unloading of a mark 20 gearbox, he will just call it 'number 4317'. Thereupon, the computer will recognise the item instantly, will know its destination, and will send it on its way via the conveyer belt. And, of course, there is no conceivable limit to the range of numbers obtainable through the use of the ten digits, 0 to 9.

Again, just supposing the computer is being used to assemble plant on the factory floor where the operator has greasy hands, and the presence of water or electricity, for example, have created a hostile environment in which it is quite impossible to operate a keyboard. All that is needed is a microphone that will pick up the operator's voice.

At this point you might well ask: Assuming that the machine knows Joe Bloggin's voice and he suddenly goes sick and Jim Jiggerboy takes over. How will the computer be trained to recognise Jim's voice? Believe it or not the re-education of the machine will take no more than a few minutes, because a facility for teaching it will have been built into its system for this very purpose. In effect, Jim will press a button in order to tell the computer that he is going to re-train it in the recognition of the way in which he pronounces numerals. The machine will respond by asking, on a screen: 'What is 1?' The new operator will reply: 'Say "one" ' – no matter how he pronounced the word "one". And he will go on: 'Say "one"; say "one"; say "one" ' – until the computer indicates on the screen that it has learned its lesson. Thereafter Jim will order: 'Say "two" ', and so forth. The entire process occupies no more than a few moments. And thereafter, when Jim goes off duty and Fred takes over from him, Fred will put the computer through the same training modes so that, almost at the press of a button, it is able instantly to recognise the respective voices of Joe, Jim, Fred *et al*.

But to come right down to brass tacks, some of the more discerning of you are bound to ask: 'How long will it be before voice recognition is so perfected that it will be in daily use in every law office?' That is a difficult question to answer, if only because it has already taken thirty or more years to advance as far as we have done. My guess is that it will take another ten, or possibly twenty years before speech recognition is absolutely perfected. But who knows? In these days technology advances at such an incredible – and, may I say? – quite unpredictable speed.

Quite apart from voice recognition, the use of laser light, instead of electricity, will soon herald the time in which complex tasks, such as the high-speed transmission of pictures, will enable solicitors to do their conveyancing business at an incredible speed – provided, of course, that our sometimes recalcitrant local authorities also follow suit.

Sick Johnny Under Bumbledom's Hand

The dead hand of Bumbledom is perennially and, of late, increasingly reaching out for further conquests. For years it has been plucking at the cornerstones of the Englishman's home in an attempt to reduce it from a castle to a State-controlled personnel habitation unit and now its latest threat is aimed against the Englishman's control over his own family. Bumbledom, in fact, reckons that its own institutional efficiency is far better than the loving care of the father and mother whom nature provided.

Now clearly, in any civilised community, a parent may not with impunity kill, maim, neglect or harm his children, even though they are his 'own'; and yet a mother may allow, and even, for the sake of peace and quiet, encourage her little Johnny to suck endless packets of horrid sweets between meals until his teeth are as riddled with decay as a rabbit-infested paddock is full of burrows. She is especially prone to quieten him in this way if, like her husband, she is trying to hold down a job. Perhaps she also fails to buy Johnny a tooth brush? Nevertheless, under our Welfare State, regular school dental inspections at least ensure that her Johnny's cavities are neatly filled free of cost, or, at little cost to her, although the damage to his gastric apparatus may be neither as early detected nor so easily repaired.

But to return to Johnny. His school may (at considerable cost to the community) teach him safety in road habits as part of the regular curriculum, with kind policemen and some realistic apparatus to impress upon his young mind that he must avoid being one of the many hundreds killed, or the tens of thousands injured, in a single month. But when Johnny's mother takes him shopping on Saturday – she is always in a hurry, of course – she instils all the bad habits again. But that does not make her responsible to Authority. Nor can she be compelled, in the school holidays, to prevent Johnny from clambering about in the clutter and rubble and traps of one of the tens of thousands of fascinating building sites that are dotted all over the country. If Johnny comes to serious harm, her responsibility for his safety may help to determine whether he can successfully claim damages from the building contractor,[78] but it ends there. The dirt that Johnny incidentally plasters all over his body and his clothes does little harm and if he swallows some, it is probably less pernicious than the sweets. In this connexion, I happened to overhear, on a London bus, a charwoman's comments on this very subject and I quote her verbatim. 'If yer don't take in dirt in yer grub, 'ow are yer going to combat normal diseases? It stands to reason!'

Charles Lamb once humiliated us by remarking that even lawyers were children once, but although little Johnny may scramble in the gutter, he is prevented by wise laws from being exposed to tuberculosis through crawling in the spittle-contaminated sawdust of a tavern whilst his parents got drunk. That, I understand, was the principal object behind the legislation which, long ago, barred children from public houses. Today, they are no longer excluded, not only because the spittle and the sawdust have long since disppeared. Then there are the numerous laws, happily quite old laws, which still prevent little Johnny from being sold to a chimney sweep, or his puny labour exploited in his own parents' home. And so I could go on multiplying examples of how the State has stepped in between him and his parents to prevent them from ill-using him. 'Necessity (said Pitt) is the plea for every infringement of human freedom'. But where, I would ask, do you start to draw the line?

The latest threat of official coercion comes from the Regional Hospital Board of Sheffield. They propose that when parents refuse permission for their child (let us continue to call him Johnny rather than Oliver Twist) to have an operation which the doctors in their wisdom consider necessary, a juvenile court should be hurriedly convened at the hospital and, by use of a streamlining procedure, should be invited to make an order, taking Johnny out of his parents' custody and placing him in the care of the local authority. Bumbledom would then be free to consent forthwith to the operation on Johnny.

The problem arises because a surgeon who operates in defiance of the parents' wishes opens himself to criminal charges of assault and battery, not to mention actionable tort, and, in the year 1960, this problem appeared to be acute in Sheffield, because in that city at that time there were some 1000 of Jehovah's Witnesses (who, I understand are opposed in principle to surgical operations), besides many Christian Scientists who hold somewhat similar views. The other side of the problem is the fact that Johnny's parents will be criminally responsible in manslaughter if they wilfully neglect to provide him with medical aid so that he dies.

All the well-known cases on this aspect of the matter – they are classic textbook examples – concern a sect known as the Peculiar People and they all follow a common pattern. Thus a child aged two had been ill and wasting away for eight or nine months. The parents, who were nothing if not affectionate, nursed their baby with kindness, keeping him well clad and properly fed, but they refused to seek skilled medical advice because, they said, to make use of it would indicate a lack of faith in God. Instead, the father called in an elder of the Peculiar People, one George Hurry, an engine driver, who anointed the baby with oil and prayed over it in literal compliance, as he said, with the injunction in the Epistle of James, Chap. V, vv. 14, 15. ('Is any sick among you? Let him call for the elders of the church; and let them pray over him, anointing him with oil in the name of the Lord: and the prayer of faith shall save the sick . . .') Unhappily, the baby died of chronic inflammation of the lungs and the father was convicted of manslaughter.[79]

The law under which the Sheffield authorities proposed to act is this. The Children and Young Persons Act 1933 provides that, if a juvenile court is satisfied that a child is in need of care and protection, it may make an order committing him to the care of any fit person, whether a relative or not, who is willing to undertake the care of him (s 62). Three things are noteworthy in regard to the making of such an order. First, the court is required to endeavour to ascertain the child's religious persuasion and to commit the child, if possible, to a person of like persuasion (s 75(1)). Secondly, the person to whose care the child is committed is given 'the same rights and powers . . . as if he were his parent' (s 75(4)). Thirdly, as you might expect, that soulless legal entity, the local authority, is by statute 'deemed to be a fit person' (s 76, as amended by s 5 of the Children Act 1948). (What, by the way, is its religious persuasion?)

Writing to the famous Mancunian newspaper which now calls itself simply *The Guardian*, a justices' clerk's assistant of many years' experience stated that he could not too strongly emphasize that a juvenile court is a court of law. Hence the proceedings would have to be commenced by way of a summons or notice to the parents, who would have to be given reasonable notice of the hearing. They would have a right to attend and be legally represented and an appeal would lie against their decision. These and other factors made him sceptical about the 'streamlining' procedure. Indeed, if I may say so, if Johnny was truly in desperate need of an operation, he would almost certainly die pending an appeal.

The Times viewed the 'well-intentioned proposal' of the Hospital Board 'with the gravest suspicion', although it conceded that 'a child's life and health comes before the prejudices of his parents'. It continued: 'Not all cases in which parents may differ with the hospital authorities are of the straightforward kind which is chosen as a model for the purposes of persuasion. There may be a difficult reckoning of risks and probabilities concerning which enthusiastic surgical opinion may argue one way and a parent's more general concern another. Again, the parent's objection may not always be one of principle; he may for good or bad reasons distrust that particular hospital; or his objection may be based on a deep, though unscientific, understanding of the child and on his responsibility for its future, neither of which is shared by the doctors recommending an operation'.

In writing to that newspaper, a correspondent, himself a parent as well as a surgeon, shared the aversion of parents to operations on their children, though 'It is,' he said, 'for the surgeon to explain, persuade, and convince; his privilege to inspire trust and confidence. His task may on occasion be difficult, even exasperating; he may encounter ignorance, panic, religious scruples, half-baked so-called scientific knowledge – antipathetic bias of every kind. His patience may be sorely tried, yet he must persevere with simple explanation of the inescapable facts and with understanding sympathy. His highest reward is public faith in his judgment and integrity.'

It occurs to me that if I am the victim of one of the five-figure non-fatal road accidents which occur during most months and I am desperately injured and unconscious, I shall be placed in a *somewhat* similar position to little Johnny with his peritonitis (or whatever it was) and his unconsenting parents.

I can only hope, in such a case, that some surgeon will be bold enough to operate on me as necessary without waiting for me to return, if I am lucky enough to return, to a condition in which I am able to give my assent. By the same token, I should have thought that some of those who have taken the Hippocratic oath would be willing to risk a charge of battery if Johnny's life is really at stake, rather than call Bumbledom in aid.

What a Din!

Charles Lamb once said: 'Not many sounds in life, and I include all urban and rural sounds, exceed in interest a knock at the door'. There is, of course, nothing intrinsically fascinating in that sound; but what does the postman bring?

One of my many Australian correspondents, a lady with a busy solicitor's practice in Victoria, wrote to me the other day in these terms. 'I found time at the end of last December to marry . . . My husband, G., is an acoustic engineer who started his own business about a year ago. We think that Melbourne is so noisy that there must be a future in this sort of work. In the multi-storeyed glass buildings that are springing up in the city there are a lot of noise problems and here's hoping that people become noise-conscious for G's sake.'

For a goodish slice of my life (actually, precisely forty years), I worked in an office overlooking Lincoln's Inn Fields, its lawns and flower beds surrounded by 400-year-old giant plane trees, the whole forming an attractive oasis which – if I may use an Irishism – would be unbelievably peaceful if it were not so noisy.

Long before World War II it became each day from 12 to

3 o'clock, a Hyde Park Corner in miniature, the air throbbing with the raucous shouts of the preachers, the politicians, the philosophers, the quacks, the hecklers and even the local sword-swallower, to say nothing of a flame-swallower. Then, after Munich, for a full year, we endured, all day long, ceaseless riveting as basements were shored-up for air raid shelters. The war, goodness knows, was noisy enough at times by day and by night. Since the peace the Fields have become, especially in summer, a sort of Lido-cum-car-park. Bands play at mid-day, ice cream vendors announce their arrival with loud jingling bells like a grossly amplified child's musical box, aircraft and, sometimes, the rattling helicopters, cruise overhead, there is the periodical scream of brakes which indicate a near collision – sometimes an actual collision – at a blind corner at the entrance to the Inn, and, of course, there is the perennial din of re-building everywhere. The skyscrapers which are altering London's profile rise like ugly fingers and each of them has a history of pile-driving, compressor-drilling, rivetting, and other horrors which have often made conversation indoors impossible unless every window is shut fast. And damn! There's the telephone again! Thought becomes an automatic rather than a deliberate and careful process.

But the plight of the folk who live beside London Airport is worse than those of the people in Lincoln's Inn. They claim that their children suffer from deafness and that their nervous systems are seriously affected so that they develop an anxiety which, in turn, infects the parents. The noise at times is said to verge upon physical pain lasting as long as twenty seconds.

Modern scientists measure noise throughout its compass from the threshold of hearing (such as Shelley's 'low, sweet, faint sounds, like the farewell of ghosts') to the threshold of feeling (where it becomes an acute physical pain) and they express the results in units of a logarithmic ratio known as decibels. Thus the rustle of autumn leaves at its loudest can scarcely amount to ten decibels, whereas a compressor-drill or a riveter may produce 100 to 120 and an airplane, at close range, as much as 130 decibels. They talk about the 'phon', which is a unit of loudness, the 'sone', a unit of noise-nuisance, and the 'noy' a unit of noise from aircraft.

When, in an appreciative, relaxed mood, I am walking in our still beautiful countryside, I am always conscious of a multitude of sounds which, to me, are most pleasurable.

Myriads of rivulets hurrying through the lawn,
The moan of doves in immemorial elms,
And murmuring of innumerable bees.

Contrariwise, some sounds exasperate me. To be far from any town and to be startled by the sudden frantic scream and roar of hedge-hopping American jet bombers fills me with an instant anger. That perhaps is excusable, but when I am passing through a placid, picturesque village and, without warning, the street reverberates with the clamorous jingle bells of a newly arrived ice cream vendor, and I begin to feel a surge of rage, I am being unreasonable. After all he wants to attract customers and the children want to be told it is time for an ice.

Thus although sound may be prejudicial to efficient work or even injurious to health, we are all, to some extent, conditioned to liking or disliking certain noises because of our previous experience of them. As G. K. Chesterton once wrote:

The folk that live in Liverpool,
    their heart is in their boots;
They go to hell like lambs, they do,
    because the hooter hoots

Church bells are anathema to some people, so that the chimes prompt them to write irately to the newspapers to ask when the anachronism of ringing them will be abolished by law and, in the same strain, no doubt the whining schoolboy with his satchel and shining morning face, as he crept, like a snail, unwillingly to school, hated the sound of the school bell – if they had a school bell in Shakespeare's day.

The Private Member who, with Government backing, succeeded, in 1960, in getting his Noise Abatement Bill through the Commons was inundated with suggestions, both rational and irrational as to particular noises which ought to be controlled. In summer-time many small steamers take tourists up and down the Thames whilst a boatman gives a running commentary by loud-hailer about places of interest. His stentorian blether irritates some people who lives beside the river and the Private Member confessed to having unwillingly overheard many inaccurate accounts of the history of the Palace of Westminster whilst he was deliberating in one of the committee rooms of the House of Commons.

The Bill provided that 'noise or vibration which is a statutory provisions[80] with minor modifications. Thus any three persons who, as the occupiers of premises, are aggrieved by noise or vibration may take a case to the justices, although it will be a sound (!) defence to any charge to prove that the best practicable means have been used for preventing and counter-acting the effect of the noise or vibration. There is an ominous but inevitable saying: 'Nothing in this section . . . shall apply to noise or vibration caused by aircraft.'

One clause of the Bill dealt in detail with loud-speakers in a street, proposing that they should be entirely forbidden between 9 pm and 8 am and forbidden 'at any other time for the purpose of advertising any entertainment, trade or business'. There followed a long list of exemptions – relating to the police, fire bridges, ambulances, local authorities, public telephone systems, transport undertakings and the like – and, the clause used phraseology that clearly also allowed both a horn or other warning instrument and a radio in a car so long as persons nearby were not given reasonable cause for annoyance. The travelling showman was also protected and the fair at 'Appy 'Ampstead will continue to belch out its multiplicity of sounds on every Bank Holiday.

The jingle bells of the ice-cream merchants have twice been before the courts. In one case[81] in which a van was filled with an electrical musical box and amplifier the Divisional Court, upholding the conviction for using a noisy instrument so as to cause annoyance to the inhabitants, decided that an instrument may be a noisy instrument whether or not it is a musical instrument. In another similar case[82] there were two vans run by rival firms, and in their competition for custom, one sounded five notes on an amplified dulcimer at frequent intervals in a fierce endeavour to drown the Anniversary Waltz played by the other, thereby sadly disturbing the daytime slumber of a night worker. The prosecution (it was held) did not have to call all the inhabitants to prove that they had been annoyed by the row, the Lord Chief Justice observing: 'They need not call any of them: *res ipsa loquitur,* or *res ipsa* something or other.' To which *The Times* reporter supplied the caption, '*Res Ipsa Tintinat?*'.

The new Bill was kind to those who use jingle bells for the sale of ice cream. The general prohibition against using a loud-speaker for advertising a trade was not to apply to one fixed to a vehicle which is being used for the conveyance of a perishable commodity for human consumption 'if it is operated solely for informing members of the public (otherwise than by means of words) that the commodity is on sale from the vehicle'. But the loudspeaker must not give reasonable cause for annoyance to people in the vicinity. However, most of the existing offences arise under local by-laws and the Bill provided that no by-law shall be held to be void for repugnancy merely because it prohibits something which the bill permits.

Such were our small attempts to fight noise in the year 1960. As for myself, by concentrating upon writing this I have managed to surround myself with a temporary wall of silence. Now that I have finished it is time for me to come out again amongst the phons, the sones and the noys and be redecibelized.

TAILPIECE

After I had written the above the House of Lords amended the Noise Abatement Bill in Committee by taking away the preferential treatment it accorded to the chimes of the ice-cream vendors – 'these instruments of cruelty' as Earl Attlee called them. Why (asked a noble lord) should not sellers of mousetraps or of old clothes or the detergent manufacturer also be exempted? Another noble lord estimated that there were millions of people under the age of fifteen years who were in favour of ice-cream bells so that members who supported the proposed amendment were old fogies.

Sir Francis Drake's Leat

From time to time vast areas of Australia are so severely stricken with drought that there is an imminent danger that a giant dust bowl will be created. I have seen, with my own eyes, and, indeed, smelt in my nostrils, the devastating effects of drought in the dead heart of Australia.

This reminded me of our own unprecendentedly severe water shortages of 1976 when people could and did walk over the dry clay beds of some of our reservoirs; the more pessimistic prophets prognosticated that conditions could not return to normal for at least a decade; prayers for rain were said in churches of all denominations; whilst the specially appointed Minister for Drought made plans for the Royal Navy to transport water to the driest areas in the West country and Wales.

'The flowers will have to wilt', he said, 'the cars to remain dirty. Water used for bathing must also be used for flushing toilets.'

A doomsday plan in some areas allocated about a quart of water to every person a day. We were suffering the driest twelve-month period recorded since 1727.

And then came the deluge! Even Noah would have felt at home. We had such rain that within two or three weeks we were back to normal, thus showing that all our prophets were false ones. A few months thereafter, a certain Minister – bless him! – was made Minister for Snow.

All these turbulent events, in their turn, reminded me of the halcyon days, whilst I was responsible (although only nominally so) for the setting up of the Land Registry's incomparable system for computing certain conveyancing records, so that, in consequence, I had to visit Plymouth every third weekend over a period of about one year. It was then that I was taken to its hinterland to see Drake's leat. This is an open, artificial conduit, stone-lined, about six to seven feet wide and two feet deep, down which torrents of water tumble for seventeen miles into the city of Plymouth.

Sir Francis Drake. Drake, he's in his hammock . . .

Take my drum to England, hand et by the shore,
Strike et when your powder's runnin' low;
If the Dons sight Devon, I'll quit the port o'Heaven,
An' drum them up the Channel as we drummed them
     long ago.

And, in the year 1980, the original Drake's drum was accepted for the nation by HM Treasury in lieu of death duties. Drake, of course, apart from all the sentimentality, was a brilliant navigator, an intrepid fighter and probably the most successful pirate in the history of this world. But my real purpose is to tell you about Drake's leat.

Following his circumnavigation of the globe in the *Pelican* (which, whilst he entered the hazardous Straits of Magellan, he renamed *The Golden Hind*), Captain Francis Drake (as he then was) returned to Plymouth and began to enter into local politics, being elected Mayor of the Borough of Plymouth for the years 1581–1582.

There is little doubt that he had an ulterior motive in

doing so, knowing, as he did, that the existing water supplies in Plymouth were by no means sufficient to provide the city with water for all needful purposes (including, strangely enough, the fighting of fires), as well as supplying water to the ships of Queen Elizabeth's Navy which were based there. The people of Plymouth then relied upon well water which came from public sources named Buckwell, Finewell, Ladywell, Waterwell and Quarrywell, in addition to a private supply from Martock's well.

Evidently, even in 1559, when Drake was aged twenty-one, there was a water shortage. The Plymouth corporation then mounted a survey for 'viewing of the ground wherebie fresh water myght have byn brought into the towne', and it is noteworthy that during 1576–1577 (just before Drake set off on his long voyage of circumnavigation) the River Mew (now called, as I believe, the River Meavy) was surveyed as to the possibility of its being able to give water to the community.

Drake had come to the conclusion that it was necessary to supplement existing resources by means of a leat which would convey water from the Meavy, over some seventeen miles, to the city. Sir Francis (as he had by then become) persuaded the Plymouth council to accept his views and thereafter, in 1584, he got himself elected as a member of Parliament in Westminster, where he was the chief sponsor of a bill to bring water to Plymouth, which received the Royal Assent in 1585 and became 27 Eliz. Cap. 20. *Inter alia* it provided:

'It shall be lawful to the Mayor and Commonalty of Plymouth in the county of Devon, and their successors, to dig and mine a Trench or Ditch, containing in Breadth between six or seven Feet over in all Places, through all the Grounds lying between the Town of Plymouth and any Part of the River of Mew, for the necessary conveying of the said River to the said Town, and to do Reparations and make all Things necessary, whereby the River may be brought and continue unto the said Town, without the Let of any Person; the said Mayor and

Commonalty paying to the Owners and Farmers of the said Grounds the Value of the Ground so digged, to be assessed by two Justices of Assise; but the said River shall not be conveyed through any Person's House, Orchard or Garden, nor to the Hindrance of the Water-course of any Mill, without the Owner's Consent.'

Thereupon Drake was able to prevail upon the Plymouth council to award him the contract for constructing a very considerable part of the conduit. One condition of the agreement was that the ships of the Royal Navy should receive all needful supplies of water and that any surplus should go to the city. Another provision was that Drake should be permitted to build six mills on the leat and use the water runing through them without payment of any rent.

Although the Act was passed in 1585, nothing was done to implement the building of the leat until December 1590, when the first sod was cut. The reason is plain. In the interim Drake was busily engaged upon the singeing of the King of Spain's beard at Cadiz in 1587 and, following the famous game of bowls on Plymouth Hoe the following year, of attacking the Armada.

The seventeen-mile-long leat was completed on the 23rd April, 1591 and, in current terms, it cost about £550,000 to build;[83] at a time when the total revenue of the city of Plymouth was about £350 (say, £30,000 today, give or take a little).

Rumour has it that, in the result, because of the number of ships to be watered as well as on account of the increase in Plymouth's population, Drake's fleet was well supplied whilst the townfolk were as short of water as ever they were before the building of the leat. Of course the arrangements did not cost Drake a farthing (or, should I say, 'a ducat'?) and he was paid for a good deal of the actual engineering work. Poor Plymouth was out of pocket! In fact, Sir Francis and his family made at least £500,000 a year out of the project. Just imagine the wrath of a present-day ratepayer at these goings-on!

The Shark that Gorged an Arm

When last I was in Sydney a friend took me to the beautiful beaches at Coo-gee. 'Coo-gee', incidentally, is an aboriginal phrase meaning 'stinking seaweed'. However, we there inhaled nothing but refreshing ozone coming off the sea.

Coo-gee is notorious on account of the fact that, during the 1930s, on payment of sixpence, you could visit the aquarium and there see the shark which had disgorged a tattooed human arm that had belonged to a member of the criminal underworld named James Smith.

The person who was charged with being his murderer, one Patrick Brady, attended the coroner's inquest, claiming that, as the law then stood, an arm is not a body and that, without a body, there can be no inquest. This is what Mr Justice Halse Rogers had to say about that plea.[84]

'This case raises a point of considerable difficulty, one as to which counsel are agreed there is no direct authority. Some few cases are recorded of a challenge of the authority of the Coroner to hold an inquest, but there is no report of any case in the history of the office which has existed for many hundred years in which the question has been raised before a Court,

223

whether the remains on which an inquest is being held are sufficient to be regarded as a corpus or body.

'Instances are recorded in which inquests have been held on parts of bodies as, for instance, where there has been an explosion and the remains are unidentifiable. Also inquests have been opened on part only of a corpse where there has been deliberate dismemberment after death. These . . . exceptional instances appear to me to afford no help in this case.

'On the evidence before me it appears that the Coroner has commenced an inquest concerning the death of one James Smith. No body identified as that of James Smith has been found, and, of course, it follows that the whole body of James Smith has not been viewed by the Coroner, but an arm found in extraordinary circumstances has been produced to him, and by certain tattoo marks this has been identified as the arm of James Smith, and there is evidence that the arm which was severed from the trunk by a sharp knife, was cut from a dead body, and the Coroner has sworn that he is satisfied that the James Smith, whose arm it was, is dead. [Therefore] it may be taken that the Coroner is satisfied that the death of an identified individual has been established, and he, having viewed part of the body of the deceased, proceeded to hold an inquest. The applicant for prohibition, who has been arrested and charged with the murder of James Smith, challenges the legality of the action of the coroner, and his challenge is based on the ground that no inquest can be held except *super visum corporis*,[85] and that no corpus has been viewed as a preliminary to the holding of the inquiry.

'The Coroner derives his authority from the Coroners' Act 1912, but that Act does not indicate the limits of his jurisdiction and says nothing generally as to the cases in which he may act, except that the practice and procedure in his Court are to remain as they were before the passing of the Coroners' Act 1904. Reference to that Act shows a similar provision, namely, that the practice and procedure were to remain as they were before the passing of that Act. [Hence, the] practice and procedure must be in accordance with the common law of England which was imported into the colony of New South Wales by the provisions of 9 George IV., Chapter 83.

'The Common Law Rules as to the duties of a Coroner are of great antiquity. The Statute *de officio coronatoris* (1276) was according to the learned author of Jarvis on Coroners "merely directory and affirmatory of the common law of England." It enacted that the Coroner "should go to the place where any person is slain or suddenly dead or wounded . . . and should by his warrants to the bailiffs or constables summon a jury out of the four or five or six neighbouring towns and make inquiry upon view of the body; and the Coroner should duly inquire into the manner of killing and all the circumstances that occasioned the party's death . . . they should examine the body to see if there be any signs of strangling about the neck or cords about the members, or burns." One may note in passing the distinction drawn in the Statute between the body and its members.

'In a treatise on "The Office of a Coroner," by John Wilkinson (1651) is set out the form of charge of a Coroner to a jury which contains this passage: "For I must tell you that Coroners have authority to inquire by their office of all manner of homicides and slaughters by men especially above all other things, and that by the oaths of men *super risum corporis* and not otherwise.' And in England by the Coroners Act 1887, the Coroner was authorised to hold "an inquiry upon the dead body of a person lying within his jurisdiction."

'I have made the foregoing brief observations on the history of inquisitions to show that the view of the body has always been an essential to the holding of an inquest. It may be suggested that in view of the fact that counsel for the respondent admits that the inquest must be *super visum corporis*, these observations are unnecessary, but it has been argued that as part

225

of a body has in this case been viewed and identity established to the satisfaction of the Coroner, that is sufficient; but the view of the body was never merely for the purpose of establishing the fact of death or the identity of the deceased.

'In Hawkins' Pleas of the Crown it is said that "If a Coroner take an inquisition without view of the body he may take a second inquisition *super visum corporis* for the first was absolutely void . . . ." Anciently it would seem the body was lying before the jury and Coroner during the whole inquest; and in truth the body is itself part of the evidence to the jury. If then they see it before but not after they are sworn, a material part of the evidence given to them is given when they are not upon oath. In corroboration of this view . . . it is to be observed that "if the body be not found, or it hath lain so long before the Coroner has viewed it that he can in no way be assisted from the view in taking his inquest or if there be danger of infecting people in digging it up, the inquest ought not to be taken by the Coroner unless he have a special writ or commission for that purpose."

. . . In [R v Ferrand] the Court held an inquest to be void because the jury was sworn by a clerk *super visum corporis* before the appearance of the Coroner. He then came and re-swore the jury without himself having seen the body . . . after several days. It was suggested that he had had no view of the body and therefore that he had no authority to proceed with the inquest. In the words of Best, J. "Upon this suggestion he goes to the church, causes the body to be disinterred, just looks at the face of the deceased and then orders the corpse to be again covered up. This was not a sufficient view of the body to give him authority to proceed. He should have had an opportunity of seeing whether there were any marks of violence, and of ascertaining from the appearance of the body what was the occasion of the death of the deceased."

'I have cited the passages from Hawkins, and the facts of *Ferrand's Case* to show both the strictness required from

226

Coroners as to a proper view and the irrelevancy of the fact that death and identity had been established. In the time of Chief Justice Holt, it was held to be an indictable offence to bury a man who had died a violent death before the Coroner's jury had sat, and in 1884, two persons were indicted for burning or disposing of dead bodies with intent thereby to prevent inquests where they should have taken place . . . But in *Rex* v *Hazlewood* . . . Lord Chief Justice Hewitt said, "It is still as in *Ferrand's Case* a condition precedent that there should be a view. A failure in that is a failure to begin the proceedings as they should be begun."

'It is clear from the cases and authorities . . . that it is idle to urge that the Coroner has had something just as good as a view of the body, or that the absence of the body will in no way impair the value of his inquiry. As the practice and procedure of his Court must follow the common law a view of the body is still essential; and it would seem that unless he is able to have such a view as may help him in his inquiry he should not enter upon an inquest. The whole matter, therefore, reduces itself . . . to the question, "Is an arm a body or corpus?"; or "How much of a body may be called a body?" Now, I am clearly of opinion that in ordinary parlance no one would dream of speaking of an arm as a body . . . . I am of opinion that the limb which has been viewed in this case cannot be called a body. Were I to hold otherwise it would follow that each leg was a body, and likewise a severed head, and consequently if the various parts were found lying within the jurisdiction of different Coroners there might be so many separate inquests. I am not concerned to decide whether a trunk without head or limbs might be called a body or corpus, but I am constrained to the opinion that any separate member cannot be so termed. Consequently, I am of opinion that there was no proper basis for an inquest, and that the Coroner should not have entered upon the inquiry.

'It appears to me to be quite unsatisfactory that the

position in regard to inquests should be left as it has been, but as the Legislature has deliberately preserved the common law practice and procedure the Court has no alternative. It must see that such procedure and practice are observed even if it finds the rules apparently out of date and hardly suited to present day conditions. In England the matter has been dealt with by the Coroners Act of 1926; but just before the passing of that Act in *Rex* v. *Hazlewood*, already referred to, the Court held that notwithstanding the Coroners Act of 1887, the common law rule with which we are now concerned, still applied. If it is thought essential that Coronial inquiries as they have hitherto existed should continue the matter should be dealt with by the Legislature. But although I am of opinion that the enquiry cannot proceed in this case I do not think that the administration of justice will be in any way impeded by this decision. An inquest is only one form of proceeding in cases where there has been a violent death and murder is alleged. Where an inquest cannot for any reason be held there is still open a proceeding before a Magistrate, and following such proceeding there may be a committal and trial. A finding by a Coroner is not a necessary preliminary to such procedure, and in a trial for murder it is not necessary to give evidence of the finding of the actual body. Confusion sometimes arises from the phrase *corpus delicti*,[86] as though the corpus in that phrase had some reference to the body of the deceased. It means merely the fact that a crime has been committed. Reference might be made to *Peacock* v *The King*, where Chief Justice Griffiths said: 'Hence results the rule in criminal cases that a coincidence of circumstances tending to indicate guilt, however strong and numerous they may be, avails nothing unless a *corpus delicti*, the fact that the crime has been actually perpetrated, be first established. So long as the least doubt exists as to the act, there can be no certainty as to the criminal agent. Hence upon a charge of homicide it is an established rule that the accused shall not be convicted unless the death be first distinctly proved either by direct evidence of the fact or by inspection of the body.'

'An inquest is merely an inquiry and it has its disadvantages as well as its advantages. As to the latter, it may often, from the publicity which it receives, enable further evidence to be procured which will assist in the administration of justice. But where an arrest has been made and a charge of murder laid, the publicity given to the evidence at such an inquiry may be gravely prejudicial to the accused, especially where evidence which would be inadmissible at a trial is received and published widely. At one time it was illegal to publish such evidence, and it might be that restrictions should again be imposed. However, that has nothing to do with the matter before me. . . .

'Counsel for the respondent admitted that prohibition was the appropriate remedy in such a case as this, and I have dealt with the matter on that footing. The case of *R* v *Staines* is an authority in support of that view.

"For these reasons I am of opinion that the rule should be made absolute . . ."'

Thus the Supreme Court of New South Wales rejected the argument that an arm is not a body and that without a body there can be no inquest. Yet although the learned judge's observations were clear beyond any peradventure, a perverse coroner's jury did not accept them and, in consequence, failed to nail the murderer.

There is a curious corollary to this tale. The friend who took me to Coo-gee (and who, incidentally, is himself a retired judge of the Sydney District Court), happened, during World War II, to be in Perth, in Western Australia, whilst serving in the Australian Army. He there met someone who had identified Patrick Brady, the alleged murderer, who was then flourishing and running a local casino.

Taxmen and Other Big Brothers

Heave up the drawbridge! Slam down the portcullis! Pour molten lead on those morons below who strive to invade my castle, my home!

It is improbable that some account of the *Rossminster* case[87] has not trickled through Alice's rabbit hole from the Podes to the Antipodes. But if I may shortly recapitulate, at 7 am one autumn morning in the year 1979, some seventy (no less) taxmen (despite all that we have heard about alleged heavy cuts in Civil Service manpower) and a few policemen simultaneously raided 'in military style' – Lord Denning's words – the homes and offices of two people who were supposedly engaged in the legitimate business of tax avoidance. They seized and took away in lorries many tons of documents, including passports, copies of our financial newspapers (which, I suppose, the editors themselves might have supplied had they been asked), kids' bank savings books and even (to her utter chagrin) the school report of an eleven-year-old girl. Incidentally, this is not the first occasion on which these marauders have stolen the possessions of mere children and the entire process smacked of what we lawyers commonly call a 'fishing expedition', coupled, perhaps, with a mania for persecution.

All this the seventy high-handed taxmen purported to do in pursuance of an English Act of Parliament,[88] having earlier applied *ex parte* to a circuit judge for a warrant. For some quite inexplicable reason, a Divisional Court did not think the actions of the taxmen amounted to an abuse of power even though it could not possibly be otherwise than such an abuse!

In the Court of Appeal Lord Denning and his colleagues said that, although those who committed fraud on the Revenue were parasites who sucked the lifeblood of society, suspicion was not enough to prove guilt. Every man was innocent until proved guilty. The warrant of search was rightly challenged because the taxmen had not chosen to specify – as by law they were required to do – a particular offence to justify the search and, in some hands, the statute might be an instrument of oppression.

In his picturesque and pungent manner Lord Denning asseverated that there had been no operation of this kind and upon this scale since the year 1783 when the King's Messengers arrested John Wilkes, the radical journalist and Member of Parliament, and seized all his papers. Lord Denning recalled how the then Lord Chief Justice had quashed the warrants as being 'worse than the Spanish Inquisition . . . a law under which no Englishman would wish to live for one hour'.

Finally, the Master of the Rolls ruled that the raids were 'an illegal and excessive use of power'. *Certiorari* would go to quash the warrant.

In the House of Lords Lord Wilberforce (whose famous ancestor devoted his life to the suppression of the slave trade) conceded that the integrity and privacy of a man's home and of his place of business was an important human right but, in recent years, it had been eroded by statutes in the belief that it should be overridden by the interest that the public had in preventing evasions of the law, and he and three other Law Lords (Lord Salmon dissenting) held that, according to a strict interpretation of the statute, the searches and seizures were valid.

In a leading article, *The Thunderer* recalled[89] that throughout our legal history there have existed two broad strands of judicial approach. There are those, like Lord Denning, who take the view that 'a judge has the duty to interpret the law, so far as he can, in a way which accords with social and personal justice, which upholds rather than destroys the civil liberties of the individual, which looks with suspicion and not equanimity on the increasing encroachment of the State and other power groups in the lives of citizens'. The other kind of judge interprets Acts of Parliament 'narrowly, supporting the words of the law in preference to the justice of the case'.

All this has been paraphrased by the man in the street by saying, in a grossly over-simplified way, that Lord Denning has done justice by breaking the law and the Law Lords have done an injustice by observing it to the letter.

Be all that as it may, it is undeniable that as we in these islands came to the year 1984, the number of Mr Orwell's animals that have become more equal than all the others has increased by a geometrical progression.

You think I exaggerate? At this very stage in space-time I am told that no one in this country knows precisely how many nosey-parkers are authorised by law (which, in practice, almost always means authorised by subordinate legislation) to invade the privacy of my home or my business premises. But I will give you a few facts. There are well over 250 different authorisations which empower some petty inspector or other to enter my premises and more than 30 of them are permitted to invade my home alone. There are more than 200 different kinds of inspectors. They can and do frequently enter the premises of one-man and other small enterprising businesses. Some need an easily obtained magistrate's warrant; others do not. Some of these over-masterful people question my neighbours about me in my absence. Clearly, any little householder or business man who has his private premises searched even before he has had his morning breakfast and got his scared children off to school, without any charge being asserted against him, is bewildered, frightened and thoroughly apprehensive. Just fancy! On an empty stomach!

It would be an enormous task for me – and quite unrewarding for you – if I were to attempt to enumerate, classify and describe with particularity all the hundreds of narks who are now empowered to force their ways into the precincts of my castle. Some, as I have said, need a warrant. Others are required to give advance warning of their invasion; others, not. Some may use force; others, not. In some instances an obstruction of the intruder is punishable with imprisonment.

I suppose that the Customs and Excise men who enforce Value Added Tax are amongst the worst offenders. Of course, many people seek both to avoid and to evade VAT. The unscrupulous evaders, in common with most honest citizens, regard it as an iniquitous imposition. Be that as it may, many ordinary little people in business up and down this country have actually described the enforcement methods of the Customs as making the Gestapo look like amateurs. It is surprising how many little men in the street have used just that kind of expression. They are referring to the searching of workers' pockets and handbags; to the prevention of staff going to the lavatory unaccompanied; to the stealing of the private belongings of little children; to the seizure of business papers and the impudent cross-examination of staff in the most offensive way in front of customers and clients.

There seem to be no limits to the harassment which is all too commonly practised but, in all this you will, I am sure, understand that I am not for one single moment impugning the proper and well-observed code of conduct of our police who are thoroughly respected by the public at large – nor, I should add, the behaviour of sheriffs and bailiffs, who are also authorised to enter our homes for the purposes of levying lawful execution.

What does Big Brother's essential work consist of? Most of the great London stores have installed television cameras in order to prevent the theft of many millions [*sic*] of pounds' worth of goods each year. British Rail uses cameras on football trains to photograph every passenger in the hope of stamping out hooliganism. Lorry drivers in the United Kingdom regard the tachograph, wholly accepted by their European colleagues as a benefit and a protection, as 'a spy-in-the-cab'. The alleged phone-tapping of the conversations of subversives and traitors make some of our politicians hot round the collar. And so forth.

I question whether Big Brother is deeply involved in these fairly innocuous affairs. However, in addition to the devastating invasions of privacy which I briefly described earlier, in 1980, I did not altogether approve of the Government expenditure of £503 in the purchase of binoculars – not, as you might suppose, to allow a few old age pensioners like me to watch at Lords the superb batting and bowling of Ian Botham more closely – but simply to enable a few Social Security spies to judge whether, by living in sin, a handful of people who were drawing benefits to which, as unmarried people, as they knew, they were not lawfully entitled, should be prosecuted.

Et domus sua cuinque est tutissimum refugium.

Sojourn in Oz

Part 1: South Australia

Marjorie, my wife, and I never cease to rejoice at finding ourselves, once again, on Australian soil and we think that to awake to the antiphonal melodies of *granilla cyanolenca* as they call, one to another, is an unforgettable experience even if, on rising, you fail to clean your teeth with white wine, as I'm told all good Adelaideians do. These splendid black and white Murray Magpies are just like our English white swans in that they are faithful to one partner for life. Small wonder that they sing so joyfully. It is also a pleasant experience to be lulled in the hot noonday sun by the song of the cicadas, and to fall asleep by night to the chirping of crickets, and at any time to listen to the bellbirds, whose song is precisely like the ringing of small bells.

'And, softer than slumber, and sweeter than singing,

The notes of the bellbirds are running and ringing.'

In viewing Colonel Light's fair city from Mount Lofty, his brilliant conception and development of the site in relation to both topography and climate are clearly evident – this, despite a wealth of ignorant opposition to his plans at the time. Of his critics he merely said: 'I am perfectly willing to bear [the

235

responsibility] and I leave it to posterity, and not to them, to decide whether I am entitled to praise, or to blame.' He conceived Adelaide as an ideal garrison town and his clever zig-zagging of East Terrace provided the means of an enfilading fire which would be totally unexpected by hostile aboriginal natives making a frontal attack.

On going to and from the Barossa Valley, that paragon of vineyards throughout the entire world, we saw all over the Adelaide Hills, many still existing bitter reminders of Ash Wednesday 1983 – blackened trees by the ten thousand, despite their sprouting green foliage, and many desolated homesteads, though some have been restored. One such Gehenna was Greenhill where, with the temperature screaming at 110°F scorching winds fanned the flames at 60 miles per hour. And, incidentally, there was evidence of an even worse plight at Cockatoo in Victoria, where every single house is newly built. Around Airey's Inlet was Joan Hammond's house, which with all its invaluable musical memorabilia was destroyed – another distressing spot.

Passing through one of the earliest areas of South Australia to be settled, a thought occurred to me about the way in which the winegrowers promote their products. People in Europe, at least, are suspicious of sherries or ports that have not emanated from Spain and Portugal, respectively, Their fears would be allayed if only Australian producers would call their quite superb wines by such beautiful and original names as Yankalilla (Australian sherry) and Ongarparinga (Australian port). Such appellations would surely match their delicate aromas and flavours. And, incidentally, in several States, I have been puzzled to know whether I'm drinking Reisling or Riesling. Better, perhaps, if they called it Coonawarra!

Then there is that little purple wildflower called Salvation Jane, so named on account of the sheep and cattle it saved during a severe shortage of fodder during a drought in South

Australia. 'This will be our salvation', said Patterson to his wife Jane. The Victorians call it Patterson's Curse because it grew so strongly there as to overwhelm everything else and could scarcely be eliminated. Indeed, even the Parliament in Adelaide proposed to get rid of it as a noxious weed; until, that is, it was rescued by the beekeepers in the State because of its high yield of honey. Wouldn't 'Salvation Jane' be a suitable name for a Clayton drink? [90]

Part 2: Victoria

When we arrived in Melbourne, two things immediately disconcerted me. Ever since Marjorie and I first visited the city thirty-five years ago, we have loved to wander, during the evening shadows, over the King's Domain and up to the Shrine, where we have frequently had a friendly chat with the policeman, in the attractive uniform of the Australian Light Infantry, with rifle and fixed bayonet, who happened to be on duty. Now, following reveille at about 5pm, there is no one there by night. No one to talk to! and who has presumed to remove Simpson and his donkey bearing a wounded comrade at Gallipoli in 1915? The place is not quite the same, although, by way of partial compensation, there is still the memorial to Edward George Honey who was the very first person to conceive the idea of two minutes' silence on Remembrance Day.

Then in the gloomy, spooky, soulless precincts of Melbourne Gaol, where Ned Kelly was hanged on 11 November, 1880, we saw the lashing triangle designed for those who were sentenced to have their backs ripped to ribbons by the cat-o'-nine-tails. This torture was last used at Pentridge in 1958 and I imagine that we in the United Kingdom abolished the 'cat' at about the same time. Be all that as it may, the thought struck me most forcibly: how savagely ruthless – or how ruthlessly savage – we all were only a bare twenty-eight years ago.

On a happier note, whilst in Victoria, we twice visited Kangaroo Ground where, although we saw no roos, the entire bush resounded to the unsurpassed ringing of the bellbirds. On another trip I was fascinated on discovering that although the Bunyip is a mythical beast, there is actually a township of that name. We bypassed it on our way to Gippsland where, amidst mile after mile of deep bushland, we visited Walhalla. It was here, on 26 December 1862, that Edward Stringer struck gold. Over the ensuing years, the total yield was 73 tons (*not* silly tonnes) which was housed in a strong vault by the roadside. At today's prices it might be worth some $A28,000,000,000.

Incidentally – and most incongruously – in the local museum which displays many of the miners' artefacts, clothing, and day-to-day documents, besides numerous old photographs, there was a facsimile copy of the warrant for the execution of Charles I, bearing the fifty-nine seals and signatures of the traitorous Roundheads. I wonder why.

Walhalla lies in an area of fearful fire risk where, on Black Friday, 13th January, 1939, virtually the whole of the Gippsland was wiped out. At nearby Woods Point many babies whose parents had placed them, for safety, in the creek, were severely scalded in the boiling waters.

High above the town is the cemetery where some 1,100 miners and the members of their families lie in their last resting place, beneath great pines. Sadly, many of the tombs house little children. Higher still, after a breathtaking up-hill scramble, the pioneers carved off the top of the mountain in order to create what is surely one of the most remarkable cricket grounds in the world. Warwick Armstrong once played here. Giant-like, he wagered that he would hit a six into the Star Hotel. But he failed to do so. Indeed, he scored no more than a miserable eleven runs.

Yet, everywhere, the countryside and the bush were, to

our English eyes, just superbly beautiful. C. J. Dennis put it
thus:

'The young green leaves is shootin' on the trees,
    The air is like a long, cool swig o' beer,
The bonzer smell o' flow'rs is on the breeze,
    An 'ere's me, 'ere,
Just moochin' round like some pore, barmy coot,
    Of 'ope an' joy, an' forchin destichoot.'

Now let me ask you, where, in Victoria, will you find
Mrs Cooke's former Boarding School for Young Ladies, housing
a naked one? The answer, in a roundabout way, is that it stands
on a site bought for £100 at the very first public auction to be
held in Melbourne in 1837, by John Batman, who founded the
city. He camped on the banks of the Yarra in 1834 and declared:
'This will be a site for a village.' Over the years the premises
were used, in turn, as a butcher's shop, a timber yard, a grain
store and (being opposite the Fish Market, now Flinders Street
Station), as a fishmonger's warehouse. In 1853 the structure was
converted to a hotel. In 1875, Henry Figsby Young and Thomas
Joshua Jackson, who had struck rich gold in Otago, New
Zealand, bought the place. Finally, in 1908, their successors,
Norman Young and Henry Jackson, paid 800 guineas for the
painting of the beautiful nude Chloe by Jules Lefebure of Paris,
which was awarded the gold medal at Melbourne's Great
Exhibition of 1880. They then hung it in what has probably
become the most famous pub in Australia, commonly known as
Young and Jacksons.

Part 3: New South Wales

I am almost ashamed to confess that it was not until our
fourth visit to Sydney, that my wife and I went to Botany Bay
where, on the 28th April, 1770, Captain James Cook and his party
landed in order to water H. M. Barque *Endeavour*. (In passing,
this ship was a bare three metres longer than the old ferry boats

239

Curl Curl and *Dee Why* that so often plied Sydney harbour over more than thirty years, whilst a Boeing 747 is rather more than three and a quarter times its total length.)

Spear-carrying aborigines of the Gwiyagal tribe menacingly disputed the arrival 'although they were but two an we, 30 or 40 at least', wrote Cook. But equally interesting for me was the recorded death of the seaman, Forby Sutherland, who was the first British subject to die on Australian soil. He was buried four days after the landing.

Then what a joy it was, after the lapse of thirty-five years to gaze, once again, upon the incomparable splendour of the Blue Mountains, with their sheer rock faces, and almost impenetrable bush which fades into the palest of blues in the far distance, and to ponder upon the bravery – not to say effrontery – of men like Gregory Blaxland, William Charles Wentworth and Lieutenant Lawson who, on the 28th May, 1813, dared to challenge the fearful hazards of a jealous and retributative Nature, by crossing the heights to reach Mount York. I'm told some of their predecessors failed to achieve the crossing because they stuck to the valleys. And just on their heels, twenty-eight men under a surveyor named Evans, laid out the road of 101½ miles from Emuford to Bathurst in desperately hard conditions within a mere six months.

Then, at Windsor, we learned about Andrew Thompson who – it was said – with extraordinary energy and enterprise, contributed more to the material advantage of the infant colony (as it then was) than any other man of his time. He served under governors Hunter, Bligh and Macquarie – nothing is said of Governor King! Men like him are surely needed today.

Parramatta, an early seat of government, was, originally called Rose Hill. What many Australians may not know is that the species of mainly red and blue parrots known as *platycercus rosellas* was originally nicknamed Rose Hillers. It was at Parramatta, only three years after the start of colonisation, that James Ruse, a convict on ticket-of-leave who was married to a convict wife, was, as a reward for his industry and honesty of purpose, granted thirty acres of land adjoining Experimental Farm Cottage by Governor Philip and provided with tools and seed, conditional upon his producing food. He redeemed his pledge by being the first person to grow wheat in Australia. Little could he have dreamed of the vast areas of the continent that are devoted to the raising of that very cereal today.

Finally, having gazed with delight once again upon the Hawkesbury River, we discovered, some two miles south of Gosford, a memorial stone to Henry Kendall, and were reminded of lines which all middle-aged Australians must surely have learned in their schooldays.

'The silver-voiced bellbirds, the darlings of daytime!
They sing in September their songs of the Maytime:
When shadows wax strong, and the thunderbolts hurtle
They hide with their fear in the leaves of the myrtle.'

Now it so happened that I was walking down – of all places in Australia – Boomerang Street in Sydney on my way to Kings Bloody Cross, when I met a fellow who told me that he was having golf lessons. Why, for goodness' sake did he pick on me? Perhaps I've got the kind of face that confiding people like. At all events, he confessed that his mentor had told him that his grip wasn't too bad. His stance, his address, were quite acceptable. His swing was at least as good as average. 'But', said the pro, 'that little white ball is far too close to your feet – after you've struck your tee shot!'

Ever since my wife and I have been *subjected* (if that is an appropriately courteous verb) to continuous and typical Australian hospitality, I have been conscious that discrimination is just as dirty a word in the Commonwealth of Australia as it is in the UK. Thus, according to a recent issue of the *Sydney Morning Herald* (which, incidentally, and to its eternal shame, buried dear old Grannie and her eighth (as distinct from fifth) column

241

all too long ago!) obesity, and obesity alone, is a bar to both social success and opportunities for employment, simply because of discrimination against fat people. The Anti-Discrimination Board of New South Wales confirmed that it had received complaints from overweight men that they are severely prejudiced against on this score. Again, incidentally, and touching prejudice, there is no mention of the fair sex. All the furore arose from a Danish study, extending over more than a decade, which demonstrated that whereas over one half of ordinarily proportioned men got jobs in New South Wales, only thirty per cent of the fat people were similarly successful.

As a matter of law, it seems that this particular handicap does not slide easily into any of the several categories of bias upon the grounds of race, sex, marital status, or physical or intellectual impairment required by law.

I was also amused to read that three male teenagers complained about sex discrimination to the Anti-Discrimination Board in a cause that will, almost inevitably, go later to the Equal Opportunity Tribunal. I say 'almost inevitably' because the New South Wales Department of Education has apparently recently decided to ban all corporal punishment as from the 1st January, 1987. Be all that as it may, these lads have asseverated, with complete truth, that, whereas they could be and, indeed, are caned, their counterparts in girls' schools could not be, and were not, similarly whacked upon their posteriors.

Counsel for the defence of the relevant authority pleaded that infants possess no rights to assert or defend a civilian claim 'in their own right' – whatever that means when translated into plain English. But the lady judge, Justice Mathews – God bless her! – thought quite otherwise.

I have been astounded at the changes that have transformed Sydney since I first saw it some thirty-five years ago. There was then the so-called 'six o'clock swill'. Almost every wife in the land had misguided forebodings that if the then existing periods allowed for drinking were to be extended to 'reasonable drinking hours', as they now have been, most women would never see their husbands until late at night. In parenthesis, I suppose that most of my readers today cannot believe that such things were ever said – or accepted. But they were. And, at the time, I was so bold as to asseverate, as long ago as 1951, that the whole concept was nonsense as, indeed, it has now proved to be.

But, even today, what on earth is the reasonable visitor supposed to do in order to quench his perennial thirst on a Sunday – which thirst, incidentally, is no less potent on the Sabbath than it is on any weekday – when most of the pubs and bottle shops are shut?

I have pondered upon how Sydney has changed since I first saw it in 1951. At random, I would say: then, there were no skyscrapers. Today, the city is replete with them. Then, most people were ashamed of being associated with criminality in the distant past. Today, they show great interest if one of their ancestors happened to be a convict, no matter what peccadillo he committed. Then, in 1951, no decent lady ever entered a pub. Today, thank goodness! every lady is accepted there.

Sydney Harbour remains, as ever, quite incomparable – a term that, on a former occasion, a Wellingtonian friend of mine just could not swallow. He took the gravest possible exception to it. *En passant*, at least you don't sink Russian ships there!

But, today, at the weekend, the harbour has many billions of dollars worth of fine yachts and other privately-owned craft. Where does all this vast wealth come from? Who owns it? How do they acquire it?

Meanwhile, THE BRIDGE, stately as ever, remains some 171 feet above water level, quite enough to let the great liners of past days pass under it although, alas, they seldom do so now. At the Manly end of the harbour the desiccated site of the formerly noble Norfolk Island Pines was sad to see.

I am writing as we fly above the Northern Territory on our way to Hong Kong. We have just said 'Farewell' to our many antipodean friends for the fourth time. We did so with sad hearts.

———————————●●●————————————

Debunking

We lawyers tend to be too literal-minded at times. Some of us need debunking.

'Then you should say what you mean', the March Hare went on. 'I do', Alice hastily replied; 'at least – at least I mean what I say – that's the same thing, you know.'

'Not the same thing a bit!' said the Hatter, 'Why, you might as well say that 'I see what I eat' is the same thing as ' I eat what I see!'

By and large, and occasionally, I am against debunking, especially in this age when the Clever Ones seek to discredit everyone and everything. How on earth do they know that Alfred didn't burn the cakes when they weren't actually there near Wareham in Dorset to see that he didn't do it? Never let us question the truth of harmless hallowed traditions that, in our tender years, we were nurtured on. Rather, let us debunk what is shallow, specious and cynical today.

In these ancient islands we are daily surrounded by real history. Thus I have just returned from a week's holiday, during which I walked around the greatest earthwork in Europe – four miles in circumference – at Maiden Castle where the Belgae were finally defeated by the Romans. I saw with my own eyes, in a nearby museum, the sword-cleft skull of one of our men who opposed the invader and the actual vertebrae of another, stricken with the steel Roman arrowhead that killed him. I saw with my own eyes the hoard of over 22,000 antoniniari coins of billion (bronze, coated with silver) that some Roman miser had buried 1,700 years ago. I saw the great giant of Cerne Abbas, cut out in the turf of a chalk down. He is at least 2,000 years old. He stands 180-feet-high and his erect penis measures 30 feet. Yet, as it happens, there was a Christian Abbey a few hundred yards away. How on earth, all through the centuries, did the church tolerate this phallic worship of Hercules round the corner? These diverse things I have described were all part of the intimate daily lives of real people.

I also stood among the ruins of the Abbey Church of St. Edmundsbury, first built in 903. The third church (1065–1097) was probably the largest, and the abbey one of the wealthiest, in Europe. Today, all that remains of the church are a few ruined stone piers rising above the greensward. Yet it was here, on the 20th November, 1214, that Cardinal Langton and twenty-five barons of England swore at the high altar to impose the provisions of Magna Carta upon King John. Then on the 15th June, 1215, in a meadow at Runnymede, lying between Windsor, where the King's forces were based, and Staines where the barons were camped, they enforced their will upon him.

Open before me, as I write, is a child's book of English history bearing, on its fly-leaf, the name of my maternal great grandmother. It has a picture (*sub nom.* 'John signing Magna Carta') of one of several armed and grim-faced barons handing to the petulant monarch a quill pen. Having disavowed debunking I must, nevertheless, point out that John certainly did not sign the charter for it is unlikely that he was able to write a single word. He caused it to be sealed.

However, at Runnymede that day the King solemnly swore to keep the matters set out in the charter 'in good faith and without deceit' and, although he had no intention of observing his oath, the first page of the constitutional history of all the English-speaking peoples was written. Many times tyranny has tried to raise its head again but it has never succeeded. 'We, too, are heirs of Runnymede', wrote John Greenleaf Whittier, the American poet. And Kipling put it thus:

'And still, when mob or monarch lays
Too rude a hand on English ways,
A whisper wakes, the shudder plays
Across the reeds at Runnymede.'

It is true that one modern writer has sought to debunk history as we were taught it by painting John white and the barons black. It is true that the barons at that time were essentially concerned with their own narrow interests. Indeed, even Sir Winston Churchill has explained the charter as being primarily a redress of feudal grievances extorted from an unwilling King by a discontented ruling class demanding its privileges. No doubt it was. But for the very first time it established that the law was above the King and that the King must not break the law. From its principles flowed the rule of law, the maxims of equity, habeas corpus, trial by jury, and the many other benevolent appendages of a freedom loving people that have been exported to many nations throughout the world. Lord Denning, when he was the Master of the Rolls, laid stress upon the effect of the *ipsissima verba* of the charter. 'It was expressed in language which has had its impact on future generations. It put into words the spirit of individual liberty which has influenced our people ever since.'

Today we sometimes complain that our laws are too rigid and our judges too hidebound by precedent. Yet sometimes the judges do demonstrate their almost perverse independence and the flexibility of the law, as witness the *Burmah Oil Case*,[91]

247

where the House of Lords refused to bow down to what they must have known was government policy. A giant amongst law lords, Lord Macmillan, once wrote that 'in almost every case, except the very plainest, it would be possible to decide the issue either way with reasonable legal justification'. To this extent, precedent is no fetter. Indeed, in referring to this land of freedom, Tennyson wrote about:

A land of settled government,
A land of just and old renown,
Where freedom slowly broadens down
From precedent to precedent.

It was in 1965 that the sealing of Magna Carta was celebrated with royal pageantry at St Paul's cathedral. There were festivities at Runnymede. Then on the actual day of the 750th anniverary we lawyers held our private ceremony at the Law Courts in the Strand in the Great Hall that so closely resembles the nave of a Gothic cathedral. The band of the Scots Guards played in one 'musicians gallery' and the trumpeters of the Household Cavalry occupied another. There were four glittering processions, each announced by a fanfare, the first including all the judges of the High Court and the Lords Justices in their magnificent robes. Finally, there was the entry of Magna Carta, when Lord Denning bore one of the four original tattered parchments, grey with age, upon a scarlet tray.

The Lord Chancellor extolled the virtues of the charter and so, too, did a number of other distinguished speakers. Then Lord Gardiner requested Lord Denning, as Keeper and Master of the Rolls and Records of the Chancery of England, to remind the assembled company of some of the more important provisions of the charter. Lord Denning thereupon read out excerpts from it, including the famous clauses 39 and 40.

'No free man shall be taken, imprisoned, disseised, outlawed, banished, or in any way destroyed, nor will we proceed against or prosecute him, except by the lawful judgment of his peers and by the law of the land. To no one will We sell, to none will We deny or delay, right or justice.'

Thereafter the Lord Chancellor requested the Master of the Rolls to keep the ancient record safe 'so that its message may continue to be an inspiration, not only to the present generation of English-speaking peoples, but to generations to come'.

'That will I gladly do.'

We then had the National Anthem, made more thrilling by a fanfare of trumpets, and the processions re-formed and filed out in reverse. A stirring moment in history had come and passed.

Many other anniversaries were celebrated at this time, such as the seventh century of Simon de Montfort's parliament. In a minor key, but not an insignificant one, it was, in 1965 just 100 years earlier that a sedate Oxford don named Charles Lutwidge Dodgson, in spinning an exciting new story for children, wrote with devastating logic:

'Take some more tea', the March Hare said to Alice, very earnestly.

'I've had nothing yet', Alice replied in an offended tone, 'so I can't take more'.

'You mean you can't take *less*', said the Hatter: 'it's very easy to take *more* than nothing'.

Do these sound rather like a lawyer's argument? Be that as it may, Lewis Carroll was a bachelor who so enjoyed the company of little girls that he used to invent wonderful stories for their delight whilst they lazed in the sunshine in some Oxfordshire meadow. The beastly minded Clever Ones have now labelled him a Humbert Humbert amongst the Lolitas. They, of course, need debunking. But the effect of Magna Carta upon countless generations of men can never be debunked.

Hustling Hong Kong

Whenever my wife and I have travelled from Australia to our home in the UK, we have stopped off at Hong Kong, as a temporary relief during the long and tedious journey.

In this busy, bustling island, we could no more stay away from the water than we could in Sydney.

During the five-minute trip from Hong Kong Island to the Kowloon Peninsula, the 'fragrant harbour' (for that is the island's native name) is bursting and babbling with every form of water transport from the fast-gliding green and white ferry boats, constantly crossing each other's paths, to multi-coloured and ornate junks with bat-wing sails and sporting a huge red duster, plus giant dredgers in crude red, green and yellow paint, dragged by tugs, with tiny sampans jittering and bobbing in the wash of the large ships. Stately transports, tankers, and vast container vessels from every maritime nation in the world lie off-shore, at anchor, waiting their turn to be called in and relieved of their cargoes. Overlooking the waterway many hundreds of tall, palatial homes of commerce and industry, and hotels, stand stately, whilst an autumnal mist from all the brooding hills hangs over the glittering sea that separates the island from the mainland.

Whilst we were in Hong Kong in 1987, Mr Justice Simon Li, who had served on the Supreme Court Bench for more than twenty years, told members of the local Bar Association, in his farewell speech on retirement, that High Court judges should be increasingly recruited from the Hong Kong Bar – something that hitherto has scarcely happened – simply because of the independence of thought which would thereby be engendered in them, rather than if they had been promoted by seniority as a matter of course from the District Court.

'I am now of the view,' said Mr Justice Li, 'that the judiciary should increasingly be drawn from among the ranks of the private profession. The nature of practice at the Bar is such that it breeds an independence of thought and spirit which particularly benefits its members for judicial office.'

Mr Justice Li went on to inform members of the Bar 'that Chinese judges would be increasingly used in the courts and that many of them had the advantage of being bilingual'. 'So,' he concluded, 'the time is ripe for encouragement to be offered to suitably qualified members of the Bar to accept judicial office, with the recognition that, for many of them, the acceptance of an appointment will involve financial sacrifice'.

Incidentally, the emblem of the Hong Kong Bar Association closely follows those of the Inns of Court in London, including Pegasus and the Pascal Lamb, but it is now proposed that there should be a fundamentally fresh design so as to recognise that, today, a substantial proportion of the members of the Bar are Chinese, locally recruited and locally trained.

Quite apart from these important and fundamental ideas, Hong Kong is an exciting city. Just walk down any one of its main streets, chock-a-block with old-fashioned green double-deck trams, blue and yellow buses, scarlet and white taxis, coaches, cars, vans, canvas-covered lorries, and all the other paraphernalia of road transport, and you will find a preponderance of brightly lit shops, selling gold, diamonds, sapphires, rubies, pearls, jade and other exquisite jewellery (often guarded by a man with a rifle), interspersed with palatial banks and other business houses, tailors and ladies' outfitters of the finest quality and, in sharp contrast, shabby little stalls, tended by ancient wrinkled Chinese women, selling fruit and vegetables, or papers and cheap books.

At intervals narrow, steep-stepped alley-ways, full of petty merchandise, rise up the hillside. The pavements buzz with activity like a bee-hive and the air resounds with harsh and raucous Chinese voices. Amongst the swirling, bustling crowds that throng the pavements stand armed police, smart in their serge uniforms and peaked caps, whilst all too many hapless, ill-clad mendicants hold out their begging bowls with skinny arms and grubby hands.

Incidentally, these pavements are virtually free of all litter. Small wonder, because according to the *South China Morning Post*, during our stay, a certain Mr Yau Kam-yuk was fined $HK400 (call it roughly £30 in our currency) just for throwing down a cigarette end in the street! We could do with a similarly condign punishment for litter-bugs here!

Pleas and Further Cross-Examinations

I suppose that many of you, like I do, re-read in later life the books that you relished as a child or a teenager. One of the latest ones to which, at the age of considerably more than the allotted span, I have been drawn again, is *Gulliver's Travels*, by no means confined to Lilliput and Brobdingnag – the learned professor at the Academy in Laputa certainly produced and used the very first word-processor! Just re-read the book and see.

'Lawyers', said the creator of this wonderful work, 'are a society of men bred up in their youth in the art of proving by words multiplied for the purpose that white is black according as they are paid.'

Of course it is our duty as lawyers to excel in the art of persuasion. Ignoring, for the moment, the reference to vulgar remuneration, of course it is the constant duty of any and every advocate to advance his client's cause, even if this involves him in seeking to establish that which is refutable or refutative. Of course he may need to prove that yellow and pink are indistinguishable, the one from the other. Similarly, in non-contentious business, it is necessary to be incisive and unambiguous, so that no lawyer worth his salt places much faith in greys.

So much for old Lemuel! In so far as he may have been perspicacious about our professional attitudes, perhaps I ought to record the fact that, many, many years before the current English Theft Act became law, there was an ingenious member of our junior Bar who invented a defence against stealing which became popularly known as 'Codd's puzzle'.

Someone had stolen a succulent duck. In his defence of the alleged thief, Mr Codd, of counsel, put before the simple, decent, ordinary English gentlemen of the jury, no less than seven condign and mutually exclusive defences which, inevitably, bemused the simple, honest chaps in the jury box because – please remember – there were no perspicacious, not to say perspicuitive ladies there in those days.

Thus, Mr Codd, in turn averred that: (i) the bird had been bought by the defendant; (ii) it was found by him; (iii) it had been given to him; (iv) unaided, it had flown into his garden; (v) then, seeing that he was completely innocent, it had been put into his pocket whilst he was fast asleep; (vi) also, especially and dialectically, that the succulent duck had never existed except in the wild imagination of the accuser's mind. But even more cogent than all the foregoing arguments, was the last one, namely, (vii) that Codd's client was ready, if need be, to make a clean breast about everything. Was he codding?

In the event, I am happy to tell you that Codd's client was acquitted so that anyone who is ever called upon to act for someone who is accused of theft would be well advised to study Codd's simple yet effective formula for the proof of innocence.

However, the incidence of theft in our courts is as nothing compared with the vast range of motoring offences that, today, are so utterly destructive of life and property. By contrast, it may interest you, if I may be allowed to quote that prolific, prodigious, French artist, Henri Matisse (1869–1954) who once said: 'What I dream of is an art of balance, of purity, and serenity.'

Possibly you may recoil from some of his modern works, but how can you fail to admire his vibrant 'Portrait with a Green Stripe' or, indeed, his 'White Plumes'?

This extraordinarily innovative artist also happened to be a pioneer in motoring at about the time when it was customary to have a man with a red flag preceding this quite outrageous monster. Perhaps most of us, in today's conditions, might well bewail the disappearance of the red flag. But, to come back to M. Matisse; once upon a time, when he set out upon a reliability trial, he was asked by a newsman what he would do should he have the ultimate misfortune of meeting a vehicle advancing in the opposite direction from his own. (This, of course, was long, long before the invention of the breathalyzer and a multitude of other hideosities.)

'Monsieur', he most gravely replied, 'should the inconceivable happen, I shall, naturally, instantly halt my own motoring car, draw it in to the side of the road, then dismount, and afterwards shelter in the nearby field until, at last, the other has passed by.'

The masses of crazy modern drivers might benefit from such wisdom if only they were able to open their minds to new ideas – which many of them are not.

It is axiomatic that driving and drink are incompatibles. But drink is acceptable if you are stationary as well as traditionally sober as a judge on the bench. The late Lord Chief Justice Goddard, whose cogent judgments and nimble quips alike enriched his judicial career, once stated that, in writing his famous *Commentaries*, Blackstone invariably worked with a bottle of port at his elbow. When he, Lord Goddard, was first elevated to the bench, he decided to emulate this practice of his most pre-eminent predecessor in office whilst preparing his own reserved judgments. However, in the event, he found that this spoiled his port, so that he gave it up (the writing, not the port!).

That outstanding advocate, indeed, that legal giant, and

one of the most devastating cross-examiners of all time (see page 16), the late Norman Birkett who later became Lord Birkett, once stated, in his older age: 'When I was young I was amazed at Plutarch's statement that the elder Cato started to read Greek at the venerable age of eighty. I am amazed no longer. Old age is ready to undertake tasks that youth shirked because they would take too long.'

I most humbly agree. Today, I do one thousand and one things which I had neither the time nor, indeed, the innate ability to do when I was young.

When one thinks about the quite incomparable quality of a first-class cross-examination, one of the most subtle arts in this world, it is difficult to match the guileless, cynical, destructive questions that Lord Birkenhead asked when he was simply Mr F. E. Smith and also merely an undergraduate in the ancient University of Oxford. Following a student's rag, he was charged with the serious offence of assaulting a policeman. Smith rejected the charge absolutely and emphatically. In cross-examining Smith the prosecuting counsel asked, somewhat jejunely:

'Do you realise that you are accusing this respectable constable of perjury?

F. E. (who, even as a student, had a far more potent brain than his questioner) was most indignant in denying this specious, yet quite ridiculous argument.

'Yes, you do, sir', asseverated prosecuting counsel. 'The constable swears you kicked him. You swear you didn't. What other possible explanation is there except that he has committed perjury?'

In his most devastating rhetoric which, even at that early age, F. E. had developed to such an extraordinary degree, he similarly pointed out that this was merely one of five possible explanations, namely:

'First, he is committing perjury. Secondly, I am committing perjury. Thirdly, he is honestly mistaken. Fourthly, I am honestly mistaken. Fifthly, and lastly, although the two assertions are apparently contradictory, it is possible, none the less, that they can be reconciled.'

Oh! One last word. It was Sir Patrick Hastings, over very many years Birkett's constant opponent, who once stated:

'If it had ever been my lot to decide to cut up a lady in small pieces and put her in an unwanted suitcase, I should, without hesitation, have placed my future in Norman Birkett's hands. He would have satisfied the jury that – (a) I was not there; (b) I had not cut up the lady, and (c) if I had, she thoroughly deserved it anyway.'

Truck

I have a friend who is serendipitious. He is retired, lives by the sea, and likes to indulge in a little beachcombing. He it was who told me that 'serendipity' is the faculty of making happy accidental discoveries, such (I suppose) as stumbling upon a pearl – even a cultured pearl – whilst admiring the litter of a favourite sow.

In this odd language of ours litter also suggests scattered rubbish. Rubbish, in turn, is trash (or truck) and truck brings to mind the oppressive system under which English farmers, little more than 150 years ago, forced their starving labourers to take their wages in bad corn or worse beer. Small wonder that they sometimes did a little retaliatory rick-burning!

Meanwhile, industrialists often made their workmen spend their earnings at the boss's store in buying commodities which they did not want, or contrived that they should be paid in a public house owned by the boss, thus ensuring a fluid return to his pocket of the money he had recently paid them.

These evils resulted, as you know, in the Truck Acts which required a workman's entire wages to be paid in current coin of the realm. The Acts cover a 'labourer, servant in husbandry, journeyman, artificer', and so forth – a descriptive string of names of manual workers which is now knotted with anomalies. A bus driver who has to do repairs is a workman; his conductor is not. Nor is a grocer's assistant, a hairdresser, a potman in an hotel, nor, indeed, an office worker, all of whom, in consequence, may lawfully be paid by cheque. But if, for example, a coal miner or a docker, each of whom is far better rewarded on average than any of the workers mentioned above, is paid by cheque, the employer is not only liable to criminal process, but can also be required to pay the worker's wages all over again without getting any credit for the money conferred by his cheque.

Some thirty years ago there was an unsuccessful attempt to get rid of these absurdities. The Cheques Act 1957, in providing that an unindorsed cheque paid by a banker should be evidence of the receipt by the payee of the sum payable, virtually abolished the need for indorsement of ninety-seven per cent of all cheques and enormously reduced the giving of receipts, to the great relief of 'inside' accountants but causing some discomfiture, I am told, to their 'outside' colleagues. From the very day of its coming into force the Act began to save industry and the business world some millions of pounds every year, not counting the assistance it gave to banks. But the original Bill, which was introduced as a private member's bill, also proposed to amend the Truck Acts so as to legalize agreements between employers and manual workers for the payment of wages by cheque. This proposal provoked protests from the trade unions which not unnaturally were echoed in Parliament so that, rather than jeopardise his entire Bill, its author was content to jettison part of it. Later, however, the trade unionists veered in their views so that the Payment of Wages Act 1960 was steered through the many troubled waters that so easily swamp a private bill. This Act authorised an employer to pay his employee's wages by cheque or by payment into a bank account at their request.

259

As you may suppose, at that time most manual workers had no banking account so that they needed to be educated and encouraged towards opening one. Past experience with some workers who had been lawfully paid by cheque suggested that they tended to defeat the system by asking their employer to cash their cheques. Alternatively, an embarrassing burden could be put upon the small local shopkeeper who neither wished to cash cheques regularly nor cared to refuse to do so. Nevertheless, obvious advantages from widespread payment by cheque would consist of a reduction in the costly process of handling large sums of money on the one hand, and the encouragement of thrift on the other. There is one other point. As surely as each succeeding Friday evening comes and the toilers in our cities buy their evening newspapers on their way home, their eyes are instantly caught by the almost inevitable headline – 'Another Big Wages Grab', or 'Terror Gang seize £150,000' or words to that effect. Universal payment by cheque helped to diminish that particular crime.

Wards of Court

I will lay odds of ten to one in pounds that not one in ten of you, my readers, can place the man whose middle name was 'Klapka'. He once wrote: 'I like work. I can sit and look at it for hours. I have to keep it by me: the idea of getting rid of it nearly breaks my heart'.

Last month I should have welcomed a few odds and ends of homely advice from Klapka for, like old J., the narrator in Jerome Klapka Jerome's 'Three Men in a Boat', I was unable, for reasons that an appellate court might possibly distinguish from his, to give myself the pleasure of writing to my friends in Australia. My inability – if that is a neutral enough term – is something that I can scarcely with justification blame upon our lately departed summer. All two days of it. Or were there three?

Of course, everyone of my age recalls the halcyon, hot, exuberant summers of his youth. Except, that is, for those poor, dehydrated, disillusioned realists whose noses have, for one or two decades, been unable to support rose-tinted spectacles. One of these chaps once recalled, in a letter to *The Times*, although I suspect the event must have been before his birth – that the August of 1588 was a bad month because of what happened to the Spanish Armada. Another correspondent referred, at second hand, to the foul weather in August 55 BC as recorded by Julius Caesar in his account of the Gallic wars. Now, summer, or no summer, in the year I first wrote this piece, in defiance of all the elements, a multitude of other sensational events ran themselves to a standstill. That best seller, the Denning Report, did more than restore sanity – it rendered null, void and pointless a multitude of the usual Stock exchange *risqué* jokes about the Keeler-Profumo affair. The preliminary proceedings in the Great Train Robbery case involving £2,631,000 ground slowly but inevitably on. We were urged, in criminal trials, to adopt the rather unsatisfactory Scottish notion of a 'non-proven' verdict. We all know that not to be believed is not necessarily to lie,[92] but why leave verdicts so unjustly vague? And whilst all these weighty matters were being pondered, a female infant named Crump burst into the kind of blazing summer light that I used to enjoy as a boy.

The device of making a young woman (of tender teenage years, or slightly above) a ward of court, so as to bar her from marrying a man whom her parents dislike, has become almost a commonplace, everyday affair. And a number of young men have been sent to prison because they have defied the Majesty of the Law by running off with their girl friends whilst a wardship order was in force. No doubt the prosperity of the blacksmith at Gretna Green is on the wane, for I imagine that that is the ultimate place at which absconding couples would dare to show their happy faces.

Now Crump (Patricia to her friends) was just nineteen-years-old. On the 23rd April, 1963 she was made a ward of court on the motion of her parents because they disapproved of her association with one Robert Bede Kearney, her first cousin, older than she by five years, and a hospital porter. He was restrained from marrying her and was ordered, from Scotland or Ireland or wherever he happened to have taken her, to return her to the custody of her parents. On the 19th June, foolishly, impetuously and with youthful defiance, these young people were lawfully married at a registry office in Stepney in the east end of London.

If lovers are fools,
It is nature that makes them such.

But that is not all. Patricia, it seems, had, in an Eve-like manner, eased the way for Robert by forging her parents' consent to the wedding. And although –

At lovers' perjuries,
They say, Jove laughs –

the Attorney-General was not amused by this contempt of court, aggravated, as it was, by wilful lying, and he applied for these newly married young people to be committed to prison. At this, the assertive Patricia retorted, in effect, that she had formed the view that it was quite hopeless to persuade a learned judge of the Chancery Division of the High Court of Justice ever, in any conceivable circumstances, to allow her to marry her Robert and that, when she was confronted with the might and jurisdiction of court 'and all its stately language, in which she was described as "an infant", her heart had failed her'. Possibly to an impartial observer, her heart had seemed to do anything but fail her.

You will notice that the offence committed by Patricia and Robert was not that of marrying, nor even that of perjury. It was simply contempt of court. The punishment for contempt ranges from an indefinite number of years of incarceration to a few minutes – as happened recently in the case of a man who publicly applauded his friend's acquittal on a criminal charge at Quarter Sessions.

In the *Crump* case, Mr Justice Faulks considered that the contempt of Patricia and Robert placed him in a considerable dilemma because, clearly, to punish them severely would fail to teach them not to commit the offence in future – something they were unlikley to do in any event! Patricia's own parents had not moved to commit their own child but they had elected to treat what had occurred as a *fait accompli*. People would have accused them of being stony-hearted if they had moved to commit their own daughter. So it came about that the Attorney-General moved and, once it became known publicly that an order of the court had been deliberately flouted, it had to be made plain that this kind of disobedience could never be disregarded.

Said the judge: 'The pecuniary position of these young people makes the imposition of a fine unrealistic and the court is left with the disagreeable alternatives of imposing no penalty at all except a lecture, which future potential offenders will, no doubt, regard as troublesome, rather than as a deterrent, or sentencing them to imprisonment, a course against which the mind of the court instinctively revolts'.

Despite this instinctive revolt his lordship sent Robert to Brixton Prison and Patricia to Holloway Gaol for twenty-eight days, as being the shortest term that was not derisive of the authority of the law. Doubtless this case will cause some disapproving parents to hesitate in future before embarking upon proceedings which may lead their own children to prison. Yet, you must add to the knowledge that 'all mankind loves a lover', the fact that we live in an unusually sloppy-thinking, somniloquent and over sentimental age. Having done that, you may well imagine what a volcano of half-baked opinions erupted in the press. 'To gaol a *pretty* girl for such a *trifling* affair is disgusting'. [My italics.] It was not long before the Home Secretary was asked to recommend that Her Majesty should exercise Her prerogative of mercy.

Mr Gerald Gardiner Q.C. (as he then was), who had some imaginative proposals for reforming many of the highways and by-ways of the law, stepped into this controversy. He alleged that the average age of puberty in girls was thirteen. That as a natural consequence of this alleged physical change and of the increased earning power of young people, one in four of all women married at the age of nineteen or earlier. That nearly one sixth of all children are born to mothers under twenty-two, some 70,000 a year being borne by mothers under twenty-one. He went on to point out such diverse facts as that liability to taxation arises as soon as anyone's work begins; that at sixteen, young people can ride a motor cycle or fly a glider; at seventeen, buy firearms, drive a car and be in sole control of an aircraft (although, if a law student, he or she cannot make a valid contract to take flying lessons[93]), and that (then not now) at eighteen, men were liable for compulsory military service. And, of course, both men and women could be hanged. It seems to me that most of these facts are irrelevant to the issue of marriage and some people who, by their skilled training, know far more than Mr Gardiner about puberty, have cast doubts upon his firm, but unsupported, assertion that, today, children mature physically earlier than we in our time did. So much rabid nonsense has been published recently about this subject that it is difficult for the layman, who is sometimes, despite the advance of years, still able to recall the emotions and temptations of his youth, to avoid a healthy scepticism about such extravagant claims. Of course there are fluctuations in physique from age to age according to the manner and place in which children are reared. Was not that great Tudor King, Henry VII, born to a girl of thirteen and a half years of age by her second husband? (Margaret Beaufort was born on the 31st May, 1443: Henry was born on the 28th January, 1457).

Perhaps the sanest comment on this subject was offered by a correspondent of *The Times* when he observed:

'The fact that a person is biologically able to produce children at the age of thirteen or so does not mean that he or she is emotionally sufficiently mature for marriage'. But Mr Gardiner summed up his case, after firmly declaring that premarital intercourse is not the right basis for marriage, by stating that 'in a time of physical change we have, by doing nothing, increased the period of restraint from four years after puberty to seven, and we cannot expect that this increased strain on young people will have no effect'. But are Mr Gardiner's premises sound?

Today, as I lay aside my rose-tinted spectacles I observe that some teenagers of decent parentage ruin property and endanger life in passenger trains, wreck gardens, smash tombstones, set fire to churches, leave their excrement and urine in the most sacred places and generally commit the most revolting acts of vandalism. Fit to marry? Even though they can fly an airplane? And in Scotland alone, which is relatively sparsely populated, they do well over two million pounds' worth of wanton damage every year. Thus, for example, in a recent period of three months 1186 railway carriage windows (worth at least £25 each) and 12,235 light bulbs were smashed in Scotland alone. Are these wicked children truly fit to marry? By such standards the conduct of Patricia and Robert becomes the merest pecadillo.

But love is blind, and lovers cannot see
The pretty follies that themselves commit.

Yet, quite properly, as you may think, the Home Secretary turned his face against recommending a reprieve for them. And in the result, I sincerely hope that Patricia and Robert will realize, as Jerome K. Jerome once wrote, that 'love is like the measles; we all have to go through it'. And that their early ordeal will bind them together with firmer knots than, all too often, a mere ceremony does.

———————————————• • ———————————————

All Children Shall be Treated Fairly

A wombat, as every Australian and not a few people outside that great country well know, is a diprotodont burrowing marsupial of the genus phascolomys. But if you subtract its ultimate preposition (which primarily expresses the position of something in space and time), you arrive at the theme about which I now wish to offer one or two ideas.

In short the WOMB.

Only a few days ago, at the time of my writing this, the highest court in our country – in the words of *The Times* –
'has opened a door which can never be shut. Previously, practitioners worked as best they could with what they knew to be inadequate statutory provisions concerning the possible ill-treatment of a child in the womb. Now they face the issue starkly in the face.'

If one really comes down to brass tacks – which, assuredly, is just what we lawyers are perennially obliged to do, day in, and day out, throughout our lives as practitioners – then it seems to me that the momentous and unanimous decision of the Law Lords [in *re D (a Minor)*] really paves the way for children who, whilst still in the womb, have been maltreated by their mothers through an abuse of drink or of drugs – as tens of thousands in this country and, no doubt, as is the case elsewhere – should have the most unmistakenly and equivocal right against their wickedly recalcitrant dams.

After that inordinately long sentence, I feel that we all ought to take a deep breath – and reflect for one moment.

Little Victoria was born prematurely. At birth, she weighed a mere five pounds and, for six weeks, she lived in an intensive care unit. During the period she was suffering from the desperately withering symptoms that are the concomitant of a withdrawal from drugs.

Throughout the entire nine months of the pregnancy, little Victoria's mother, aged thirty years, was so deeply addicted that, as a matter of course, she habitually took drugs far in excess of the amount that her medical adviser prescribed for her.

The local authority had obtained, from a magistrates' bench, a care order which allowed it to have custody of Victoria. Then her mother went all the way up to the House of Lords in an attempt to regain the keeping of her child.

But the Law Lords said, 'No'.

Indeed, Lord Brandon of Oakbrook stated that because Victoria's mother persisted in taking excessive amounts of narcotic drugs throughout the period of her pregnancy, the magistrates were entitled to hold that thereby the child's development and health had been avoidably impaired.

Lord Justice Goff supplemented this view by asseverating that there was no reason why the magistrates should not be entitled to have regard to the events before little Victoria was born, or to the state of events at her birth.

The Law Lords could also say that it was likely, on account of the addiction to drugs of Victoria's mother and father, that her health would continue to be impaired.

Some lawyers believe that this momentous decision will

have the most far-reaching effects insofar as it paves the way for making any woman who does harm to her unborn baby, by taking drugs of any kind – especially, restricted ones – liable to prosecution.

If I may now change tack – I would like to say something about the 126,000 children who, each year, in England and Wales (because so many of our monthly and yearly statistics ignore Scotland and Northern Ireland), are born illegitimate. The Law Commission, in a recent report, has declared that it is time to end the long-established and almost imperishable stigma of bastardy – and even to obliterate the word 'illegitimate' in our laws, as well as in our legal documents in regard to people who, through no fault of theirs, happen to have been born out of wedlock.

The Law Commission has called upon our Government to adopt its draft Bill which is aimed at ensuring that all children are, by law, treated alike, whether their parents be married, or unmarried.

But, seeing that, in the early days following its creation, I frequently gave evidence to this same Law Commission, and, as frequently, suggested a multitude of novel ideas for the reform of our laws, which almost without exception it accepted and adopted, but which the Government of the day never implemented in any way at any time, I am in no way sanguine that the latest draft Bill will ever be passed into law.

It is fairly obvious, in this day and age, during which the somewhat unrealistic but persistent prejudices of an earlier Victorian era have been swept aside, that the legal position of a child who happens to have been born of unmarried parents, should be wholly equated with that of one who has been begotten by married parents.

And now this has come about. The Family Law Reform Act 1987 is described as 'an Act to reform the law relating to the consequences of birth outside marriage. . . .'

These momentous words have helped to remove the illogical and unfair stigma of bastardy.

All this, as every well-informed wombat assuredly knows, can only be in the best interests of modern society in general and, in particular, innocent children.

———————————▶ ● ◀———————————

Litter

It is said that when, during the junketing which followed the peace that ended the Napoleonic Wars in 1814, Field Marshal von Blücher looked down upon London from the top of St Paul's Cathedral, he remarked, 'Was für Plunder'; which has nearly ever since been rendered as 'What a place to plunder!' In fact what he said was 'What rubbish!'

I don't suppose that he was referring to the state of the streets though he might well have done so even though, for very many years, London prided herself on being far tidier than most other English cities.

It is significant that when last the platform immediately below Nelson's figure at the top of the column in Trafalgar Square was cleansed, some four tons of refuse blown up there by the wind was removed. The city itself spends huge sums every year for keeping each mile of its streets clean and the clearing of the royal parks in London costs up to £400,000.

At Windsor, which attracts so many visitors, there are vast dustbins marked 'litter' in fifteen languages. It is, perhaps, unfortunate that the Hungarian inscription refers to 'nonsense'. But it is the English rustic beauty spots which suffer most from discarded rubbish. Modern manufacturers of foodstuffs and sweets and cigarettes place so many fussy and unnecessary wrappings around their goods that when we English have a picnic we often leave an untidy mess behind us. If we could but adopt the happy Australian habit of boiling a billy we would probably burn up our waste paper, but you will appreciate that in our soaking summers, we will seldom be able to do so, if only for the reason that we can never find tinder for our fires.

Under our laws an offence is committed when 'any person throws down, drops or otherwise deposits in, into or from any place in the open air to which the public are entitled or permitted to have access without payment, and leaves anything whatsoever in such circumstances as to cause, contribute to, or tend to lead to, the defacement by litter of any place in the open air . . .' There is a saving for acts done with the consent of the owner or person having control of the littered premises. Applied literally, these provisions would seem to involve me in a prosecution if I happen to be the owner of the five-pound note which an unusually serendipitious friend of mine picked up in the roadway last week. *A fortiori* I am guilty if I incautiously flick a match or a cigarette end into the gutter, or toss a bus ticket from the public pavement into my neighbour's front garden. Yet if I am so unmannerly as to dump a dozen empty beer bottles over my garden wall into my neighbour's premises, I do not offend against the Litter Act because the public are not admitted to either of our gardens. What rubbish! The existence for many years of local bye-laws has had no noticeable effect. The police cannot be expected to observe or prosecute more than a handful of offenders and the suggestion which has been made that we all owe a duty to the community to report upon our untidy fellows seems hopelessly impracticable and certainly un-English.

Ever since the law was passed almost every church, chapel or registry office has posted a notice prominently at the entrance, forbidding the throwing of confetti at weddings. This provoked some typically light-hearted correspondence in *The Times*. One gentleman who candidly disclosed that he was in the rice trade suggested that the throwing of rice – a practice now out of fashion, though certainly symbolic of fertility – would provide food for the birds which would quickly eat it up. One bridegroom, retorted another correspondent, had had to return from his honeymoon so that a doctor could remove a grain of rice from his ear. Another writer preferred the softer qualities of English wheat or Scottish oats. Yet another favoured the use of soap flakes which, in our climate, would soon wash down the church paths. Finally a correspondent, writing on the notepaper of a famous soap firm, asked whether any manufacturer could possibly resist the lure of selling 346,903 more packets of soapflakes – that being the number of weddings in the previous year.

This correspondence was touched off by a certain Archdeacon who, by analogy with the ancient Jewish custom of showering sweets upon the bridal pair, advocated in his parish magazine the throwing of sugared almonds which, he considered, children could afterwards retrieve and eat.

Just imagine the gleam of triumphant serendipity that would light up the eyes of any small boy (like all his kind, not too fastidious about hygiene) who suddenly came upon the recently abandoned scene of half a dozen sugar-almonded weddings!

Horror Comics

During the year 1955, for six months or so, on and off, our press constantly and consistently mounted an attack upon what, in my boyhood, went by the name of 'penny bloods', or 'penny dreadfuls' but which, owing to a vastly changed economy, are now known as 'horror comics,' procurable, in 1955, at prices between 6d and 2s 6d. Parliament, at about that time, and certainly since, has concerned itself with them. Indeed, the Children and Young Persons (Harmful Publications) Act 1955 (of which, more hereafter) is directed against horror comics. The pertinent word is 'harmful'. Therefore I asked myself, what, if anything, is harmful in the illustrated trash that our children and adolescents can, if they are so inclined, look at and read?

Being sceptical about this subject, as also about many things that are written about that frail but precocious entity, the modern child, and having a genuine interest in him and also in what is said about him, I thought I would examine the question for myself by procuring a few horror comics. The handful of papers and magazines that I managed to buy seemed, to my sophisticated adult mind, to be innocuous, although lurid, especially when my thoughts turned back to my own childhood.

I tried to imagine the effect upon the rudderless mind of a child of a stepmother who, during an economic crisis, coldbloodedly deserted her husband's two children in order that she and he might have more to eat. Then I calculated the effect of the ensuing sordid tale of torture and attempted cannibalism by an adult; of homicide (even though justifiable); and of larceny of extremely valuable property by juveniles which was alleged to result in lasting happiness for them and for others. Yet that is simply a paraphrase of the well-loved fairy-tale of Hansel and Gretel, written by those princes of childhood's fiction – the brothers Grimm. Then think of the torture, violence, murder, and other crimes that are the very essence of such children's entertainment as 'Punch and Judy,' 'Treasure Island,' or 'Buffalo Bill.' My own father, as he dandled me on his knee used to repeat –

Fe, fi, fo, fum,
I smell the blood of an Englishman:
Be he alive, or be he dead,
I'll grind his bones to make my bread!

and my father would grate his teeth to emphasize the giant's words. What is there in Superman's travels through space that is more horrifying than this?

Having got thus far, I was fortunate in having my eyes opened by a collection of horror comics acquired by the National Union of Teachers (either by confiscation or by way of gift) from urban children whose ages ranged from six to fourteen. It immediately struck me that 'horror comic' was so inadequate a description as to be misleading because neither comedy nor mere horror embrace half of what I saw. I had expected a vivid illustration of all kinds of violence, torture and death. I was not altogether surprised at seeing moronic creatures more frightful than Frankenstein mauling scantily clad women. But I was not prepared for the depravity, the utter morbidity, and the

275

revolting aberrations of mind and of body that were depicted again and again. Nor had I anticipated that there would be illustrations containing hidden pictures. As children I suppose we were all familiar with this kind of thing but in what I saw there was this difference, that the hidden matter was salacious.

I was dismayed by the constancy with which the end of each picture story – as distinct from a phrase in it – showed the triumph of evil over right. Typical of these was the story of a girl aged about eight, which portrayed the shooting of her father and the trial of her mother and her mother's lover for murder. Following a conviction, both were exhibited in the electric chair. Finally, the orphan, having dried her tears, winks cunningly from the page as she confesses how she cleverly contrived three deaths in order that her rich aunt might pity her and adopt her. No summary can convey the disgust which this series of drawings created in me.

At this critical time there was published a book by a German-born American psychiatrist, Dr. Frederic Wertham, entitled *Seduction of the Innocent,* which not only exposed the terror and obscenity and madness that are to be found in horror comics, but also made two important points. First, that the unwholesome diet is repeated so often that a child hungers for it and will even forsake football and cricket for it. Secondly, that there is a nexus between horror comics and juvenile crimes of violence.

The book is undoubtedly sensational. It mentions an adult writer who, in the guise of 'teenage dope slave', purports to describe the beneficient effects of morphine; 'One needleful of joy-juice and you get so satisfied with the world you forget your obligations.' Again, Dr. Wertham asked one boy, 'What do you want to be when you grow up?' Without hesitation the child replied, 'I want to be a sex maniac.'

Now although (if I may express a personal opinion) some modern psychology seems to be blighted by arrogant guesswork about human behaviour, and although our American friends have a sense of hyperbole that we in England cannot match, it is unquestionable that Dr. Wertham should be urgently heeded. In 1955, in the United States more than sixty million horror comics were published each month, and £55 million worth of them were sold. We have imported many of them. Here indeed is big business. Is it not significant that this industry – for it is such – has bitterly attacked Dr. Wertham for his criticisms of it? As a review in one of our more conservative newspapers put it: 'It is unbelievable that any profit motive, however great, can tempt citizens to produce material that must not only contribute to the corruption of their society but provide such terrifying evidence of corruption already existing.'

The declared object of the Children and Young Persons (Harmful Publications) Act 1955 was to 'prevent the dissemination of certain pictorial publications harmful to children and young persons.' It was directed against any book, magazine or other like work which consists wholly or mainly of stories, told in pictures, with or without the addition of written matter which portrays the commission of crimes, or acts of violence, or cruelty, or incidents of a repulsive or horrible nature, in such a way that the work as a whole would tend to corrupt a child or young person into whose hands it might fall 'whether by inciting, or encouraging him to commit crimes or acts of violence or cruelty or in any other way whatsoever'. There was a maximum penalty of four months' imprisonment or a fine of £100 (or both) on summary conviction for printing, selling or hiring a work, or importing plates for producing a work to which the Act applies.

In the House of Commons the Home Secretary said that as a result of the publicity already given to horror comics their publication in this country had been severely curtailed. It was, however, very difficult for parents and teachers to ensure that children did not get hold of these comics without their knowledge, and the government felt it was necessary to ask the House to pass a bill to support parents and teachers, by empowering the courts to prevent the continued circulation of such copies as might still be on the market and to prevent the resumption of their publication.

There was strong criticism of some of the wide and rather vague definitions in the Act, including suggestions that magistrates would be faced with a difficult task of interpretation and that freedom of utterance was at stake. It would be laughable, if it were not lamentable, that literary men of the calibre of the late Sir Alan Herbert should take the stand that an Act to purify the pictorial reading of little children is a threat to the liberty of authors, publishers, printers, and booksellers. In this context, it is slightly ridiculous to blether about obscene, corrupting, and horrifying literature or art being less obscene, less corrupting and less horrifying if it is presented in a manner which has literary or artistic merit. A few views like those of APH were aired in parliament, but a writer to *The Times* said of them: 'Surely this is absurd; surely [such a work] becomes more dangerous if presented with literary or artistic merit, precisely because the danger is less readily recognized. A lethal dose of arsenic concealed in a peppermint cream is more dangerous than a hundred doses in a hexagonal fluted bottle labelled "Poison" .'

Perhaps I am over-simplifying the problem, but it seems to me that in dealing with children, literary and artistic merit is of secondary importance and that the onus of proving his point lies heavily upon anyone who alleges that perpetual and exclusive reminders, visual and verbal, about deceit, hatred, brutality, rape, torture, death, homosexuality and madness are not harmful to children. 'It were better for him that a millstone were hanged about his neck, and he cast into the sea, than that he should offend one of these little ones.'

Some 2,380 years ago Plato recommended that Homer should be bowdlerised to protect the morals of children in

Athens. In 1955, Sir Richard Livingstone, when lecturing on the subject of tolerance cited 'Plato's ideal' in these weighty words: 'We do not wish our rulers to grow up among representations of moral deformity, as in some diseased pasture where, day after day, feeding on every poisonous weed, they would little by little, gather insensibly a mass of corruption in their very souls.' The lecturer added: 'How far should we tolerate these forces which debase our civilization and make money by doing it? The adulteration of food is forbidden; should we permit the adulteration of food for the spirit and mind, whose health is even more important than bodily health?'

Sinistrality

Are you larboard or starboard? When I was a child, most potentially left-handed children were compelled, when writing, to use their right hands at school to the detriment, as the psychoanalysts – or, are they psychologists? – now claim, of those kids' balanced mental outlook. Most countries now recognise that sinistrality (if, for once, I may depart from my normal habit of using short, simple, Anglo-Saxon words) must be recognised and, indeed, welcomed. Not so, apparently with Italy, Yugoslavia and all the Iron Curtain countries, saving only the Czechs, for some reason which entirely escapes my thinking.

In passing, as a young cricketer, I had no conceivable difficulty in bowling, with equal facility, from either hand, nor with batting similarly, although, in later years I largely lost this capability. And, like every match-winner, I could catch with my left hand or my right hand without any conceivable difference or difficulty. But, of course, so too, can thousands of other dexters.

Touching cricket, a left-handed cricketer wrote to *The Times* claiming that, in truth, he ought to be called a right-hander because, as he said, 'one is called left-handed if one has his front foot (the right one) forward, shoulder (right) forward, and the top hand, which is supposed to be the one which does the work, is also the right hand.'

This stance provoked another correspondent to claim that the right-handed golfer used his left hand predominantly in controlling his club, and therefore, that 'if one can persuade a true left-hander who wishes to take up golf to approach the game in a right-handed manner, his stronger left arm and hand will give him a significant advantage over his right-handed opponent.

During most of their working lives, lawyers in every country, are primarily concerned with the recognition of human rights, their maintenance and enforcement. But, so far as I am aware, not a single one of them, has ever interested himself in human *lefts*. Therefore, it is almost inevitable that I should now bring to your attention the considerable importance of being sinister – perhaps 'sinistral' would be a happier word.

I first became interested in sinistrality when, at the age of six or so, my dear father, who was a great biblical scholar, read to me the story of Ehud, a left-handed man of the tribe of Benjamin. Ehud, as you will recall, was sent to pay tribute to Eglon, the enormously stout King of the Moabites, who was then cruelly harassing the children of Israel and, because Ehud was left-handed, he was not suspected by Eglon's guards of carrying a dagger in his left hand beneath his robes. In the result, when the room was cleared of all observers, Ehud plunged his weapon into Eglon's fat belly and thereafter escaped unharmed.

There are, of course, a multitide of biblical vindications of right-handedness and, apparently, left-handedness was consequentially denigrated. To quote but one example (from *St Matthew*, ch. 25, vv. 31–33): 'The Son of Man . . . shall set the sheep on his right hand and the goats on his left.' Contrariwise, of course, in the book of *Judges*, ch. 20, v. 16, it is said of the Benjamites that 'among all this people there were 700 chosen men lefthanded; everyone could sling stones at an hair breadth, and not miss'.

My interest in this subject was considerably enhanced because one of my sisters is left-handed. Earlier on, she was a missionary in Northern Rhodesia (now Zimbabwe), where her African friends watched, with no little apprehension, whilst she fed herself with her left hand because, as you probably know, all normal people there commonly use the left hand for cleansing themselves after an evacuation of their bowels.

Many of us do not, I believe, realise what a considerable handicap left-handed people suffer in a right-handed world. In the West End of London there is a shop for them. It sells scissors, tin-openers, potato peelers and many other artefacts that are so constructed as to enable left-handers to operate them with just the same facility as those of us who are dexterous use the tools that are specifically designed for us. I don't suppose you've ever thought of the difficulty that a left-hander has to overcome in winding a wrist-watch provided for a right-handed person. Or, indeed, envisaged the peculiar hazard that bedevils a left-handed violinist in an orchestra who, at all times, is in danger of poking his bow into his right-handed neighbour's eye. I am told that there is some similar difficulty – surely not quite so potent – when, at a Chinese dinner, someone uses chopsticks in the wrong hand. Then, again, our pen-nibs never work properly for them – perhaps of diminishing importance in the age of the ball-point pen. Even the ordinary cheque book has stubs on the wrong side for them. And, of course, the leads to a telephone handpiece wind themselves into an indescribably horrible mess whenever the apparatus is used alternately by left and right hands.

Incidentally, it occurs to me that, in a largely right-handed world, the fact that dexterity indicates adroitness, both manual and mental, is wholly unfair. This is odd when one considers – as is the proven fact – that many, and possibly a preponderance of all computer analysts and programmers, whom I always regard as clever people, are naturally sinistrals.

Nevertheless, left-handedness cannot be all that unimportant if only because, among the numerous dialects in these islands, there are no less than eighty-eight words in some 313 localities that describe it explicitly. Obviously I shall not set out all eight-eight of them here. But let me give you a tiny sprinkle of examples, such as bullock-handed; cack-handed; clicky; coochy-gammy; cow-pawed; gammy-palmed; keggy; scroochy; south-pawed (like those who box the wrong way round); quippy; watty; and widdershins. I like that last one, the best of the lot: widdershins.

Perhaps you will agree to pause for a minute or two in order to reflect why, after dinner, the port is passed round in a clockwise direction. Or why (as is apparently the fact) sixty per cent of cats are southpaws. Or why ninety per cent of parrots are similarly afflicted. Or why – and this is a jolly one – some forty per cent of boys (not girls) who are born by breech delivery are also sinistral. Also, remember that some of the greatest men the world has ever known were in this same category – Alexander the Great, Cicero, Charlemagne, *et al*.

Perhaps, the best possible thing is to be ambidextrous as suggested by one wag who wrote to *The Times* last year to say that he shaved both sides of his face simultaneously with a razor in each hand. The potential saving in time, he told us, 'would be significant, probably curing all the nation's economic ills'.

In conclusion, a piece of fantasy. Has it ever occurred to you that if sundials had first been invented in the antipodes, instead of in our hemisphere, all the world's clocks today would operate in an anti-clockwise manner? I ask this deliberately provoking question in order to shake all of you out of any kind of complacency, as is essential in this age of modern technology if we are to survive.

TAILPIECE

I have a friend, an able professional man, who confesses

that he is wholly unable to tell left from right. Therefore, to enable him to avoid leading a totally disorientated life, he wears a ring on his right little finger. He thereby knows that that side of him is starboard. He claims that 28 per cent of the population suffer from a similar disability – but that is something that I would never believe in a trillion years. It could scarcely amount to 0.28 per cent.

Souvenir Land

For the most part I have never much enjoyed poetry, yet there are one or two gems which I read and re-read almost compulsively. One such is Coventry Patmore's 'The Toys'. In case you do not know it, let me start:

'My little son, who look'd from thoughtful eyes
And moved and spoke in quiet grown-up wise,
Having my law the seventh time disobey'd,
I struck him, and dismissed
With hard words and unkiss'd,
– His mother, who was patient, being dead.
Then, fearing lest his grief should hinder sleep,
I visited his bed,
But found him slumbering deep,
With darken'd eyelids, and their lashes yet
From his late sobbing wet.'

The father in this simple episode goes on to describe how greatly he was disturbed on seeing the little lad's collection of trifles by his bedside, set out 'with careful art' – a box of counters, a red veined stone, a piece of glass abraded by the beach, several shells, a couple of French copper coins, and so forth. It is a simple, possibly sentimental poem: do read it if you have never yet done so. It has a good denouement. My purpose in mentioning it is to demonstrate that, from childhood onwards, people love to amass things and that some adults are more assiduous collectors of keepsakes than are kids. There are many reasons why children preserve inconsiderable trifles. It is sometimes more difficult to explain why adults do so, even allowing that:

'Who hath not saved some trifling thing
More prized than jewels rare,
A faded flower, a broken ring,
A tress of golden hair.'[94]

Or, I might add, a tiny sod of English turf, which, from 1972 onwards became commonly known as 'souvenir land'. Souvenir land was the bane of my life during 1965 to 1972. The sale of Souvenir Land became the ultimate in gimmickry. In 1969 some Australian friends of mine who were staying in a London hotel showed me a flashy brochure which they had found placed, like a Gideon bible, by their bedsides. The outer cover depicted, in vivid chromolithograph (or other ilk), a company of the regiment of guards, led by their band, marching forth from King Henry VIII's gateway in Windsor Castle. This splendid wrapping served to introduce an invitation, by a noble marquess, for any commoner, and especially any commoner amongst our American cousins, to buy a 'private estate adjoining Windsor Great Park and almost within bowshot of Windsor Castle'. Reading on, it appeared that the estate would consist merely of 'one square foot of England'. Virgin land where I live in Hampstead is worth never less than £500,000 a plot. So possibly a square foot of land near Windsor Castle is worth acquiring -- especially if you can buy more than one!

Mind you, so far as potential purchasers were concerned, the noble lord was probably more conscious of the historical, than of the monetary value of his offer, for he describes how this place 'has seen much of the glorious pageant of England's past'. It lies 'in the heart of Royal Berks, a county woven into the tapestry of English history, called 'Royal' from the presence of Windsor Castle, the home of England's monarchs for nearly 1,000 years'. He goes on to state: 'Here is a unique gift opportunity. This is giving on a grand scale at a modest price. What better Christmas, birthday or anniversary gift for the man who has everything. Everything, that is, but a piece of English real estate. This is more than just a passing souvenir. You are presenting a gift of lasting historic interest. You can assure your good friend, the recipient, that only a short gallop away from his property is Runnymede, where King John signed the Magna Carta . . . . This is the gift that will truly last for ever; for – and we have this on good authority – there'll always be an England.'

Most moving, no doubt, but probably a little hyperbolical as regards the bowshot. After all, Henry VIII, by statute, required his people to give up such pursuits as football and hockey in order to build up our nation's military strength, and to practice with the long bow. Although the people of that age (saving the King, who was a vastly strong man, as several extant examples of his personal armour amply demonstrate) were extremely short by today's standards, Henry decreed[95] 'that no person above the age of twenty-four shall shoot with the light flight arrow at a distance under two hundred and twenty yards'. I imagine that not even His Majesty could have despatched the heavy war arrow that far. I am also a little sceptical about the 'short gallop' because this particular souvenir land lies, as the crow flies, which is a somewhat longer distance than the horse might, more than four and a half miles from Windsor Castle. By comparison, the Grand National, which one would scarcely regard as a short gallop, is run over four miles and 856 yards. And the 'private estate'? A square foot of land which any commoner today may walk over daily, and probably does. Not that that matters much.

There were numerous similar offers of souvenir land for sale between 1965 and 1972, as the pile of leaflets, pamphlets and advertisements, some plain, some gaudy, which I now have in front of me, testify. The price of one square foot of English soil varies between £2 and £15 or so. You were invited to own a tiny part of a prehistoric encampment near Stonehenge; a square foot of a cider-apple orchard in the West Country; a 'souvenir to cherish' in Kent, the garden of England; an oak tree in Sherwood Forest where Robin Hood and his merry men, Friar Tuck, Maid Marion *et al* ran loose; a morsel of marshland which Shakespeare may well fastidiously have contrived to avoid; or a small part of rugged Snowdonia – to commemorate the investiture of HRH the Prince of Wales. Land beside Loch Lomond was also up for sale. Then there was a 'liberty estate' at Bury St Edmunds where, it was claimed, one million plots were available. Although, in connection with Magna Carta, we tend to train our thoughts on Runnymede, it was at the high altar of St Edmundsbury – once the largest cathedral in the whole of Europe – that the English barons under Archbishop Stephen Langton swore to extract a charter of their liberties from King John.

We should, perhaps, realize that if and so far as these initial schemes succeeded, the acquisition of a large number of souvenir plots might well become a status symbol.

Earlier I referred to souvenir land as having been 'the bane of my life'. Actually, at the constant risk of being served with a writ of *mandamus*, I was lucky in preventing it from becoming baneful by refusing adamantly (despite the threat) to entertain all transactions dealing with it. This I did because of the incalculable amount and cost of the work involved. I was aware of the existence of twenty-seven estates of souvenir land in England and Wales. Most of them were of far greater extent than a mere acre and a single acre may be split into 43,560 plots, each comprising 144 square inches. The true cost, at that time, of issuing a certificate of title for each would be not less, and sometimes far more, than £10, whilst the fee properly chargeable at most of the material times was one shilling.

Now just imagine the task of demarking upon the ground, in rough undulating terrain, usually covered with gorse or scrub, bramble and sapling, the exact location of tens of hundreds of thousands of minute patches each of 144 square inches. Just imagine the job of having to delineate upon plans such a vast number of plots, not only in relation to one another, but also in their relative juxtaposition to established features already existing on the site. Just imagine the utterly ruinous expense of producing separate certificates of title for each trifle of land.

Had these developers of souvenir land been allowed to pursue their way unhindered, Pelion would have been piled upon Ossa, and inevitably the ordinary business of providing people with registered titles to their homes would have had to be shut down because of the overwhelming tidal-wave of work. Furthermore, HM Land Registry would have been rendered bankrupt within a short period of time. Now, perhaps you will understand why, in the face of a threat of *mandamus*, I once lived on the razor's edge.

Nevertheless, seeing that the sellers of souvenir land set up their offices in American ports of departure to the United Kingdom, there were valuable dollars to be earned. One wag wrote to *The Times* stating that: 'According to my maths, the entire nation's salvation lies in this venture. The Government's duty is clear – they must nationalize [the developers], then sell the entire United Kingdom which, at four dollars a square foot, will realize £3,751,900,612,571. The nationalized company must then declare itself bankrupt and the income must be distributed to every man, woman and child –which will give £73,800 per head.' Although, according to my off-the-cuff calculations, this man's figures were billions below the true mark, perhaps he had the grain of an idea for keeping us solvent. But who would have the impertinence, however impoverished, to sell a portion of

> 'This royal throne of Kings, this sceptred isle,
> This earth of majesty, this seat of Mars . . .
> This precious stone set in the silver sea . . .
> This blessed plot, this earth, this realm, this England'?

It was against this background that a Bill (now the Land Registration and Land Charges Act 1971) was introduced into the House of Lords to regulate (*inter alia*) the sale of souvenir land. Lord Hailsham then stated: 'Clause 4 removes a minor nuisance from the troubled life of the Chief Land Registrar . . . [The sale of souvenir plots] is innocent enough in itself, and it is even beneficial if and when it makes a modest contribution to our balance of payments. But it causes quite a disproportionate amount of trouble . . . To make the Land Registry investigate each title and issue a separate certificate in respect of each tiny plot would call for a totally unjustifiable increase in the Registry's manpower resources . . . Clause 4 operates to bless souvenir buyers by . . . a harmless practice without clogging the administrative machinery.'

And the ex-Lord Chancellor, Lord Gardiner, reiterating much of what Lord Hailsham had stated, said: ' I am also delighted that souvenir land has been dealt with, because I know personally what a nuisance this was being to the learned Registrar . . . I am sure that this legislation will give the Land Registrar a happier Easter.'

And it did! For now the law is that no one is allowed to register the title to souvenir land; no one may transfer or mortgage it on the register. Yet today people may lawfully deal with it off the register and their lawyers may produce the most handsome and impressive-looking Olde Indentures, tricked out in medieval language, in ancient script, all of which will not only greatly please our American cousins, but will also lead to legally enforceable transactions. They are to be effectual without registration once the Chief Land Registrar has declared the existence of a 'souvenir land scheme' and noted the declaration on the register.

Touching this subject, an old friend of mine, no longer with us, a London lawyer named George Dodsworth, wrote to *The Times* to point out that, as the pitch at Lords is to be relaid over the next four years, the MCC might replenish its coffers by inducing a multitude of cricket lovers to buy, and cherish in a corner of their gardens, a small piece of the sacred turf lying in front of the very cathedral of cricket. This promoted another cricketer to confess that some fifteen years ago he had actually made a lawn from pieces, measuring about two feet square, taken from no less than twenty-three major first-class cricket grounds, and that he established a map to identify every single one of the plots. As an ex-playing cricket enthusiast that somehow appeals to me. But the fact that in a shop near where I worked during forty years, daft people can buy a tin of London smog, or a tin of water culled from nearby the white cliffs of Dover, fills me with despair about the sanity of adult human beings.

———————————●●●———————————

Sherlock Holmes was not Consulted

About eighteen years ago there was an incredibly clever burglary at a branch of Lloyd's bank in Baker Street, in London, some three-quarters of a mile from Lords cricket ground and only the throw of a cricket ball away from 221B Baker Street, an address which no longer exists, but which is the veritable site from which Sherlock Holmes was alleged to have stunned the civilised world by his logical and irrefutable deductions. I apologise to anyone who may be hurt by that word 'alleged' because, although I myself, in my simple way, believe that Sherlock Holmes was merely an exceptionally clever detective who subsisted within the elastic imagination of Conan Doyle, I am well aware that thousands – possibly millions – of people living upon the American continent are convinced (*vide* all their many Sherlock Holmes societies) that he was a real person. There are some of them here, in England too! Who am I, who was not there at the relevant times, to contradict them? They have studied their hero minutely. Many books have been written about him. I have merely read Conan Doyle for fun.

But coming down to hard brass tacks, is there no merit in reading these stories? In parenthesis, the word 'story' in Middle

292

English originally meant an historical narrative. I believe that it was not until the year AD 1500 that a kind of fictional connotation was attached to the meaning. However, to answer my own question: Sherlock Holmes, once observed[96] that 'it is of the highest importance in the art of detection to be able to recognise, out of a number of facts, which are incidental, and which vital. Otherwise your energy and attention may be dissipated instead of being concentrated.'

Do you know, when I was a teenager, I had an almost idolatrous regard for all those old men (as they then seemed) in wigs and silk gowns who sought to expound our laws before His (as they then were) Majesty's justices, who then, to me, seemed even older than the KCs. Occasionally, as a new boy in the law, I was distressed because some point which appeared to my childlike mind to be so simple, and so compelling, was converted into a complex issue on account of past history and the untold number of precedents of our judge-made laws. Perhaps the one thing, above all others, which I should like to possess today is a childlike mind. Be that as it may, as an ordinary traveller on the Hampstead tube and an occasional jet-flyer to the antipodes (both direct descendants of the man on the Clapham omnibus), as well as a lawyer, I would like to associate myself warmly with the plain statement of Mr Sherlock Holmes set out above.

The facts of the recent crime, as they became known months after the event, were these. In the small hours of a Sunday morning an enthusiastic radio ham chanced to change the frequency of his wavelength and thereby, instantly, and by a quirk of fate, he was able to pick up an extraordinary series of conversations. These took place, first, between the members of a gang who were in the course of robbing a bank of enormous sums of money; secondly, by a wretched, complaining look-out man on some roof-top who was tired of peering through binoculars, afraid to go to sleep, and quite desperately fearful of not waking up in the morning; and, thirdly, by a female 'controller' in some unidentified command post. These exchanges over the air involved six or seven people but, to the ordinary listener, many of them were enigmatic because of the continual use of esoteric criminal slang. Nevertheless, our radio enthusiast got into touch with the Post Office and Scotland Yard.

Unhappily his efforts had little effect. As happens all too often, people who are made aware of the imminence of serious crime are sceptical, and therefore are often afraid of making fools of themselves. According to the newspaper reports, the bank people were hoity-toity. Their alarms, as they said with calm complacency, were proof against any burglar. If the door of their strongroom was shut (as it undoubtedly was) and the circuit not broken (as was also undoubtedly true), all must be well. Anyhow, a most complicated procedure, involving a solemn supplication to the high priests of the bank, needed to be invoked if, during the weekend, any doors were opened specially to please the police. Scotland Yard, for their part, apparently thought that they could trace the source of any radio signals without outside help. In fact, their detectives began an intensive and systematic search of 750 banks within the inner London area. Double checks were carried out on some 150 banks within the radius of one mile from Baker Street. Yet, if only the Post Office had been called upon, in due time, to use their detector vans, which contain some of the most sophisticated equipment in the world for tracing radio signals, the criminals must have been caught whilst their crime was still-born.

Believe it or not, at about 1530 hours on the Sunday some detectives, together with several bank security officers, searched the inside of the very premises upon which, behind fifteen-inch-thick vault doors, the criminals were lying low. On account of their observer's radio contacts, the intruders on the other side of the safe doors maintained an absolute silence. There were no signs of an external entry through the bank because there had been none. I feel sure that, at this point, Sherlock Holmes must have turned several times over in his fictional grave.

What had happened? Soon after the employees of the bank had gone home on the Friday evening, the thieves entered the tradesman's entrance of an empty leather goods shop, two doors away. Apparently the business was up for sale: the premises had been closed for at least two weeks. The intruders carried in with them drills, numerous cylinders of oxygen, thermic lances (for piercing any substances, including reinforced concrete and hardened steel), two-way radio sets, tubular ladders, *et al*, besides sufficient supplies of food and, as I believe, drink. They thereupon set to work to drill a passage under an intervening shop, of some forty feet in length and, thereafter, upwards through three feet into the very vaults of the bank, from which, eventually, they extracted some £1,500,000 worth of valuables and money.

One of the burglars, evincing an almost Sherlock Holmes-like perspicatiousness, had previously opened an account at the bank, secured to himself a box in its safe deposit and, as an unobjectionable customer, had descended into the vaults, where he had taken numerous measurements with the aid of his umbrella. Another of the crooks had previously contracted to buy the shop from which the illegal entry was eventually begun and held the keys.

Would Sherlock Holmes have been out of his depth in tackling such a crime? How would his magnifying glass have matched up with the modern short-wave radio and the use of thermic lances? The short answer is that Sherlock Holmes was always up-to-date in his own day and age. Anyhow, in order to answer my own questions I would like to remind you of one of his most triumphant cases.[97] Of course, my summary of it makes poor reading in place of Conan Doyle's original text but, perhaps, on that very account, I may be able to persuade you to go to the source itself.

An advertisement had appeared in the *Morning Chronicle* of 27th April, 1890. [I stick to 1890, although counsel in the recent case referred to the year 1880.] It announced that 'on account of the bequest of the late Ezekiah Hopkins of Lebanon, Penn., USA, there is now another vacancy open which entitles a member of the League to a salary of four pounds a week for purely nominal services. All red-headed men who are sound in body and mind and above the age of 21 years are eligible . . . .' Candidates for this job with the Red-Headed League were recommended to present themselves at an address in Fleet Street at 11 am on a certain Monday morning.

This advertisement was brought to the notice of a certain Mr Jabez Wilson, who, whilst he possessed a full flaming red head of hair, had an ever-diminishingly successful pop-shop at Saxe-Coburg Square, just outside the walls of the city of London. It was his bright assistant, Vincent, whom he had recently taken on at half the normal rate of wages, who almost compassionately pressed his employer to apply for the job. In fact Vincent took his boss to Fleet Street at the appointed time, when the roadway was beseiged by thousands of people with heads of every colour ranging from brick to lemon and straw to orange. But Mr Jabez Wilson was a veritable redhead and when, eventually, he and Vincent got into the bare room where another ultra red-headed man conducted the interviews, he was accepted for the job – but only after, to his intense discomfort, it had been amply proved that he was not wearing a wig!

As to the job, it appeared that a deceased and eccentric American millionaire had bequeathed a suitable sum to provide £4 a week for a suitable red-headed male who would religiously copy out the Encyclopaedia Britannica from 10am to 2pm daily in the Fleet Street office [incidentally, providing his own pen, paper and ink] on the strict and absolute condition that he would never leave the premises during the prescribed hours upon any pretext whatever. Not much of a job: but a most welcome supplement to the income which Mr Jabez Wilson's failing pawnbroking business yielded. And he was assured that young Vincent would manage the job at Saxe-Coburg Square competently during the slack hours for, of course, the best transactions took place well after 2 pm when Jabez would be back in his own office. Incidentally, he had no objection to Vincent, who was a keen photographer, slipping downstairs under the pop-shop in order to develop his plates, so long as the counter was never neglected.

Then suddenly, after eight weeks of profitable employment, when Mr Jabez Wilson had nearly finished copying all the entries under A from Ency. Brit., he arrived on a Friday morning to find a notice on the door of the miserable little Fleet Street den announcing that the Red-Headed League had been dissolved.

After failing totally to trace his late employer, he consulted Mr Sherlock Holmes who, in no time at all, thought it 'possible that graver issues hang from it than might at first sight appear'. 'Grave enough!' said Mr Jabez Wilson. 'Why, I have lost four pounds a week.' 'As far as you are personally concerned', remarked Holmes, 'I do not see that you have any grievance against this extraordinary League. On the contrary, you are, as I understand, richer by some £30, to say nothing of the minute knowledge you have gained on every subject which comes under the letter A. . . .'

Subsequently Holmes, accompanied by the ever-faithful Dr Watson, visited the shabby-genteel Saxe-Coburg Square where the ever-enigmatic sleuth thumped the pavement with his stick in order to discover whether there were any hollow passages under the roadway. Later, they turned into the busy thoroughfare in which the Coburg branch of the City and Suburban Bank had their premises.

Do you remember the sequel? Sherlock Holmes, Watson (with revolver), the manager of the bank (which, at that time, happened to be holding a fortune in golden Napoleons), and a high official from Scotland Yard descended into the vaults of the premises late on a Saturday night. Eventually, in the early hours, Vincent and his red-headed accomplice emerged from the bowels of the earth – only to be caught red-handed.

In the real life story which recently unfolded itself, neither Sherlock Holmes nor Dr Watson were in the vaults, ready to make their arrests. It is possibly a matter for regret that they had not been consulted. Nevertheless, nearly sixteen months after the event, six men were indicted with crimes arising out of that weekend enterprise. Three of them pleaded guilty to charges of having entered the bank in question and stealing cash and jewellery therefrom to the value of at least £1,500,000. Several others denied any kind of complicity.

In the result three men were sent to jail for twelve years, another for eight. All were extremely lucky if only for the reason that the total plunder, which ultimately turned out to be worth well over £3,000,000, and thus was far greater than that of the Great Train Robbery, after which several of those convicted were sent down for thirty years.

Only 260 out of the 268 owners of the robbed deposit boxes in the bank came clean, and there was speculation that the odd eight boxes contained valuables belonging to criminals, because those eight refused to disclose even their names. Personally I deplore this kind of Swiss bank situation. Why should banks not insist upon knowing what is put into their deposits? And the odd thing is that the newspapers keep suggesting that Mr Big (whom Sherlock Holmes named Professor Moriarty) lived near my early childhood home and that he was an ordinary commuter. Obviously he was able to command considerable loyalty from his minions.

There I must leave the matter, save possibly for one

amusing incident. When one of the accused who had pleaded 'Not guilty' was being questioned about a person whom I shall call 'X' he told the police that he did not know X. When, thereafter, he was faced with a photograph taken at X's wedding in which he appeared, he dismissed the whole affair by stating: 'I go to thousands of weddings a year. My memory is dreadful.' Sherlock Holmes, of course, could have made a fairly devastating analysis of all those weddings.

Notes

1 (1884) 14 QBD 273.
2 A W Brian Simpson, *Cannibalism and the Common Law*, University of Chicago Press.
3 (1953) 107 JP 24.
4 [1954] 1 WLR 261.
5 (1931) NI 209.
6 (1860) 8 CB (NS) 515.
7 *Walsh* v *Holst & Co Ltd & Ors* [1958] 3 All ER 33 (CA).
8 Cf *Adams* v *Lancashire and Yorkshire Rly Co* (1869) LR 4 CP 739.
9 In Mr Dooley's opinions: 'Cross-examinations'.
10 Per Lord Justice Denning (as he then was) in *Jones* v *National Coal Board* [1957] 2 QB 61, 65.
11 Montgomery Hyde, *Trials of Oscar Wilde*, (1960), pp 120, 150.
12 Lewis Carroll, *Through the Looking Glass*, Ch VI.
13 Glim, Summer 1957: That was the Question. Lord Birkett gave me permission to quote this passage.
14 *Tulk* v *Moxhay* (1848) Ph 774, an early case dealing with the enforcement of restrictive covenants.
15 *Nicholson* v *Westmorland CC*, The Times 25 October 1962.
16 *Hillas & Co Ltd* v *Arcos Ltd* (1932) 147 LT 503.
17 *Adamastos Shipping Co Ltd* v *Anglo-Saxon Petroleum Co Ltd* [1959] AC 133, at 158.
18 *Church of Jesus Christ of Latter-Day Saints* v *Henning*, The Times 31 May 1963.
19 Law of Property Act 1925, s 184.
20 *Wing* v *Angrave* (1860) 8 HLC 183.
21 *Re Alston* [1892] P 142.
22 *Re Benyon* [1901] P 141.
23 *Re Howard deceased* [1944] P 39.
24 *Re Lindop* [1942] Ch 377. Cf *Re* Cohen [1945] Ch 5.
25 *Per* Cohen J in *Re Pringle* [1946] Ch 124, at 127.

[26] *Hickman* v *Peacey* [1945] AC 304.
[27] *Williams* v *Williams* (1882) 20 Ch D 659.
[28] In earlier times Mainprize was the action of procuring the release of a prisoner by becoming surety.
[29] Judges 16:20.
[30] In an address to The English Association.
[31] *Gatehouse* v *Vise* [1956] 3 All ER 772.
[32] Henry Luttrell (1765–1861).
[33] Income Tax Act 1952, s 109.
[34] *Soul* v *Irving*, The Times 19 November 1963.
[35] *Gollins* v *Gollins* [1962] 3 WLR 1344 (CA); [1964] AC 644 (HL).
[36] In *Kaslefsky* v *Kaslefsky* [1951] P 38, at 48.
[37] *Per* Lord Thankerton in *Thomas* v *Thomas* [1947] AC 484, at 488.
[38] *Per* Langton J in *Spence* v *Spence* [1939] 1 All ER 52, at 56.
[39] *Lines* v *Lines*, The Times 16 July 1963.
[40] *Hall* v *Hall* [1962] 1 WLR 478.
[41] *Buchler* v *Buchler* [1947] P 25, at 47.
[42] *Draper* v *Draper*, The Times 28 October 1954.
[43] *Willan* v *Willan* [1960] 1WLR 624.
[44] *T* v *T* (1961) 105 SJ 933.
[45] *Williams* v *Williams*, The Times 15 March 1958.
[46] *Bohnel* v *Bohnel* [1960] 1WLR 590.
[47] *Williams* v *Williams* [1963] 3 WLR 215.
[48] *Good's Case* (1626) Popham 211, at 212.
[49] *Bolsom* v *E Karmois* [1956] 2 WLR 625, at 636.
[50] *Bonitto* v *Fuerst* [1944] AC 75, at 82.
[51] *Hills* v *London Gaslight Co* (1857) 27 LJ Ex 60, 63.
[52] *Green* v *Premier etc. Ltd* [1928] 1 KB 561, at 566.
[53] *Ex parte Bull*, The Times 29 March 1963.
[54] *Southam* v *Smout*, [1964] 1 QB 308.
[55] *Russian and English Bank* v *Baring Bros* [1936] 1 All ER 526.
[56] *Semayne's Case* (1604) 5 Coke Rep 91.
[57] *Ryan* v *Shylock* (1851) 21 LJ Exch 55.
[58] F P Dunne, *Mr Dooley on Criminal Trials*.
[59] In *Cooksey* v *Haynes* (1858) 27 LJ (Ex) NS 371.
[60] *Hughes* v *Budd* (1840) 8 Dow QB 315.
[61] *Mounson* v *West* (1588) 1 Leon 132.
[62] *Bushel's Case* (1670) 6 Howell's State Trials 999.
[63] *Gorman* v *Barnard* [1940] 2 KB 570, 584.
[64] *Hale* v *Cove* (1725) 1 Strange 642.

[65] *Straker* v *Graham* (1839) 7 Dow 223.

[66] F P Dunne, *Mr Dooley on Expert Testimony.*

[67] Majority verdicts were introduced into England and Wales by the Juries Act 1974, s 17.

[68] This refers to the events of 1921–22, not to the current troubles.

[69] *Hilder* v *Associated Portland Cement Manufacturers Ltd*, The Times 21 July 1961.

[70] *Bolton* v *Stone* [1951] AC 850.

[71] *Castle* v *St Augustine's Links Ltd & Anor* (1922) 38 TLR 615.

[72] *Shaw* v *DPP* [1962] AC 220

[73] *R* v *Mella* (1960), not officially reported.

[74] *R* v *Straker* (1962), not officially reported.

[75] *R* v *Clayton & Halsey* [1963] 1 QB 163.

[76] *Gale on Easements*, in any of its many editions, is an authoritative legal textbook. An easement is the legal right to use another person's land for a specified purpose as, for example, a right of way, or a right of drainage.

[77] *Gollins* v *Gollins* [1963] 3 WLR 176, 186.

[78] *Phipps* v *Rochester Corporation* [1950] 1 QB 450.

[79] *R* v *Downes* (1875) 1 QBD 25.

[80] Public Health Act 1936, Pt III.

[81] *Raymond* v *Cook* [1958] 1 WLR 1098.

[82] *John* v *Heath*, The Times 24 April 1958.

[83] £850 in 1558: my figures are based on a formula kindly supplied to me by the Bank of England Economic Intelligence Deparment.

[84] The Weekly Notes (Australia), vol 52, pp 100 *et seq*; 21 August 1935.

[85] 'Upon a view of the body'.

[86] 'The whole body [or nature] of the offence.'

[87] *Inland Revenue Commissioners* v *Rossminster Ltd and Others*, The Times 14 December 1979.

[88] Tax Management Act 1970, s 20 (C) (3), as amended by the Finance Act 1976.

[89] *The Times*, 18 December 1979.

[90] A Clayton drink is a non-alcoholic beverage by means of which teetotal wowsers indicate that they are, at least, actually drinking.

[91] *Burmah Oil Co (Burma Trading) Ltd* v *Lord Advocate* [1965] AC 75.

[92] *Howarth* v *Howarth*, The Times 5 July 1963.

[93] *Hamilton* v *Bennett* (1930) 94 JP Jo 136.

[94] Mrs E. C. Howarth, an American (1827–1899).

[95] 33 Hy VIII, cap 9.
[96] *The Memoirs of Sherlock Holmes*, 'The Reigate Squires'.
[97] 'The Adventure of the Red-Headed League'.